Demand analysis
for marketing decisions

Demand analysis
for marketing decisions

G. DAVID HUGHES
Burlington Industries Professor of Business Administration
University of North Carolina, Chapel Hill

 1973

RICHARD D. IRWIN, INC. Homewood, Illinois 60430
IRWIN-DORSEY INTERNATIONAL London, England WC2H 9NJ
IRWIN-DORSEY LIMITED Georgetown, Ontario L7G 4B3

© RICHARD D. IRWIN, INC., 1973

First Printing, April 1973

ISBN   0-256-01479-5
Library of Congress Catalog Card No. 72–98123
Printed in the United States of America

For Beth Ann

Preface

Marketing managers' decisions in the key areas of products, prices, channels of distribution, promotion, and public policy start from a common point—an understanding of the needs of buyers and consumers. The process for understanding these needs is known as demand analysis—the heart of the strategy of the *marketing concept.* This text applies the theories, models, and measures from the four behavioral disciplines that are most frequently used for demand analyses. These disciplines are demography, economics, sociology, and psychology. A simple model of demand is developed in Chapter 1 and elaborated upon throughout the remaining chapters. Variations on the model by each discipline provide the information needed for marketing decisions. This basic model of demand is like the basic model in accounting—assets equal liabilities plus net worth—in that it provides a basis for generating information for decisions.

The text is *multidisciplinary,* not *interdisciplinary,* because it treats each discipline separately, rather than integrating them. Experience with other approaches has revealed a pedagogical advantage to this separation: The reader familiar with one discipline can review that material quickly and read slowly those chapters new to him.

Application and theory are kept separate by having two chapters on each of the disciplines. The first gives marketing applications and the second presents theories, models, and measures. Chapter 1 explains the place of demand analysis in the marketing plan. The applied and theoretical material for each discipline appear in Chapters 2 through 9.

Chapter 10 focuses on the need for planners to understand the philosophy behind measurement and model building. (Readers who enjoy abstraction may find Chapter 10 a useful preview to the concepts presented in Chapter 2 through 9.) Chapter 11 examines recent trends that may bring about changes in the characteristics of demand.

It should be noted that in the practice of marketing there is no distinct separation between the disciplines or between application and theory. The distinction has been used for purposes of clarity and pedagogical efficiency. The sequence of material represents an evolution of seven years' work which included classroom testing and the comments of more than 15 marketing professors who served as reviewers of many drafts of outlines and complete manuscripts.

The text is designed to get the student involved in relevant issues. Discussion questions at the end of each chapter encourage individual or team projects and in many cases require personal observations in retail, wholesale, and manufacturing institutions. An annotated bibliography of more than 150 secondary information sources is provided in Appendix A. These sources permit low-cost demand analyses for course projects and for use after the course is completed. Reading questions at the end of each chapter help the student test his knowledge of the text material.

Suggested cases from five recent case texts are annotated with discussion questions that are relevant to demand analyses. Thus, for each chapter, students and the instructor may work together, selecting those cases that best meet the needs and interests of the students.

Suggested readings for each chapter and a bibliography of more than 500 items will enable the advanced student to explore specific concepts in more depth. Answers to objective questions appear in Appendix B so that the student may check the accuracy of his thinking.

This text is written in anticipation of a possible restructuring of marketing courses to present material more efficiently by eliminating the duplication of discussions of demand in courses such as marketing management, advertising management, marketing research, and consumer behavior. This restructuring may shorten some of these courses to mini courses, or leave room for material or projects that have been excluded for a lack of time. Thus, a restructuring would produce a new course titled "Demand Analysis," for which this text would be most appropriate. When restructuring is not possible the text could be used for a behavioral science approach to marketing management and as a supplement to courses in advertising, consumer behavior, and marketing research. A course titled "New Methods in Marketing" could be created by using this text and one of the excellent texts on marketing science and marketing, because these texts generally exclude an in-depth treatment of the behavioral sciences.

Several philosophies have guided the writing of this book. There is an attempt to reflect the excitement of marketing by getting the reader involved and, wherever possible, using real examples, without a disguise. The unifying theme is the demand model, so the reader will find it easy to organize new knowledge and relate it to marketing management decisions. Great effort has been spend in digesting and integrating the concepts, thereby reducing lengthy descriptive passages.

Many people have participated in the writing of this book. As noted, many students and reviewers, known and unknown, have made important contributions. Professor Lee E. Preston was a source of encouragement, change, and refinement through all drafts. Professors D. G. Morrison, Francesco M. Nicosia and Vithala R. Rao made many important contributions during final drafts. My wife Betty continued to serve with patience and understanding the role of the nonrandom reader who insists that style and clarity are important. To all of these individuals I am profoundly grateful.

Chapel Hill, North Carolina   G. David Hughes
March 1973

Contents

Behavioral theories: *Motivation. Need hierarchy. Cognitive balance.* Communication theories: *Selective exposure. Selective perception.* Models of attitude change: *Balance and congruity models. St. James model. A multidimensional unfolding model.* Behavioral models: *Early psychological models—Hull, Spence, and Hilgard. Recent psychological models —Atkinson and Fishbein. Marketing models.* Measuring attitudes: *Identifying attributes. Measuring attribute beliefs. Instruments for measuring attitudes. Nonverbal instruments to measure attitudes.* The buyer as an information processor.

Planning scientifically. The role of measures and models in science. Measurement: *Measurement defined. The functions of measurement.* Models: *Models defined. Identifying the structure of the model.* Systems: *Systems defined. Methods for representing systems. Laws, theories, and systems.* Advantages and disadvantages of a measures, models, and systems approach. The development of a science of marketing. Three views of the marketing system.

New trends in the determinants of demand: *Demographic trends. Changing determinants of GNP. Changing values.* New trends in management styles: *A shift from problem solving to problem anticipation. A concern for societal goals.* New trends in demand analysis techniques.

1

Demand analysis for marketing decisions

The task facing the marketing executive is the profitable matching of the supply of his firm to a segment of demand in a continuous state of uncertainty. New technology and competition keep the supply side of exchange uncertain. The uncertainty of demand may be traced to the capriciousness of consumers' wants. To accomplish his task the executive has at his disposal the tools of the marketing mix—product, price, promotion, and distribution.

Marketing mix decisions begin with an understanding of demand. Plans for an existing product are based on the product's share of the market. Market share, in turn, is determined by buyers' perceptions of the attributes of this product relative to the attributes of competitive products. These perceptions are part of the psychological dimensions of demand. Trends in the size of existing market segments are analyzed by locating potential demand in time and space using population data. Thus, demographic variables are central to product planning. Planning for new products requires additional sociological and psychological variables to detect unmet needs and to promote the product once it has been developed. In addition to identifying social needs, social analysis reveals the process by which a group adopts new products. Similarly, psychological analysis identifies psychological needs and the mental processes of learning about a product and deciding whether to accept or reject it. Pricing plans are based on economic concepts such as the ability to buy (income) and the effect of price changes on the number of units sold (price elasticity). Distribution plans require a knowledge of the location of demand in time and space.

Promotional plans begin with an understanding of the communication process, which includes the effect of various sources of information and the
mental processes of perceiving, assimilating, and acting on new information. Communication research has its origins in sociological and psychological research. In summary, marketing decisions require an understanding of the demographic, economic, social, and psychological dimensions
of demand. Demand analysis consists of the application of demographic,
economic, social, and psychological theories, models, and measures to the
determination of human needs and the means for meeting these needs.

SOME BASIC MODELS OF DEMAND

The demand for a product or service is composed of two elements—the
number of people (N_t) and their rate of usage (R_t), both in time period t.
Generic[1] demand (G_t) is computed by multiplying the number of people
times their usage rate, thus,

$$G_t = N_t R_t. \qquad (1\text{--}1)$$

This equation emphasizes a fundamental point in demand analysis: an increase in demand may be the result of more people using the product,
the present number of people using it at a greater rate, or an increase
in the number of people *and* an increase in the usage rate. To project
generic demand to time period $t + 1$ it is necessary to project N and R
to $t + 1$. Thus,

$$G_{t+1} = N_{t+1} R_{t+1}. \qquad (1\text{--}2)$$

Demand analysis, in basic terms, consists of instruments to measure N and
R and models to project them to future time periods. These instruments
and models have been borrowed from the fields of demography,[2] economics, sociology, and social-psychology.

A demand analysis begins by refining the concept of N_t. Instead of
considering the entire population, the marketing planner is concerned with
determining the number of people who share a common need. This need
may be physical, social, or psychological.[3] The identification of clusters

---

[1] Generic demand, known also as primary demand, is the total demand for
a class of products such as automobiles, bars of soap, or savings institutions. Brand
demand, known also as secondary demand, is the demand for a specific brand,
such as Ford or Chevrolet cars.

[2] To facilitate exposition, demography will be treated as a separate discipline,
despite the fact that it is frequently regarded as a branch of sociology.

[3] Because a demand analysis focuses on the needs of the individual, it is central
to the philosophy of the *marketing concept,* which states that the needs should
be identified before a product is developed.

of the population sharing a common need is known as *market segmentation*. Segmentation facilitates product development, pricing decisions, distribution, and promotion (Frank, Massey, and Wind, 1972).

Market segmentation may be described graphically with the aid of the Venn diagram in Figure 1–1. The entire population is represented by set *A*.

FIGURE 1–1

A Venn diagram of market segments for new automobiles

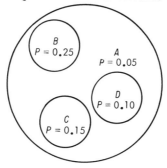

A = The entire population of the United States. The annual buying rate (i.e., the probability of buying a new car) is 0.05.

B, C, D = Segments of the population with varying probabilities of buying a new car. If segment *B* is males, ages 25–35, with an income of at least $7,500, the buying probability is 0.25, or five times that of the average U.S. resident. Market segmentation attempts to identify clusters of individuals with higher than average buying or usage rates. The total expected demand is the sum of the product of the number of persons in each segment times the average probability of buying within that segment, thus,

$$\text{Expected potential}_t = \sum_{i=1}^{n} N_{it}P_{it}$$

where *N* is the number of persons, *P* is the probability, there are *n* segments, and the estimate is for time period *t*.

The annual buying rate of this group for new automobiles is approximately 0.05. Segment *B* is a subset of this population. If members of this group are male, are between the ages of 25 and 35, and have an income greater than $7,500, the buying rate of this group will be about 0.25, or five times that of the general population. Market segmentation, therefore, may be regarded as an attempt to identify the characteristics of members of a market who have high buying or usage rates. If an automobile manufacturer develops a market strategy toward market segments *A*, *B*, and *C*, its potential market is the sum of the product of the number of people in these segments times their respective buying rates. This potential generic demand may be expressed algebraically as follows,

$$G_t = N_{Bt}R_{Bt} + N_{Ct}R_{Ct} + N_{Dt}R_{Dt}, \tag{1-3}$$

which in more generalized form reduces to

$$G_t = \sum_{k=1}^{n} N_{kt}R_{kt} \tag{1-4}$$

where there are n market segments (k). Equation 1–4 was the basic model used by the Port of New York Authority when forecasting the number of trips made on airplanes. The characteristics of travelers led to the formation of 130 segments of business travelers and 160 segments of personal travelers. This air travel model is discussed in Chapter 2.

To estimate the number of people and their physical needs, we begin with data collected by demographers, such as censuses of population, housing, and business. For example, the numbers of people in the age classifications of 0–3, 16–20, and 66–80 represent the potential generic demand for diapers, youth clothing, and retirement communities, respectively. To project N_t into the future, we must consider the rates of birth, death, and immigration. Furthermore, we must evaluate the forces that alter these rates, such as economic and social conditions. Examples in Chapter 2 illustrate how demographic data identify potential demand. For instance, a large crest in the number of persons reaching the driving age encouraged the Ford Motor Company to develop the Mustang for the youth market.

Demographic variables do more than simply locate persons in time (N_t). They help to explain variations in rates of usage (R_t). For example, the rate at which businessmen travel on airlines can be explained by knowing their age, occupation, and education (Chapter 2, the Port of New York Authority).

In developed economies, such as the United States, there is little variance in death rates and migration, which means that most of the fluctuations in the size of the population are due to variations in birth rates. The problems associated with measuring birth rates and the economic and social forces that alter these rates are examined in Chapter 3. Models for the projection of population through geographic space are also considered in that chapter.

The forces which determine usage rate (R_t) are very complex. They may be summarized briefly by stating that usage rate is some function of variables that are demographic (D_t), economic (E_t), social (S_t), and psychological (P_t). Algebraically this relationship is expressed as follows:

$$R_t = f(D_t, E_t, S_t, P_t). \tag{1-5}$$

The primary purpose of this book is to determine with greater precision the variables, their functional relationships, and models for projecting them over time, thereby enabling projections of R_t to R_{t+1}. It will become evident that the measures and models available for a demand analysis are frequently very crude, so that this analysis may be more of an art than a science.

Economic variables to be considered during a demand analysis begin with measures of general economic conditions. Then industry conditions are examined. And finally, the economic potential of the market segment is considered. Product price, personal income, and expectations for future income are important variables in this last stage of an economic analysis. The Mustang provides an example of the three stages of economic analysis for product planning (Chapter 4). Also included in that chapter are examples of using economic demand analyses to assist with the tactical decisions of allocating promotional effort for consumer and industrial goods.

A theoretical discussion and practical examples of price and income models appear in Chapter 5. That chapter includes also the concept of *market share*. Market share is simply the percent of industry sales that was made by a brand. In a high-volume industry, such as packaged grocery products, a small change in market share translates into a large change in sales. The demand for brand j in time t (B_{jt}) may be expressed as follows:

$$B_{jt} = M_{jt}G_t \qquad (1\text{--}6)$$

where M_{jt} is the market share for brand j in time t, and G_t is the generic demand in time t. The importance of market share in some industries has resulted in the development of econometric models that relate a firm's market share to the marketing effort of the firm relative to the effort of the industry. One equation that is considered in Chapter 5 may be expressed in shortened form as follows:

$$M_{jt} = \lambda M_{j(t-1)} + f\left(\frac{ME_{jt}}{ME_{It}}\right) \qquad (1\text{--}7)$$

where λ estimates the cumulative effect of the relative marketing effort prior to the present time period, ME_{jt} is the marketing effort of firm j, and ME_{It} is the marketing effort of the industry. The ratio ME_{jt}/ME_{It} is the share of marketing effort expended by firm j relative to the total effort. An example and some of the limitations of this approach are discussed. One of the limitations is that it tends to ignore the fact that promotional effort also expands generic demand. Promotional expenditures may vary generic demand through Equation 1–5 as an economic variable that influences usage rates.

Society influences demand by prescribing acceptable behavior for meeting individual and group needs. Social concepts such as culture, personal values and beliefs, social class, life cycles, and role are explored for measures and models that will explain and predict demand. Social communication networks are examined because of their influence on the adoption of innovations. These concepts and networks are examined in Chapter 6. The theories, measures, and models of these concepts and networks are discussed in Chapter 7. Included in this discussion are instruments to measure psychographics and activities. An analysis of these instruments reveals that they are really measuring situation specific personality variables.[4]

The usage rate of a product or service will be influenced by the social concept known as the *rate of adoption*. This rate will vary among groups and among individuals. As more people in a group adopt an innovation there will be a snowballing effect because adopters in one period exert an influence in subsequent periods. The rate of adoption and the snowballing effect may be expressed by the following equation:

$$\delta y / \delta t = k y (1 - y) \tag{1-8}$$

where $\delta y / \delta t$ is the rate of adoption, y is the cumulative proportion of individuals who have adopted the innovation, and k is a constant that represents the receptivity of the group. This model and other models related to the adoption process will be discussed in Chapter 7.

Psychological approaches to a study of demand emphasize the attributes or benefits that the buyer perceives in a product or service. Brands are mapped into n-dimensional space where the dimensions are these attributes or benefits. Competitive brands appear close together in this space. Opportunities for new brands may appear as holes in the space where no present brand exists. Brand preference may be represented in terms of the distance of a brand from an ideal brand. Examples in Chapter 8 include metric and nonmetric mapping of brands as well as measures of awareness and attitudes that are useful for product development and promotional strategies.

Instead of modeling market share (M_{jt}) using economic variables, as in Equation 1–7, share may be modeled using psychological variables. Market share is a function of brand preference, which is related to the Euclidean

---

[4] Because personality may be defined as patterns of behavior for coping with one's environment, instruments for measuring activities seem more appropriate to a discussion of social influences than to the discussion of cognitive information processing, the subject of Chapter 9.

distance between a given brand (B_j) and an ideal brand (I) as
projected into n-dimensional attribute space. Thus,

$$M_{jt} \approx f(P_j) \tag{1-}$$

$$\frac{1}{P_j} \approx b_0 + b_1 d^2_{Ij} \tag{1-10}$$

$$d_{Ij} = \sqrt{\sum_{i=1}^{n} S_i(I_i - B_{ij})^2} \tag{1-11}$$

where P_j is the preference rank of brand j, d_{Ij} is the Euclidean distance
between the ideal brand (I) and brand j, S_i is the salience or importance
of attribute i in the buying decision, I is the projection of the ideal brand
along attribute i, and B_{ij} is the projection of brand j along the same
attribute. This psychological market share model will be discussed in
Chapter 9.

Psychological variables tend to be important in those industries in which
competition is keen and a few market share points can mean brand success
or failure. Psychological models of demand attempt to explain how buyers
mentally process brand information and change their brand preferences.
The most commonly used models have been adapted from learning theory
and communication theory. Implementation of these models requires techniques to identify salient product attributes and instruments to measure
awareness, attitudes, and subjective probabilities of buying. These models,
techniques, and instruments are discussed in Chapter 9.

THE MARKETING PLAN

The demand analysis is one step in the development of a marketing
plan. It follows the identification of organizational goals and precedes the
selection of a marketing mix. The information required for the development of a marketing plan comes from numerous sources, both internal
and external to the firm. In this section we consider the position of a demand analysis in the marketing plan, the types of marketing mix decisions
that require a demand analysis, and some of the sources of information
that are used during a demand analysis.

Positioning demand analysis in the marketing plan

In Figure 1–2 it will be noted that a demand analysis lies between the
identification of the goals of an organization and the development of a
strategy, which includes the selection of a marketing mix. The analyses
of demand and competition reveal marketing opportunities. Feedback

FIGURE 1–2
The relation of demand analysis to long-range planning

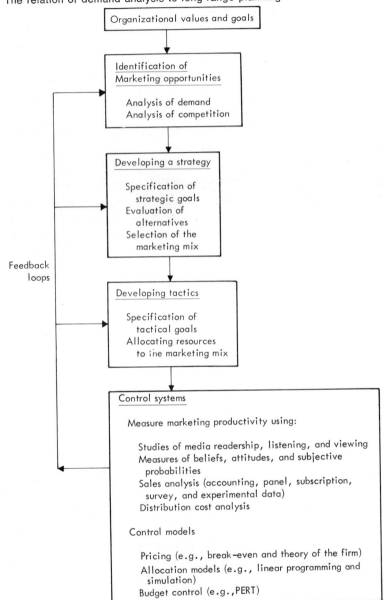

loops from control systems aid in the revision of the estimates of potential demand and competitive influences.

Market potential is an unmet need plus the ability to purchase. The measurement of potential should not be confused with forecasting. A forecast predicts sales, given an existing product or service and a projected marketing strategy.[5] An analysis of potential identifies an unmet need, which leads to the development of a strategy. A marketing opportunity is a potential that is not being met by a competitor.

The importance of measuring market potential can be demonstrated by noting that 20 percent of an average company's current sales comes from products that it introduced within the past five years, the cost of successful new products must include the cost of failures, and the failure rate sometimes runs as high as 80 percent for all products introduced. Yet, a survey of 125 members of The Conference Board's Senior Marketing Executive Panel revealed that inadequate market analysis was the primary cause of new product failure; 45 percent of the companies cited this cause (Hopkins and Bailey, 1971).

Marketing plans focus on those functions of an organization which (1) determine consumers' needs, (2) develop products or services to meet these needs, and (3) distribute and sell these products in accordance with the goals of the organization (Plattes, 1971). The goals of a business organization may be profit maximization or maintaining a return on investment. The goals of a health-care organization would be expressed in terms of maintaining or improving the health of society. A nonprofit organization such as a governmental agency may have as its goal maintaining the power to act in the future.

The strategic goals of companies and organizations are not limited to the maximization of profits. Studies of corporations by economists, management scientists, and organizational theorists have revealed additional goals such as maximization of growth and market share with a minimum-profit constraint (Baumol, 1967), avoidance of loss (Drucker, 1954), survival (Alderson, 1957), maximization of the executive's lifetime income (Monsen and Downs, 1965), maximization of profit subject to a constraint on sales (Osborne, 1964), return on investment (Lanzillotti, 1958), and creation of a corporate image (Boulding, 1956). Nonprofit organizations have similar goals, such as survival, maximization of power, and retaining the power to act.

Tactical marketing goals give direction to the implementation of marketing strategies. Measures of productivity reveal whether the system has ex-

---

[5] For a recent review of forecasting techniques, see Chambers, Millick, and Smith (1971).

ceeded or fallen short of the goals. Control models provide a means for the early detection of deviation and for the redirection of effort. If the system has fallen short, additional resources may be added. If it has exceeded the goals, it may be possible to reallocate excess resources to other projects.

Tactical goals must be expressed in terms of the magnitude of the goal and the time required to achieve the goal. For example, a well-stated goal would be, "Increase sales 8 percent during the next year," or, "Increase the market share of product A by 2 points during the next six months." Failure to express goals with such precision renders control systems useless. Yet many companies do not define their marketing goals in terms of magnitude and time. The tactical goals of the Humble Oil Company, for instance, were to increase sales faster than 3.5 percent, the annual growth rate in the industry, to increase the ratio of premium to regular gas sales, to switch customers from other brands, and to increase the sale of tires, batteries, and accessories in proportion to increases in the sale of gasoline (*Marketing Insights,* November 28, 1966). These goals are better than none, but they lack specificity with regard to time and degree. What level of "faster than 3.5 percent" is acceptable? When would the system be declared out of control? If the defined goal were a 4.5 percent increase in sales per year (1.0 percent above the industry growth rate), productivity measures would give more specific control to the system. Brand switching should be expressed in terms of changes in market share. All of the goals should have included a deadline for accomplishment so the control systems could track progress over time.

In many cases the most important dimensions of a plan are measured only vaguely. Objectives are not defined precisely. Potential is not measured. Strategies fail to assess the impact of competition and its potential reaction. Methods of control are not coordinated with objectives. But measurement is vital; ". . . because what we measure and how we measure determines what will be considered relevant, and determines thereby not just what we see, but what we—and others—do, measurements are all-important in the planning process" (Drucker, 1959).

Demand as a prerequisite to marketing mix decisions

Many of the decisions to be made when developing a marketing mix strategy depend on a knowledge of the characteristics of generic and brand demand. Frequent marketing mix questions requiring this knowledge are summarized in Table 1–1 according to the four disciplines that contribute to an understanding of demand. Reading down the columns of this table

TABLE 1–1
Frequent marketing mix questions requiring a knowledge of demand

	Multidisciplinary dimensions of demand contributing to the mix decision			
Marketing mix	*Demographic*	*Economic*	*Social*	*Social-psychological*
Product/service	What are the needs of the individual that can be identified by age, education, geographic location, and other demographic variables?	Are general business and industry conditions favorable to a new product introduction? Is the product income elastic?	What needs does society emphasize? Do buyers conform to social norms? Will life styles predict usage?	
Price	Will youth discounts develop later loyalty? Do regional brands create problems in pricing policies?	Is the product price elastic? Is a discount to the channel more effective than one to the consumer?		
Distribution	What channels of distribution will be required to reach buyers in each geographic location?	What is the best sales force incentive system? What is the best discount structure for the channel of distribution?		
Promotion	How should sales territories be defined? What media are required to reach prospects in various locations?	Can promotional expenditures be related to sales? What is the cumulative effect of past promotions? What is the return on promotional effort?	How will innovators and social communication networks influence the acceptance and usage rates of a new product?	How is the brand perceived in attribute space relative to competitive brands? What copy strategy would improve attribute awareness, attitudes, and brand preference?

reveals the relative importance of each discipline to each element in the marketing mix—product/service, price, distribution, and promotion. Demographic and economic variables contribute to each element. Social variables contribute largely to product and promotion decisions. Social-psychological variables make their greatest contribution in promotional decisions, especially the positioning of a brand among its competitors. Social-psychological variables, therefore, tend to be more important in highly competitive industries. Reading across the rows of this table reveals the complexity of promotional decisions. Answers to key questions are sought in all of the disciplines.

Information systems for planning

A continuous flow of information is required for the development and execution of a marketing plan. The information may be generated within the firm, marketing research may be required, and low-cost secondary information may be used. Table 1–2 illustrates the types of studies conducted by several departments of a typical integrated oil company. This table represents an expansion on the long-range planning steps noted in Figure 1–2. An examination of the types of studies (shown in the rows) reveals the decisions made by oil company marketing executives. The participating departments (columns) illustrate that the generation of marketing information within a market-oriented company requires the cooperation of many departments.

The marketing decision process is facilitated by a flow of timely information presented in the correct form. Because of the complexity of market information and the variety of primary and secondary sources of such information, many firms are developing marketing intelligence systems. A flowchart of the system used by Mead Johnson, a drug company, is shown in Figure 1–3. The sources of information, which appear in the left-hand column, include primary, secondary, and syndicated sources. A primary source is a study conducted by the company, in contrast to secondary sources such as government and trade publications. Special consumer studies, for example, are a primary source. Syndicated sources are systems for continuously collecting data about specific product classes. The movement of proprietary drugs is monitored at the retail level by marketing research firms which audit the inventories of a panel of food and drug stores. The movement is monitored at the consumer level by panels of consumers who report all purchases in a weekly diary. In addition to supplying brand sales and market share data, consumer panels provide demographic, economic, and social-psychological data about consumers.

TABLE 1–2
Departments in an integrated oil company that participate in marketing studies

Types of studies	Market research	Eco-nomics	Adver-tising	Org. and cost control	Product engi-neering	Public relations	Whole-sale	Retail
Organization								
Development of organization changes				X			X	X
Sales compensation analysis	X			X				X
Comparisons of organization, wages and salaries with other companies	X							
Demand Analysis								
Economic studies								
Business conditions and forecasts		X						
Petroleum products forecasts	X	X						
Special markets	X						X	X
Capital budget coordination	X						X	X
Market potentials								
By product	X	X					X	X
By territories	X	X						
By class of trade	X	X						
Potential competition	X	X						
Profit potentials	X						X	X
Consumer surveys								
Buying habits			X		X			
Motivation	X		X			X		
Attitudes			X					
Industrial surveys								
Buying requirements	X	X					X	
Buying influences	X						X	
Attitudes	X						X	
Sales								
Potential	X	X					X	X
Territory determination				X				
Quotas				X				
Forecasts	X	X					X	X
Product mix	X						X	X
Market share	X	X					X	X
Competitive Analysis								
Competitive activity	X	X	X		X		X	X
Competitive reaction	X							X
Competitive price structures	X						X	
Supply and manufacturing capabilities		X						
Marketing Mix								
Product								
Product line analyses					X			
Packaging analyses					X			
Product name studies			X		X			
New products								
Development					X			
Testing					X			
Packaging			X		X			

TABLE 1–2 (Continued)

Types of studies	Market research	Economics	Advertising	Org. and cost control	Product Engineering	Public relations	Wholesale	Retail
Name.					X			
Acceptance evaluation			X		X			
Marketing method studies	X				X		X	X
New use studies					X			
Prices								
Development of pricing recommendations	X						X	X
Price structure development	X						X	X
Trends; relationships (time/area)	X		X				X	X
Reseller discounts or commissions	X						X	
Advertising and promotion								
Advertising effectiveness			X					
Media evaluation			X					
Copy testing			X					
Sales promotion effectiveness			X					
Public relations								
Public attitude studies			X			X		
Employee attitude studies						X		
Dealer attitude studies						X		X
Distributor attitude studies							X	
Stockholder attitude studies						X		
Distribution: Service stations								
Location studies								X
Potentials calculation								X
Performance analyses	X							X
Layout and design studies								X
Operation studies	X							X
Premiums and giveaways	X							X
Return on investment analysis	X							X
Competitive construction	X							X
Control								
Profitability analyses								
By product	X				X		X	X
By area	X			X			X	X
By channel	X			X			X	X
By customer classes	X			X			X	X
Distribution cost analysis	X			X			X	X
Sales methods of distribution policy	X			X			X	X
Discounts and allowances	X						X	X
Transfer value negotiations	X							

Source: American Petroleum Institute (1957), pp. 159–61, adapted.

FIGURE 1–3

Mead Johnson's marketing intelligence system

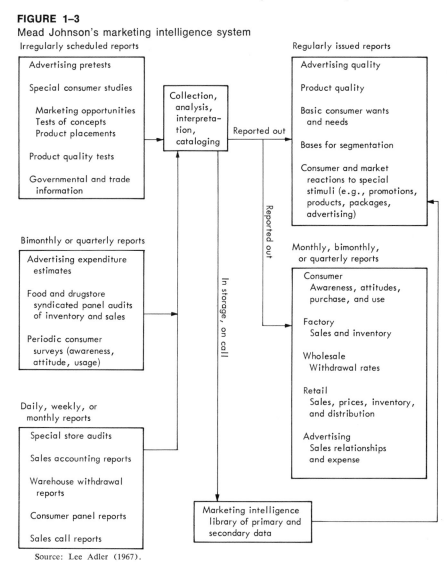

Source: Lee Adler (1967).

Figure 1–3 indicates that Mead Johnson subscribes to retail and consumer panel data. Company accounting, salesmen, and warehouse records complete the sources of information. The output of the information, the right-hand column of Figure 1–3, consists of reports in the form needed by marketing decision makers.

Marketing planners in the United States and Europe are fortunate in having invaluable sources of data that are readily available at nominal costs. The Mustang case, in Chapter 2, is an example of how readily available data can generate an idea that will lead to a successful new product. These data are collected and published by the Bureau of the Census, by media, by publishers of directories, and by research organizations that make their data available on syndicated bases. An annotated bibliography of research sources for demand analysis may be found in Appendix A. The reader who has never explored these published sources will be amazed to learn the magnitude of published information and its ready availability. The more than 150 sources annotated in the appendix represent those sources that are most relevant to a demand analysis. There is no attempt to exhaust the published data that may be relevant to all marketing studies.

The benefits of planning

A survey of 90 manufacturing companies revealed the following benefits of business planning: (1) improved definition of objectives; (2) better communication among the functions, staff, and decentralized units; (3) earlier awareness of opportunities; (4) stronger commitments to goals because of participation in planning; (5) reduction in crisis management; (6) better managerial performance through the discipline of the plan; (7) better evaluation of managerial performance; (8) greater capacity for managing change; and (9) improvement in earnings (Egerton and Brown, 1971).

Planning may be defined as anticipatory decision making (Ackoff, 1970) or the anticipation of changes for which decisions will be required (Hilton, 1970). The planning process is not without its limitations. There is the danger of planning's being regarded as a panacea and a substitute for sound judgment. There is the difficulty of reconciling corporate and divisional objectives. Failure to execute plans and to follow-up with reviews may be the result of planning's becoming an end in itself. Perhaps the greatest danger is the tendency of plans to become rigid and therefore insensitive to change. When the latter occurs, planning violates its reason for being—the anticipation of change.

MARKETING'S ROLE IN SOCIAL CHANGE

The marketplace of a nation mirrors its political philosophy toward change. Nations that tend toward broad distribution of political power and genuine choices for leadership tend also toward a broad distribution of wealth and choice in the marketplace (Lipset, 1959). The marketplace in a developing economy performs functions beyond those of simply distributing goods. Marketing methods can be used by many organizations other than profit-oriented firms. These broader roles of marketing should be considered.

Economic development

The function of the marketplace is not limited to that of distributing production. The marketplace stimulates production when the producer is able to share in the benefits of increased productivity and quality. For example, the lack of a grading system and a pricing system associated with the grading system can reduce the quality of output. A farmer who does not receive a higher price for improved products will allow quality to deteriorate to the minimum acceptable level. Similarly, if an increase in productivity means only a surplus that cannot be stored or distributed to distant markets, lower prices will leave the farmer where he was before improvements in farming techniques, except that he will be able to produce previous quantities with less effort. The economy will not advance.

The obvious difficulties in getting incentives back to producers include (1) a lack of capital at low interest rates, (2) inadequate transportation and storage, and (3) the lack of facilities for handling and grading. Less obvious difficulties include (1) defective communication systems and a lack of market information; (2) a lack of coordination between production and marketing; and (3) a shortage of trained marketing personnel who are competent, honest, and politically independent (Abbott, 1962). Establishing a viable marketing system in a developing and unstable economy can be a substantial challenge.

As the physiological needs of a population are met, its social-psychological needs emerge. To maintain freedom of choice the marketing manager must provide ". . . a choice that is not confined to price alone, but that explores the full dimensions of the consumption experience" (McKitterick, 1957).

Marketing nonbusiness services

The philosophy of the *marketing concept* requires that the development of products, services, distribution, and promotion evolves from an understanding of human needs. This philosophy has been practiced by manufacturers for several decades, by retailers for over a century, but only recently adopted by nonbusiness institutions (Kotler, 1970). A survey of postal patrons played a key role in the reorganization of the U.S. Post Office (Arthur D. Little, Inc., 1968). The Federal Housing Authority studies the need for housing in local communities. A request for federal funds for a new transportation system requires supporting evidence in the form of a demand analysis (Fertal et al., 1966). Marketing techniques have been applied to the marketing of health services (Zaltman and Vertinsky, 1971; and White, 1970), the management of programs for family planning (O'Connor, 1970; Urban, 1970; and Farley and Leavitt, 1968 and 1970), politics (Hoover, 1970), fund raising (Mindak and Bybee, 1971), and religion (Engel, 1970). Thus demand analyses can play an important role in many forms of social change, as noted recently by Kotler and Zaltman (1971).

Marketing media stimulate social change. The mass media bring innovations to all social strata simultaneously. It is no longer necessary for new products to trickle down from the elite to lower social classes. Television, more than any other medium, has made viewers aware of new life styles and aware of means for changes in the system that will enable them to participate in these new styles. Chipman (1965) observed that "revolutions are brought about not because people are poor but because they discover that they can alleviate their poverty." Television has brought into the homes of many segments of society a desire for a better life style and an awareness that change is possible.

The need to understand the individual

When an economy and a society are guided by the decisions of individuals, an understanding of these decisions is a prerequisite to an understanding of the economic and social systems that they control. Developing an understanding of these decisions is an enormous task. In the United States, for example, the marketing system is the product of billions of decisions in many different environments. These environments include 62 million households, 2.9 million farms, 312,000 manufacturing establishments, 1.8 million retail establishments, 311,000 wholesale establishments, and 1.2 million service establishments (U.S. Bureau of the Census, 1970). To these decisions in the private sector of the economy we must add the decisions by federal, state, and local governments to complete the domestic decision processes. The economy is influenced also by decisions in other countries through imports and exports. Demand analysis is the process for attempting to understand these decisions.

Understanding the individual decision process is greatly complicated by the fact that the individual may have many motives for behaving. *Physiological* man is interested in supporting life, so that value is in *use*. *Economic* man exchanges goods to maximize their *utility* to him. Utility is not limited to the physical functions of a good, as is implicit in the value of use because utility allows for differences in tastes. *Sociological* man behaves in a manner that is consonant with his perception of his several roles in the groups with which he associates. Thus, his values are determined by *role expectations*. *Psychological* man strives for tension reduction by processing information in ways that will bring into equilibrium his beliefs, attitudes, goals, and behavior. The value system of psychological man may be described as *cognitive consonance*. To understand buying motives, therefore, it is necessary to understand the buyer's values at the moment he is making a decision. An individual will attempt to optimize different values in different decision situations. By considering each discipline separately the planner can select the appropriate models and measures after he has identified the buyers' value systems. For example, a housewife may use physiological and economic values when selecting a brand of food for the family, but she will use sociological and psychological values when buying for guests. The appropriate models and measures to describe and predict her behavior differ in these two cases.

FROM A DEMAND ANALYSIS TO PROMOTIONAL TACTICS

In practice the marketing planner does not consider each discipline separately; instead, he must consider them simultaneously and also the relationships among them in order to understand the motives that lead to demand. To illustrate how the many dimensions of demand lead to the development of strategy and tactics we will consider a hypothetical example of a bank's offering a new service and the development of a promotional plan for a specific market segment.

Developing a strategy from a demand analysis

Assume that a bank wants to identify the market segment that will generate the greatest revenue for a new service it is introducing. The service enables users of regular checking accounts to use their accounts as a bookkeeping system, thereby facilitating family budgeting and completing of tax forms. Each check and each deposit slip can be assigned one of 10 account numbers by checking one of 10 small boxes on these forms. The bank's computer, in addition to charging or crediting the customer's account, will record the amount of the transaction in the subaccounts designated by the customer. Monthly statements will show the usual checks and deposits plus the balances in each subaccount.

Table 1–3 illustrates the type of multidisciplinary data that would be

TABLE 1–3

Market segments for a new banking service

Behavioral characteristics	Segments		
	Personal accounts		Business accounts
	Anxious	*Affluent*	*<5 employees*
Demographic			
Age	42	42	39
Education	High school	Two or more years of college	Heterogeneous
Residence	Urban and suburban	Suburban	Suburban
Occupation	Blue collar and clerks	Executives, salesmen, and engineers	Lawyers, small retailers, and craftsmen
Economic			
Income.	$10,000	$21,000	$18,000
Acceptable monthly charge	$0.10	$0.50	$1.00
Social			
Dominant beliefs about banks	Safe, stable	Facilitate transactions	Basic to financial management
Life style	Worrier	Outgoing optimist	Very mixed
Reference groups	Relatives and friends	Professional and business	Professional and business
Sources of information about innovations . . .	TV, relatives, and friends	Business associates and trade papers	TV, friends, business, trade papers, and journals
Life cycle	Youngest child <15	Youngest child 10–15	Youngest child 10–15
Social class	Upper lower	Upper middle	Mixed
Psychological			
Criteria of good money management	Security	Growth and to avoid inflation	Profit and keep capital working
Attitudes toward Bank A	Friendly, convenient locations	Working-class bank, not convenient	Old-fashioned convenient locations
Bank B	For rich people, not convenient	Modern, most convenient	Modern, business oriented
Bank C	Vague image, little known	New bank, aggressive	Out for new business, innovative
Attitudes toward new service	For those who need a budget	Income tax aid, help plan family finances	Supplement to present accounting
Subjective probabilities of using service by—			
Present depositors . . .	0.20	0.15	0.10
Depositors switching from other banks. . .	0.05	0.01	0.01
Noncustomers opening an account	0.07	0.00	0.00
Market characteristics			
Bank A market share. . .	30%	20%	20%
Number of accounts (all banks).	40,000	10,000	1,200
Prospects with no checking account	30,000	0	0

generated by conducting a demand analysis of potential subscribers to this new service. Two major segments are identified, personal and small business checking account customers. The personal account customers are segmented further into two additional segments. An examination of the profiles of each suggests that the first may be called the *anxious* segment and the second may be labeled the *affluent* segment.

A comparison of the columns for the individual accounts demonstrates how the dimensions of demand reveal motivations for using bank services. In this case age does not distinguish the segments, education and residence reveal some difference, but occupation provides a clearer basis for explaining differences in motivation. The income of the affluent is twice that of the anxious segment. The importance of the new service to the affluent segment is reflected in their willingness to pay more for the service.

Sociological and psychological variables reveal sharper distinctions between the first two segments. Worriers view banks as institutions for security while the affluent see them in their facilitating role. Additional comparisons may be made to reveal differences in behavioral styles, reference groups, sources of information, life cycle stage, class, attitudes toward the three commercial banks serving the community, attitudes toward the new service, and the subjective probability of using the service.

An examination of Table 1–3 by the management of bank A can lead to several quite different strategies, each based on a different perception of an appropriate goal. The ego of the management may suggest a modernization program to correct the image among small businessmen that the bank is old-fashioned. The desire to be the largest bank in the community would require a strategy to increase the bank's market share by switching customers from other banks and by attracting a larger share of new residents. A goal of maximizing bank revenue requires strategies for selling more services to present customers and attracting new customers.[6] The data in Table 1–3 provide the basis for analyzing the expected revenue for each segment.

The expected revenue for each segment is summarized in Table 1–4. This analysis reveals that a goal of improving the image among small businessmen would be inconsistent with the goal of maximizing expected revenue by a factor of 50 to 1. Similarly, a strategy designed to attract the affluent because they have a greater need for the service and would pay more is also inconsistent with the goal of maximizing expected revenue. In terms of revenue, the greatest advantage of the new service is its promotional value that will attract new customers. Banks' other business, such

---

[6] Whether a strategy of revenue maximization results in profit maximization depends on the shape of the revenue and cost curves (Baumol, 1967).

TABLE 1–4
Expected revenue generated by a new bank service; bank A

| | Monthly expected revenue generated by segments | | |
| | Personal accounts | | Business accounts |
Type of prospect	Anxious	Affluent	<5 employees
Present customers (accounts × share × probability of use × monthly charge).	$240	$150	$24.00
Customers who switch New service (accounts × (1 – share) × probability of using × monthly charge)	140	40	9.60
Other services*.	1,400	160	50.00
New depositors New service	210	. . .	. . .
Other services	2,100	. . .	. . .
Total expected revenue	$4,090	$350	$81.60

* Estimated monthly revenue per customer is as follows: anxious, $1; affluent, $2; small business, $5.

as safe-deposit boxes, auto loans, and mortgages, generates more revenue than the new service.

Assuming that bank A has a goal of maximizing revenue, a marketing strategy and tactics should be developed for promoting the new service to the first segment. The best strategy would be one that reinforces the beliefs and attitudes presently held by the segment. To accomplish this reinforcement the promotional message should present the service as a new convenience that reduces worry and enhances the security of sound money management. The influence of friends could be incorporated by using testimonial ads. Later promotion might emphasize the need for, good money management by children.

Developing promotional tactics from a demand analysis

The initial goal of promotion is an informational one—making the anxious segment aware of bank A's service. The second-stage goal should reflect some action on the part of the prospect, such as requesting more information or subscribing to the new service. After the segment becomes aware of the service, the promotional goal should shift from being informative to being persuasive. The success of the latter goal could be measured by changes in subjective probabilities of subscribing.

Possible tactics are summarized in Table 1–5. The messages for each planning period reflect the profile shown in Table 1–3. The media stress

TABLE 1–5
A promotional plan for a new bank service; bank A (market segment: anxious)

Promotional mix	Planning periods (P)		
	P_0 to P_1	P_1 to P_2	P_2 to P_3
Promotional goals	Make 20% of the community aware of the new service	Make 40% of the community aware; sign up 20% of the aware group	Make 60% aware; sign up 30% of aware group (i.e., 18% of prospects); increase probability of use to 0.25
Messages	"New security and convenience for family money management"	"Reduce worry over family money management"	"A friend will thank you for recommending this new service" "Youth accounts for young money managers"
Media	TV, in-bank promotions, training bank personnel, direct mail with bank statement	Same as previous period but drop direct mail and add sales contest for bank personnel	Same as previous but add premium to present customers who bring a friend or open a youth account
Research	Measure effectiveness	Measure effectiveness	Measure effectiveness Estimate the elasticity of lower service charge

the importance of TV and friends as sources of information about innovations. The promotional goals during the initial planning periods measure promotional effectiveness in terms of prospect information processing and observable behavior during later periods. Planning periods need not be of equal intervals. During the early stages of a new product introduction close monitoring may require short periods of a few weeks or a month. Once the product becomes established the planning period may be increased to three or six months. Research should be included in the tactical plan to provide feedback for revision of strategies and tactics.

SUMMARY

Planning for change in business and nonbusiness organizations requires an understanding of demand. In the marketing plan, analysis of demand is a prerequisite to the development of strategies and tactics that enable the organization to attain its goals. After the plan has been executed, feedback loops from control systems enable the revision of initial demand estimates.

The demand for economic goods and services is the result of decisions by individuals who are trying to meet their physiological, social, and individual needs within their economic limitations. Measures of potential demand are made by identifying the determinants of these decisions. The process of demand analysis draws on theories, models, and measures from demography, economics, sociology, and psychology.

READING QUESTIONS

1. What is a demand analysis?
2. What are the components of demand?
3. What marketing decisions depend on a demand analysis?
4. Is a demand analysis the same as a forecast?
5. What are the advantages and disadvantages of planning?
6. Do you agree with the bank promotional strategy outlined in Table 1–5?

CLASS DISCUSSION QUESTIONS

1. Arrange a debate between two teams to debate the following statement: Marketing is a capitalistic phenomenon.
2. Select a product or service and develop tables like Tables 1–3, 1–4, and 1–5.
3. Develop a marketing intelligence system like Figure 1–2 for an organization with which you are familiar. Appendix A of marketing information sources should be consulted.
4. ". . . the present trends towards aggregation of the population in a few megalopoli by the turn of the century are indeed reversible; they are not natural forces, or a natural consequence of the industrial revolution, or a natural expression of social preference." (Williams, 1971, p. 8.) Discuss the marketing implications of reversing this trend.
5. In a discussion of national and corporate goals, Williams (1971) envisions four possible futures for society: (*a*) nonsurvival, (*b*) technocracy, (*c*) meritocracy (a more humanistic technocracy), and (*d*) a person-centered society. Discuss the role of marketing in each of these futures.

SUGGESTED CASE BOOKS

BLACKWELL, ROGER D.; ENGEL, JAMES F.; and KOLLAT, DAVID T. *Cases in Consumer Behavior*. New York: Holt, Rinehart & Winston, Inc., 1969.

BOYD, HARPER W. JR., and DAVIS, ROBERT T. *Marketing Management Casebook*. Homewood, Ill.: Richard D. Irwin, Inc., 1971.

BURSK, EDWARD C. *Cases in Marketing Management*. Englewood Cliffs, N.J.: Prentice-Hall, Inc., 1965.

————, and GREYSER, STEPHEN A. *Advanced Cases in Marketing Management*. Englewood Cliffs, N.J.: Prentice-Hall, Inc., 1968.

NEWMAN, JOSEPH W. *Marketing Management and Information: A New Case Approach.* Homewood, Ill.: Richard D. Irwin, Inc., 1967.

SUGGESTED CASES

Austin Company. Boyd and Davis (1971), pp. 46–54.

The Austin Company made a special paste solder for sealing joints in air, fuel, and hydraulic lines. Sales were highest in the industries classified as electrical equipment, machinery, and fabricated metal products. A survey revealed that Austin's market share was 8.3 percent but that only 1.9 percent of the users expressed a preference for Austin products.

1. Identify marketing and communication goals for Austin Company.
2. What additional information about solder users is necessary to develop a marketing plan?

Mead Johnson (B): Cultural influences on the use of diet foods (Metrecal). Blackwell, Engel, and Kollat (1969), pp. 113–20.

A new Metrecal promotional campaign requires an evaluation of the motivations for using diet foods.

1. Develop a table, like Table 1–3 in this text, to summarize the demographic, economic, social, and psychological dimensions of the major market segments identified in this case.
2. If you worked for Mead Johnson, what internal sources of information could you use to refine the table developed in question 1?

SUGGESTED READINGS

BARNETT, NORMAN L. "Beyond Market Segmentation," *Harvard Business Review,* Vol. 46, No. 5 (January–February 1969), pp. 152–66.

BEATTIE, D. W. "Marketing a New Product," *Operational Research Quarterly,* Vol. 20, No. 4 (December 1969), pp. 429–35.

BERENSON, CONRAD. "Marketing Information Systems," *Journal of Marketing,* Vol. 33 (October 1969), pp. 16–23.

CLAYCAMP, HENRY J., and LIDDY, LUCIEN E. "Prediction of New Product Performance: An Analytical Approach," *Journal of Marketing Research,* Vol. 6, No. 4 (November 1969), pp. 414–20.

FRANK, R. E.; MASSY, W. F.; and WIND, Y. *Market Segmentation.* Englewood Cliffs, N.J.: Prentice-Hall, Inc., 1972.

KELLEY, EUGENE J. *Marketing Planning and Competitive Strategy.* Englewood Cliffs, N.J.: Prentice-Hall, Inc., 1972.

KOTLER, PHILIP. *Marketing Decision Making: A Model Building Approach,* chap. 18, "The Marketing Information System"; chap. 19, "Planning and Control Processes in Marketing Organization"; chap. 20, "Implementing Management Science in Marketing"; and chap. 21, "Developing the Corporate Marketing Model." New York: Holt, Rinehart & Winston, Inc., 1971.

LEVITT, THEODORE. *The Marketing Mode—Pathways to Corporate Growth.* New York: McGraw-Hill Book Co., 1969.

LUCK, D. J. "Interfaces of a Product Manager," *Journal of Marketing,* Vol. 33 (October 1969), pp. 32–36.

NORTH, HARPER Q., and PYKE, D. L. " 'Probes' of the Technological Future," *Harvard Business Review,* May–June 1969, pp. 68–82.

ROBINSON, PATRICK J., and LUCK, DAVID J. *Promotional Decision Making: Practice and Theory.* New York: McGraw-Hill Book Co., 1964.

SCHREIRER, F., and NICOSIA, F. M. *Marketing Research: A Behavioral Approach.* Belmont, Calif.: Wadsworth Publishing Co., Inc., in press.

SEVIN, CHARLES H. *Marketing Productivity Analysis.* New York: McGraw-Hill Book Co., 1965.

SMITH, S. V.; BRIEN, R. H.; and STAFFORD, J. E. *Readings in Marketing Information Systems.* Boston, Mass.: Houghton Mifflin Co., 1968.

STASCH, S. F. *Systems Analysis for Marketing Planning and Control.* Glenview, Ill.: Scott, Foresman and Co., 1972.

STURDIVANT, F. E., et al. *Managerial Analysis in Marketing.* Glenview, Ill.: Scott, Foresman and Co., 1970.

THURSTON, PHILIP H. "Make TF Serve Corporate Planning," *Harvard Business Review,* September–October 1971, pp. 98–102.

URBAN, GLEN L. "Sprinter Mod III—A Model for the Analysis of New Frequently Purchased Consumer Products," *Operations Research,* Vol. 18, No. 5 (September–October 1970), pp. 805–54.

2

Illustrative cases in demographic demand analysis

The cases presented in this chapter illustrate how demographic data are used to estimate the number of persons in a market segment (N_{kt}) and their usage rate (R_{kt}). It will be recalled from Chapter 1 that the product of these variables ($N_{kt}R_{kt}$) is the generic demand for a product or service. Each case should be read with the following questions in mind: First, how were the important variables identified? (Most of the cases in this chapter seem to rely on intuition and experience. Examples in later chapters will illustrate applications of multivariate statistical methods for variable identification.) Secondly, was the relationship among these variables expressed as a verbal or an algebraic model and how was this relationship determined? And finally, what was the source and the cost of the data? (These cases illustrate that demographic demand analysis tends to cost the least of the four disciplines.)

The four examples fit several classifications. There are three cases that analyze demand for consumer goods or services and one that analyzes demand for an industrial product. Two cases (Mustang and the electronics firm) focus on the private sector of the economy, and two are concerned with demand that influences both the public and private sectors of the economy (Port of New York Authority and housing in Tulsa). Three examples examine the demand for products, and one considers the demand for a service. The cases vary also according to planning horizons. The forecast for housing in Tulsa was for one year, while the Port of New York Authority made a 10-year forecast. (Longer forecasts are more sensitive to demographic variables than short forecasts, so assumptions about demographic variables must be tested.)

CONSUMER PRODUCTS

The first three cases illustrate demographic demand analysis for consumer products or services. The Mustang case is a classic illustration of the development of a new product to meet the needs of a market segmented by age. The Port of New York Authority procedure for forecasting airplane trips illustrates how demand can be estimated for many segments which are defined demographically. This case illustrates also the need to test long-range forecasts for their sensitivity to the assumptions made about demographic rates. The Tulsa case illustrates that demand analysis for housing is more of an art than a science and that the analyst must be creative in seeking out unusual sources of information—a survey by letter carriers in this instance. At the conclusion of these cases some generalizations and limitations of demographic market segmentation will be discussed. These cases were selected because they represent products and a service that are familiar; the reader can use his intuition to follow the demand analysis. Discussion problems appear at the end of the chapter, with suggested solutions in Appendix B, so that the reader may test his ability to identify variables for a demographic demand analysis.

Segmentation by age—the Mustang[1]

In 1963 the planners at the Ford Motor Company examined readily available demographic data in search of new product opportunities. The data (Figure 2–1) revealed that the crest of postwar babies had reached the driving age, and therefore $1\frac{1}{4}$ mililon young people would soon be prospects for new or used automobiles. Figure 2–1 illustrates the ease with which market segments defined by age can be forecasted. Crests and troughs move across age classifications with great certainty, so that a projection of N_t to N_{t+n} is simply a matter of advancing the number of persons in each age classification by n years.

The rate of product usage (R_t) is influenced by demographic variables, and the Mustang case illustrates this influence. Instead of measuring buying or usage rates for automobiles, we will estimate annual probabilities of persons in segments buying a new or used car. Three demographic vari-

---

[1] The author gratefully acknowledges the cooperation of Robert J. Eggert, of the Ford Motor Company, in making this material available. For a discussion of forecasting in the automobile industry see Eggert and McCracken (1966).

FIGURE 2–1

The 1963 Mustang analysis: Young people reaching driver age

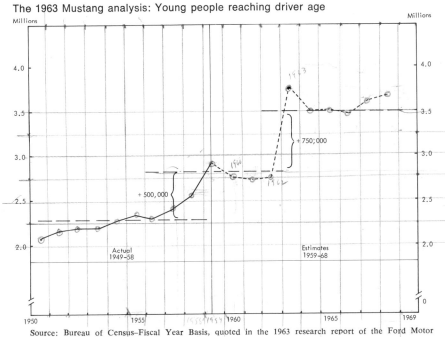

Source: Bureau of Census–Fiscal Year Basis, quoted in the 1963 research report of the Ford Motor Company.

ables influencing probabilities of buying automobiles are age of the head of the spending unit, years of education, and geographic location.

The possibility that the motoring needs of the age segment 18–24 were not being adequately met is suggested by the data in Table 2–1. The probability that the head of a spending unit will buy a car each year is 0.31, if he is between the ages of 18 and 24. The probability of his buying a *new* car, however, varies widely among age segments. The probability of a person 18–24 buying a used car is 0.27, but only 0.04 for a new car. Thus, a head of a spending unit in the 18–24 segment is seven times as likely to buy a used car. It seemed reasonable to conclude that the proportion of persons 18 to 24 buying a new car could be increased if a car were designed specifically for them.

College graduates were three times as likely to buy a new car as were high school graduates (18.6/6.3, Figure 2–2), but the high school market bought the largest percentage of new cars (27.8) because there were over three times as many high school graduates (25.2/7.8). This finding emphasizes an important point in estimating demand: market potential is the probability of buying times the number of persons in the market.

TABLE 2–1

The 1963 Mustang analysis: New and used car annual buying rates by age groups (1959–61 average)

Age group of head of spending unit	Percentage in each age group buying each year		
	New car	Used car	New or used
18–24 years	4*	27	31
25–34 years	10	23	33
35–44 years	11	21	32
45–54 years	10	17	27
55–64 years	7	9	16
65 years and over	4	5	9
All age groups	8.6	16.7	25.3

* This means that for every 100 spending units in the 18–24 age group, four buy a new car each year and 27 buy a used car each year. Obviously, many of those cars represent a replacement of the car previously owned. Nevertheless, each represents a sales opportunity.
Source: Survey Research Center, University of Michigan, quoted in the 1963 marketing research report of the Ford Division.

Because income, age, and education tend to be correlated, it is necessary to examine the effect of education on expenditures for new cars while holding income and age constant. Figure 2–3 reveals that in all segments except one (over 50, over $7,000), the person with a college education spends more for new cars than the person without a college education. Additional data (not shown here) indicated that college enrollment would approach nine million by 1980, more than double the enrollment of 1960.

FIGURE 2–2

The 1963 Mustang analysis: Annual new car buying rates by educational level (January 1962 annualized)

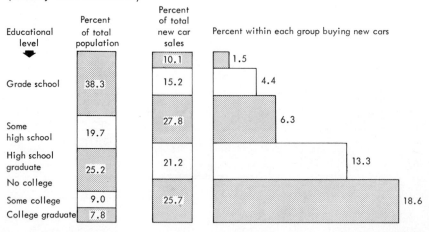

Source: National New Car Buyer Study, January 1962 and 1960 Census, quoted in the 1963 research report of the Ford Motor Company.

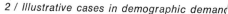

FIGURE 2–3

The 1963 Mustang analysis: Average annual household expendi?
by age of head of household, income, and education

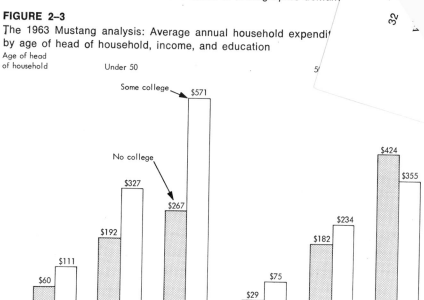

Averages: No college $166, College $378   No college $131, College $226

Source: *Life* Magazine Study of Consumer Expenditures, 1956, quoted in the 1963 marketing research report of the Ford Motor Company.

Additional demographic data indicated that the likelihood of car ownership for households in the suburbs approached certainty for incomes of $7,500 and over, while the likelihood in metropolitan areas was only 0.80. The trend toward the suburbs should increase the demand for all automobiles. It will also alter the location of dealerships and the media used for advertising.

The procedure used for identifying important variables for the Mustang analysis seemed to be a combination of Ford's extensive experience in marketing automobiles, intuition into the desires of the 18- to 24-year-old market segment, and a statistical technique known as the Automatic Interaction Detection algorithm. This technique will be illustrated in Chapter 4, but at this point it should be noted that it is a computer technique that identifies the characteristics of market segments with the highest probability of buying a product.

The implicit model was the basic demand equation presented in Chapter 1, thus,

$$B_{m(t+6)} = M_{m(t+6)} N_{y(t+6)} R_{y(t+6)} \qquad (2\text{--}1)$$

here $B_{m(t+6)}$ is the brand demand for the Mustang for the sixth year after the present decision period (Figure 2–1), $M_{m(t+6)}$ is the market share for Mustang, $N_{y(t+6)}$ is the number of persons in the youth segment (ages 18–24), and $R_{y(t+6)}$ is their probability of buying a car. Because the Mustang was the first car designed for this market, its initial share was expected to be close to 1.0 until competitors could design a youth car.

Some of the most important data in the Mustang analysis was low-cost data published by the Bureau of Census, The Survey Research Center of the University of Michigan, and *Life* Magazine. Thus, demographic analysis leading to important new products may be based on inexpensive available data.

Long-range demographic forecasting

The demand for airline services has many planning implications for the private and the public sectors of the economy. The public sector plans would include passenger and airfreight terminals, parking, ground transportation, and public utilities. Private facilities requiring planning include restaurants, hotels, and the industries which are attracted to a community because it has efficient air service.

Expansion of airport facilities in the New York metropolitan area is based on long-range forecasts of air traffic prepared by the Aviation Economics Division of the Port of New York Authority, the self-supported planning and development agency for the terminal and transportation facilities in the greater New York City region. Until 1955, the division followed the usual practice for estimating trips. This consisted of estimating passenger miles as a function of national income. These total miles were divided by an estimated average length of a trip to arrive at an estimate of the number of trips. This technique is known as the national income method.[2]

Because economists at the Port of New York Authority noted many weaknesses in this approach, they developed a new approach called the market analysis method (Port of New York Authority, 1957, 1960). This method considered air travel as a commodity that must compete with other goods and services for a share of the consumer's dollar. Therefore, a decision to purchase air travel would be influenced by demographic, economic,

---

[2] For descriptions and bibliographies of other methods see Federal Aviation Administration (1970); Schriever and Seifert (1968); Schultz (1971); and Quandt and Baumol (1966, 1969). The procedure developed by the Port of New York Authority is appropriate to this discussion because (1) it considered demographic, sociological, and psychological variables, as well as economic ones; (2) it made a valid 10-year prediction; (3) a sensitivity analysis was performed on assumptions; and (4) it illustrates the problems of identifying and measuring variables without losing the reader in unfamiliar statistical methods.

sociological, and psychological variables. A survey was used to identify the most influential demographic and economic variables and to determine their functional relationships to air trips. The validity of the method was established in 1965. The 1955 estimate of the originating and terminating trips at the New York airports for 1965 was 21.0 million. The observed trips in 1965 were 20.72 million, 98.6 percent of the forecast. The national income method forecasted only 18 million trips.

The demand for airport facilities can be segmented into domestic and overseas travel, domestic and overseas cargo, business and private flying, and helicopter traffic. The domestic travel market, the focus of this forecast, can be segmented further into business and personal travel. These segments were further divided into cells of individuals who shared characteristics that were important determinants of air travel. A survey identified the most important determinants of business trips as the flier's occupation, income, and industrial classification. The determinants of personal trips were age, occupation, income, and education. Classifications within each of these determinants generated 130 cells for the business-trip forecast and 160 cells for the personal-trip forecast. Thus, the market analysis method is not one forecast but the sum of forecasts for 290 cells, which tends to reduce the effect of an error in data or assumptions.

The steps in the market analysis method for forecasting personal air trips are as follows: First, the cell population must be projected to the n-th period ($N_{k\,(t+n)}$) using appropriate demographic variables and models. An estimate of the percent of persons in the cell who have flown before (F_k) must be projected to $t + n$. The number of trips per 1,000 fliers (R_k) must also be projected to $t + n$. The estimated trips for those who have previously flown is the product of these three projections ($N_{k\,(t+n)}\,F_{k\,(t+n)}\,R_{k\,(t+n)}$). Each year some nonfliers ($1\text{-}F$) will become fliers and will make fewer trips (R'), on the average, than long-term fliers. The number of "nonfliers" trips for a year is the product of the rate of nonflying at the beginning of the year ($1\text{-}F_{k\,(t+n)}$) times the population projection ($N_{k\,(t+n)}$) times the projected rate of trips ($R'_{k\,(t+n)}$). The computation for total projected personal trips may be expressed in the following generalized form:

$$\text{Total personal trips}_{t+n} = \sum_{k=1}^{160} [N_{k(t+n)}F_{k(t+n)}R_{k(t+n)} + N_{k(t+n)}(1 - F_{k(t+n)})R'_{k(t+n)}] \quad (2\text{-}2)$$

which reduces to

$$\text{Total personal trips}_{t+n} = \sum_{k=1}^{160} N_{k(t+n)}[F_{k(t+n)}(R_{k(n+t)} - R'_{k(t+n)}) + R']. \quad (2\text{-}3)$$

Equation 2–3 simplifies the calculations. The model for estimating business trips was simplified by the fact that most businessmen were fliers, thereby eliminating the right-hand element in Equation 2–2, which computes the trips made by the newly converted fliers.

To illustrate the application of Equation 2–3 consider the following example (Port of New York Authority, 1957, p. 109):

$$N_{k(t+n)} = 12{,}853 \text{ persons (in thousands)}$$
$$F_{k(t+n)} = 0.04$$
$$R_{k(t+n)} = 50 \text{ trips per thousand persons who had flown before period } t+n.$$
$$R'_{k(t+n)} = 10 \text{ trips per thousand persons who will fly for the first time during period } t+n.$$
$$\text{Personal trips}_{k(t+n)} = 12{,}853[0.04(50-10)+10]$$
$$= 12{,}853(11.6)$$
$$= 149{,}095 \text{ trips for cell } k.$$

Total personal trips is the sum of this calculation in the 160 personal cells.

Forecasting techniques are based on many assumptions which should be made explicit and the critical ones tested through sensitivity analysis to determine the effect of an erroneous assumption on the forecast. The developers of the market analysis approach identified the following assumptions (Port of New York Authority, 1957, p. 20):

1. Population growth in the United States will follow Projection A of the Bureau of the Census.
2. Employment by occupation and industry in 1965 and 1975 will conform to preliminary estimates of the Bureau of Labor Statistics for those years.
3. National income will increase at a rate of 3 percent per year for the period 1955–65 and at an annual rate of 3.75 percent for the period 1965–75.
4. All economic strata of the population will benefit proportionately from the expected rise in national income.
5. Each of the 160 personal-travel market classifications of the population established herein consists of "fliers" and "nonfliers." The *rate* at which "nonfliers" will become "fliers" in each cell will remain constant throughout the term of the forecast. Likewise, the frequency of air trips per traveler within each classification will remain constant.
6. In each of the 130 business-travel market classifications, it is assumed that the air trips per 1,000 population will increase in accordance with the estimated trend from 1935 to 1955.

The effect of changes in these assumptions was tested (ibid., p. 60). If the annual growth rate were 4 percent, the 1965 forecast would have increased 8 percent. If the proportion of nonfliers remained constant instead of decreasing at a logarithmic rate as assumed, the 1965 forecast would have been 9 percent less. If personal trips per 1,000 persons did not remain at the 1955 levels as assumed but increased at the arithmetic rate established by the trend from 1935 to 1955, personal trips would have increased by 20 percent. If the trips per 1,000 persons in the business cells remained constant, the 1965 estimate would have been reduced by 19 percent. The fact that the trips observed in 1965 were 98.6 percent of those forecasted suggests that either the assumptions were tenable or the errors were compensating.

The forecasting method by the Port Authority is of interest for several methodological reasons. It demonstrated excellent use of primary and secondary data. The 1955 model was validated by running it backwards to check estimates with previous observations. Sensitivity analysis was performed on key assumptions, thereby identifying those variables which should be observed closely during the forecasting period so that the forecast can be modified if necessary.

The demand for basic needs—housing

The need for housing is very basic to the well-being of a community as well as each member of the household. New housing construction also has a substantial economic impact on a local economy through its effect on the construction industry, retailing, the tax base, the need to expand public services (schools, hospitals, water treatment, and police and fire protection), and the demand for mortgages. To help the local housing authorities meet this demand in an orderly manner, the Federal Housing Administration (FHA) initiated in 1965 comprehensive analyses of local housing markets. These analyses demonstrate the complexity of supply and demand for housing, the variety of information sources that must be used, and the need to project data to a common point in time. As an example, the demand for housing in Tulsa will be examined (Federal Housing Administration, 1967).

Housing plans attempt to match the demand for housing with about a 5 percent excess in supply to facilitate mobility and choice. Thus, in very simple terms, the decision to build is based on the following equation:[3]

$$S = 1.05D \qquad (2-4)$$

---

[3] At higher levels of aggregation, more sophisticated techniques, such as econometrics, have been applied with varying degrees of success (Campbell, 1966).

where S is the supply of housing in a community, D is the demand, and 1.05 is the factor to assure sufficient supply to permit a choice. The change in demand for housing (ΔD) is based on the projected change in the number of households (ΔN). There is no need to estimate usage rates (R) because each household needs housing, so R is assumed to be 1.0. The change in the number of households is computed by dividing the projected change in population (ΔP) by the projected average number of persons in a household (H_{t+n}), thus

$$\Delta D = \Delta N = \frac{\Delta P}{H_{t+n}}. \tag{2-5}$$

The change in population (ΔP) is computed by projecting the births, deaths, and net migration to period $t + n$. Because migration, from other parts of the country and from other countries, is sensitive to economic conditions, it is difficult to project migration rates far into the future. Demand for housing can be segmented into the demand for rental housing (D_r) and the demand for the purchase of housing (D_p), which is generally single-family dwellings.

The FHA analyst concluded that the seven-year trend of births and deaths would continue in Tulsa, so the natural increase in population for 1968 would be 4,800 persons. He estimated a 5,050 net gain from migration, an extrapolation of the annual rate of 2.2 percent. The net gain from migration was due largely to expansion of firms engaged in aerospace manufacturing and metal processing and, to a lesser extent, growth in the oil and gas mining industries. Future migration estimates must reflect national changes in these industries and expansion plans of local plants.

The second step in computing the increase in households was to estimate the size of the average household. Computation of an average household unit was complicated by a change in the Census of Housing definition of a household. An average of 3.07 was used, which reflected a decline from the 1960 average of 3.11. This decline was attributed to a lower birth rate and to an increase in one- and two-person households. Dividing the total estimated population increase by the estimated size of a household unit yielded an estimate of approximately 3,200 households for 1968.

Single-family units represented 88 percent of the new units in 1960 and 65 percent in 1966. Given this rate of change, it seemed reasonable to assume that in 1968 the demand for new housing would be divided into 60 percent for single-family units for purchase and 40 percent for rental housing. Therefore, for 1968, the estimated demand for single-family housing was 1,920 units and the demand for rental units was 1,280.

The supply of housing is determined by the vacant housing that will be available ($V_{k(t+n)}$), plus new construction ($C_{k(t+n)}$), less inadequate, substandard housing ($I_{k(t+n)}$) that may be demolished as part of urban renewal. Thus, housing supply for segment k is

$$S_{k(t+n)} = V_{k(t+n)} + C_{k(t+n)} - I_{k(t+n)}. \tag{2-6}$$

In the case of Tulsa, vacancy was estimated by using the 1960 U.S. Census of Housing and a vacancy survey conducted in April 1967 by area postmasters in cooperation with the FHA. Reconciliation of data from these sources was difficult because of differences in definition, area delineations, and methods of enumeration. The 1968 vacancy projections were 1,500 units for sale and 5,600 units for rent. But 1,400 of the rental units were considered substandard because of inadequate plumbing.

Using Equation 2–4, the rental housing market conditions for Tulsa in 1968 may be expressed as follows:

$$(5,600 - 1,400) > 1.05(1,280)$$
$$4,200 > 1,344.$$

Because the projected supply greatly exceeded the projected demand, the recommendation of the FHA was that no rental units be constructed in 1968. The 1968 market condition for sale units was as follows:

$$1,500 < 1.05(1,920)$$
$$1,500 < 2,016.$$

Thus, the FHA recommendation for 1968 was to build additional single-family housing units for sale.

Estimates of new construction in Tulsa were based on the U.S. Bureau of the Census C-40 Construction Reports, building permits issued by local officials, and estimates by the local electric company. There was a decline in the number of units constructed from a high of 5,790 units in 1965, to 4,700 units in 1966, and about 1,500 units in 1967. The sudden drop was due largely to a shortage of mortgage money.

The policy of civic and bank officials in Tulsa for 1968 should have been to take action that would assure the building of at least 600 single-family units for sale. The policy could have been implemented through the granting of building permits and mortgages.

The actual recommendation of the FHA was to build 2,375 single-family units in 1968. While the report provides no rationalization for this excess supply, two possible explanations are worth noting. First, an excess supply will lower sale prices, making home ownership available to households now in rental units. This goal seems to be consistent with FHA policies. Secondly, the additional units would tend to improve the quality of available single-family units and drive the poorer quality ones out of the market. In summary, a demand analysis for housing can lead to policies that will improve housing conditions in a community.

Some generalizations on demographic segmentation for consumer goods

Age is one of the most popular demographic variables for segmentation because the data tend to be low-cost and because crests and troughs are predictable as they move across age classifications. As noted earlier, the approaching crest of youth in the driving age led to the development of the Mustang. Conversely, Transamerica Corporation abandoned a proposed merger with a publisher of high school materials because this crest was moving away from the high school segment ("Where We Go . . . ," 1967).

Teen-agers are important as a present market, a future market, and a buying influence. As a present market, their income is largely discretionary. Because they are anxious about personal identity and peer group influence, they spend heavily on grooming aids. The best generalization is probably that this is the most capricious of all market segments. The marketer who intends to develop this segment must be prepared to spend adequately for marketing research and retain flexibility for rapid changes in taste.

Some marketers base their strategy on the assumption that teen-age brand loyalty will carry into adult consumption patterns. There is some evidence that this assumption is invalid because young adults tend to reject earlier brand preferences as immature. Thus, successful promotion to the teen-age market may damage the future young-adult market.

Teen-agers also influence purchases that they do not make themselves. The presence of a teen-ager increases the probability that a family will buy a new car, and they serve as the family source of information on innovations and new styles.

An additional age segment that has been identified by marketers of leisure and travel is the "empty nest"—parents whose last child has left home. The availability of more discretionary income modifies purchasing patterns to include more travel, clothing, decorating, and luxuries.

The senior citizen market continues to grow and is more affluent now than in previous years because of social security and retirement benefits. Some products, such as medical equipment, must be designed for the elderly, but for many marketers a product that is obviously for the elderly can be a strategic error. A baby food manufacturer whose market segment was only a few years wide viewed with envy the 10- to 15-year wider geriatric market. He developed a chopped food line for senior citizens with dental and digestive problems. The product was a failure. In a youth-oriented society, such as in the United States, this failure could have been predicted. Senior citizens continued to buy baby food "for their grandchild," rather than identify with old age. This is an example of good marketing demography and bad marketing psychology.

The Danes had a similar experience with public housing. Initially, separate units were provided for the elderly, but these proved to be unpopular. Then apartment units were designed with special wings for the elderly containing additional soundproofing, ramps, etc. The occupants of the apartment building reflected the age distribution of the community. The elderly enjoyed the presence of young people, and young couples appreciated the availability of baby sitters.

The influence of education on expenditures for new cars was noted in the Mustang case. Education also influences the early adoption of new products. In a study that held the effects of income constant, rates of ownership of electric toothbrushes, dishwashers, clothes driers, blenders, diet foods, and corn oil margarine for college educated persons greatly exceeded the ownership rates of persons with no college education (New Focus on Potential Markets, 1965). Other studies indicate that college-educated consumers account for 55 percent of airline revenues, spend more for shelter and household furnishings, and buy luxury appliances (Colvin, Nilson, Rashmir, 1967). The college-educated person influences the buying patterns of others through his role as an opinion leader.

Geographic location influences the tastes of a population. For instance, in the United States the Westerner is more oriented toward the present and the future, less constrained by tradition, more willing to take chances, more curious and adventuresome, and, as a result, has more readily accepted new products such as frozen foods, cake mixes, color TV, electric carving knives, and electric toothbrushes (*Sunset,* 1967).

The geographic mobility of a population strains the public and private transportation systems for persons and goods. Planning for transportation systems requires measures of trip characteristics (purpose, length, time of day, and orientation to central business district), tripmaker characteristics (auto ownership, residential density, income, workers per household, distance to central business district, and employment density), and transportation system characteristics (travel time, travel cost, parking cost, accessibility of travel mode, walk, wait, transfer, and parking delays). Most of these data require primary research, which increases the cost of planning transportation systems (Fertal et al., 1966; Schneider, 1965; Perle, 1964).

Limitations of demographic segmentation for consumer goods and services

Several limitations of demographic segmentation must be made explicit. In the first place, a segment may constrain a marketer to a narrow age classification that does not provide room for growth. Such was the case with the baby food manufacturer and the publisher of high school texts. When dips in these age classifications appeared and sales volume dropped, they had no other segments to take up the slack.

Secondly, a formerly successful strategy of segmentation can be a curse if tastes change. Take the example of a manufacturer of compact economy cars. The firm built its image on the advantages of economy by appealing to the educated, rational man who was in the early stages of family formation. But then tastes changed. Economy cars were replaced by sporty ones, and the manufacturer was stuck with the wrong image. To change the image it developed a sports car and promoted it widely.

And finally, as a product is made more desirable for one segment, it becomes less acceptable to adjacent segments. A fashionable product to one segment may appear to be too expensive to another segment. There is even the danger of the strategy being resisted by the segment toward which it is directed. A food product that was promoted as the "in beverage" for youth was rejected as immature by youth.

INDUSTRIAL PRODUCTS—AN ELECTRONICS FIRM

To this point the discussion has been limited to the demographic dimensions of the demand for consumer goods and services. The demand for industrial goods (equipment, supplies, parts, and semifinished components) and industrial services also has demographic dimensions, the most common of which are the Standard Industrial Classification (SIC) and the number of employees.

For illustrative purposes, assume that an East Coast manufacturer of parts for the electronic components industry (SIC 367) is considering opening a sales office in California. Planning requires an estimate of the number of salesmen needed. Using sales call reports for existing territories, the manufacturer might establish that the number of employees in a firm reflects its purchases of parts, which could be related to the required annual sales calls, as shown in columns 1 and 3 of Table 2–2. By consulting

TABLE 2–2

Estimating the required sales calls for a new territory

Number of employees (1)	Number of firms* (2)	Number of calls per year† (3)	Total calls (2 × 3) (4)
Less than 20.	248	6	1,488
20 to 49	69	12	828
50 to 99	41	17	697
100 to 499.	59	26	1,534
500 and over.	17	52	884
	434		5,431

* U.S. Bureau of the Census, 1965.
† Estimated from sales call reports in present territories.

County Business Patterns for California (U.S. Bureau of the Census, 1966) the sales manager would learn that the 434 electronic components manufacturers were distributed as shown in column 2. If a salesman makes four completed calls a day, or 1,000 calls per year (250 working days), it would be necessary to hire five salesmen and a sales manager. The latter would carry a territory of about 400 calls.

This information provides the planners with a quick means for estimating the budget required for a sales force in California. Other applications of SIC data and a discussion of their limitations appear in Chapter 4.

SUMMARY

The demographics of demand consist of locating unmet needs in time and space. A strategy of market segmentation according to demographic data is common for consumer goods and services. Segmentation by age has numerous adherents in marketing; but it can be a dangerous strategy if the segment is too narrow, if a crest is replaced by a trough, or if successful promotion to one segment jeopardizes another segment. Additional demographic dimensions that have been found to be relevant to demand include the number and age of children, educational levels, occupation, and geographic location. Two demographic dimensions used frequently in industrial marketing are Standard Industrial Classifications (SIC) and number of employees.

Demographic data are more readily available in secondary sources than are other demand variables, and therefore demographic demand analysis is generally the lowest cost demand analysis. Demographic segments have the danger of being traps when there are quick shifts in tastes. Demographic segmentation facilitates building promotional strategies because media report circulations according to demographic classifications.

READING QUESTIONS ————————————

1. What are demographic variables? What are their advantages and disadvantages for market segmentation?
2. What assumptions are implicit in the Port Authority model of the demand for air travel? Do you think these assumptions are reasonable?
3. Is demographic demand analysis limited to the demand for consumer products?

CLASS DISCUSSION QUESTIONS ————————————

(Suggested answers to the first three questions may be found in Appendix B.)

1. Home videotape recorders have been described as the Polaroid of home movies and may emerge as the next major item in household electronics after color TV. What demographic variables would you include in an analysis of the market potential for *home* videotape recorders?
2. Identify the several market segments for paint and state the variables that you would use to estimate the industry potential by county.
3. State the variables that you would use when measuring the potential for fire insurance.
4. What demographic variables would you include in an analysis of the market potential for *industrial* videotape recorders?
5. Assume that a demand function can be described by the simple additive form of multiple regression:

$$\text{Sales} = a + b_1x_1 + b_2X_2 \ldots b_nX_n.$$

For one consumer product and one industrial product:
a) Identify the demographic variables of demand,
b) Show the proper signs, and
c) Write the demand function using assumed values for coefficients that reflect your estimate of the relative importance of each variable by writing the equation using standard variables (zero mean and unit standard deviation).

6. Do the conditions which led to the success of the Mustang in the 1960s exist in the 1970s?
7. Update Figures 2–1 and 2–2 using recent issues of *The Conference Board Record* and *Current Population Reports, Series P-25*. What are the marketing implications of recent trends?

8. Adapt the market analysis method of the Port of New York Authority to the problem of forecasting future needs for health-care services. What variables would you include and what would be your sources of data?

9. What airline marketing strategies are suggested by the sensitivity analysis of the models for forecasting personal round trips?

10. Using the most recent census data, identify a site in your community for a take-out food service. (For one possible approach see U.S. Department of Commerce, 1966, p. 74.)

11. Design an information system that will help planners in your community monitor the need for houses and apartments.

12. Quinn (1971) ranks the public markets for 1970–75 as follows (rankings are from the largest to the smallest market potentials): medical- and health-care, education systems, roads and highways, sewage treatment, subsidized housing, air de-pollution, airport development, mass transit, water supply systems, industrial water de-pollution, and air-control facilities. Select one of these markets and identify the relevant variables and sources of information (consulting Appendix A).

SUGGESTED CASES

Gem Appliance Company. Bursk (1965), pp. 24–27.

Located in Tel Aviv, this company was considering adding an electric dryer to its product line.

1. Does the implicit demographic model that explains dryer sales in the United States apply to Israel? If not, what variables would you consider when analyzing the market potential?

2. Do you recommend the introduction of an electric dryer?

Genesys Systems. Boyd and Davis (1971), pp. 111–24.

Technological obsolescence of engineers is a severe problem in industries where technology changes rapidly. The "half-life" of an engineer, the period during which half of his knowledge is obsolete, ranges from 5 to 9 years after his college education. Part-time programs and night courses have not successfully met the need for additional education. Genesys Systems was formed in 1967 to implement an educational TV system that would link the classrooms at Stanford University with classrooms in cooperating companies. Talk-back systems gave the advantages of classroom presence without the time lost for commuting. Genesys has replicated the system at other universities.

1. Conduct a demographic demand analysis for Genesys that will rank, according to market potential, the market segments for its educational television systems.

SUGGESTED READINGS ───────────────

ECKLER, A. ROSS. "Profit from 1970 Census Data," *Harvard Business Review,* July–August 1970, pp. 4–16, 174–77.

HOINVILLE, G. W. "Transport Research for Town Planning," *Commentary (The Journal of the Market Research Society),* Vol. 9 (July 1967), pp. 147–60.

LINDEN, FABIAN. "The Family Market—Young and Old," *The Conference Board RECORD,* Vol. 7 (August 1970), pp. 26–30.

─────. "Young Adults," *The Conference Board RECORD,* Vol. 8 (April 1971), pp. 53–56.

PARKER, G. G. C., and SEGURA, E. L. "How to Get a Better Forecast," *Harvard Business Review,* March–April 1971, pp. 99–109.

PETERS, WILLIAM H. "Using MCA to Segment New Car Markets," *Journal of Marketing Research,* Vol. 7, No. 3 (August 1970), pp. 360–63.

WISEMAN, FREDERICK. "A Segmentation Analysis on Automobile Buyers during the New Model Year Transition Period," *Journal of Marketing,* Vol. 35 (April 1971), pp. 42–49.

3

Models and measures
of population in time
and space

Examples in the previous chapter illustrated that estimates of generic and brand demand require estimates of the number of persons (N) in a specific classification (k) at a specific time (t). These classifications may be defined in a variety of ways, such as age, educational levels, and geographic location. Because the marketing decisions for the selection of promotional media and channels of distribution are dependent on the geographic location of the population, it is necessary to consider the available measures of population in space and the models that project the migration of the population through space. Forecasts of demand require a knowledge of the measures of the components of population and models for projecting these components over time. The models and measures of population in time and space that are relevant to marketing decisions will be considered in this chapter.

The basic population model may be expressed as follows:

$$N_{k(t+1)} = N_{kt} + B_{kt} - D_{kt} \pm I_{kt} \tag{3-1}$$

where $N_{k(t+1)}$ is the number of persons in geographic segment k in period $t + 1$, B_{kt} is the number of births in period t, D_{kt} is the number of deaths in period t, and I_{kt} is the net migration in period t. The value of I_t would be minus when emigration exceeds immigration. The geographic segments (k) may be defined in terms of countries, states, cities, counties, Standard Metropolitan Statistical Areas (SMSA), or according to postal ZIP codes.

In the United States the rates of net migration and death are quite constant, so that most of the variation in the net growth rate of the population is due to the variation in the birth rate. The influence of birth rates may be noted in Figure 3–1, which plots more than 30 years of these rates.

FIGURE 3–1
Annual rates of net growth, births, deaths, and net immigration: 1935–71

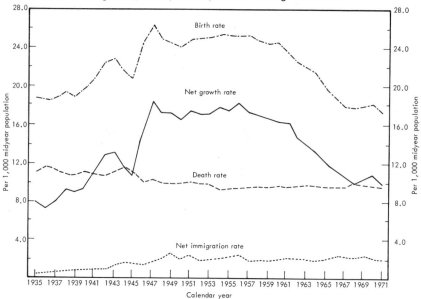

Source: U.S. Department of Commerce, Bureau of the Census, *Current Population Reports,* Population Estimates and Projections, Series P-25, No. 481, April 1972 (Washington, D.C.: U. S. Government Printing Office, 1972), p. 1.

During the last two decades the death and immigration rates were flat, so that variations in the net growth rate followed variations in the birth rate. It becomes evident, therefore, that marketing planners should understand the forces that determine birth rates.

PROJECTING POPULATIONS OVER TIME

Population projections[1] have long been a concern of public administrators. There is evidence that Thomas Jefferson and Abraham Lincoln made

---

[1] The term *projection* is generally reserved for those population predictive models with demographic variables—rates of birth, death, mobility, etc. When social and economic variables are included among the independent variables, the result is known as a *forecast* (Peterson, 1961). But this distinction in terms is generally lost upon users of these statistics, who are more concerned with what they portend than how they were derived.

projections when advising Congress. Many of the 19th century projections were astoundingly accurate. Estimates by Bonynge in 1852 were within 3 percent of subsequent census enumerations until 1910 (Dorn, 1950). The apparent precision of 19th century projections was the result of two offsetting errors—an undetected decline in the natural rate of increase, and an increase in immigration (Peterson, 1961, pp. 273–77).

Aggregate projective models

A model for estimating the size of the population from aggregate data developed by Pearl and Reed (1920) was based on experiments on the growth rate of fruit flies which received fixed amounts of food while living in a closed bottle. Their numbers followed an **S**-shaped curve—increasing at an accelerating rate (Figure 3–2) to a point of inflec-

FIGURE 3–2
The growth curve

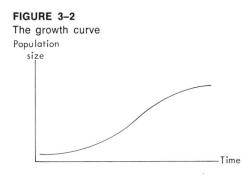

tion, where growth continued at a decreasing rate until it approached the asymptote which represented the maximum population that the food supply would support.[2]

Early estimates by Pearl and Reed were impressive. Projections for 1920 and 1930 were within 1 percent of the census. But the projections for 1940 and 1950 underestimated the population by 3.5 percent and 4 percent respectively. It would appear that during its later applications, this **S**-shaped curve, known also as the logistic curve, failed to reflect the underlying forces that determine population growth.

The success of the logistic curve may be mere coincidence, because it based population growth on a single determinant, the abundance of food,

---

[2] This **S**-shaped curve, known also as the logistic curve, was first suggested by the Belgian mathematician Verhulst, in 1838 (Dorn, 1950, p. 317). It has been used in marketing to describe the life cycle of a new product and the diffusion of innovations (Chapter 7).

which is not a critical factor in the demographic environment of the United States:

The growth rate of the human population did not decline because of hunger, as with the fruit flies, but because parents decided to have fewer children. For a period mortality fell faster than fertility, and the population increased rapidly; then fertility fell faster and the curve began to flatten out. That is to say, the **S**-shaped curve, to the degree that it has actually described the growth of human populations, has done so because of the demographic transition, not because of the biological determinants that Pearl posited (Peterson, 1961, p. 277).

The application of the logistic curve to growth or time-series data provides a classic example of the lack of communication among scientists in different disciplines. The logistic curve has been the subject of at least seven independent discoveries, five of which occurred prior to the well-publicized discovery by Pearl and Reed. The failure of the logistic to predict the population accurately demonstrates the danger of blindly applying methods borrowed from other fields, and emphasizes the need to explore the underlying forces of change (Lloyd, 1967).

Recent aggregate population projections failed to detect crucial turning points. During the last two decades the U.S. Census Bureau, the most official of the U.S. population projectors, consistently lagged behind the facts, thereby shaking the faith of market researchers who use its projections. Mayer (1967) has noted:

As population continued to climb rapidly after 1947, the bureau had to keep revising its projections upward. Projections about future growth were at their highest in 1958, just when actual growth had passed its crest, and they have been chasing the facts back down ever since. Back in 1958 the bureau's "B" projection, the one then most widely used in market research, anticipated a population of 236,400,000 by 1975. Since 1958 the "B" projection itself has twice been revised downward; yet its assumptions now seem unduly optimistic to many marketing men, and the projection being fed into most business plans for the future nowadays is the Census "C." This yields a population in 1975 of 219,400,000—17 million less than was thought most probable in 1958. Thus, businessmen generally are looking forward to only about half the addition to population that they once expected to take place between 1967 and 1975.

About the time that Pearl and Reed were developing their logistic model, demographers realized that aggregate models did not provide valid projections, and began to turn their attention to the components of population change: birth, death, and immigration. This interest encouraged demographers to improve the measures of these components. Thus, crude birth rates were refined to include general fertility and age-specific birth rates.

Refining the measures of fertility

As was observed in Figure 3–1, most of the variation in the net growth rate in the United States is due to variation in the birth rate. It is not surprising, therefore, that the failure of the aggregate projective models led to the development of improved measures of fertility.

Fertility rates measure the number of births per unit of population. The fineness of the rate is determined by the precision with which the unit of population is defined. A crude rate ignores the fact that the probability of birth varies according to sex and age.

The *crude birth rate* of a population for a given area is the ratio of registered births for the year (B) divided by the midyear population (P) times 1,000, so that the rate is expressed as the number of births per 1,000 population, $(B/P \times 1,000)$. The crude rate ignores the obvious facts that births occur only among women and to those in the childbearing ages. A finer measure of fertility, the *general fertility rate,* restricts the denominator P to the population of women in childbearing age, either 15 to 44 or 15 to 49 (Barclay, 1958). Examples of these rates may be found in Table 3–1.

To reflect the fact that the probability of giving birth varies within age classifications, *age-specific birth rates* were developed. This is not a single rate but a set of seven rates, one for each of the five-year intervals between 15 and 49. To obtain a single rate for the entire population of women in childbearing ages, these seven rates are added and the sum multiplied by five. This weighted sum is known as the *total fertility rate.*[3] The age-specific and total fertility rates are insensitive to variations in the age compositions of the population.

Sources and limitations of fertility measures

Fertility measures are derived from two classes of data, published sources and interview surveys. Published sources are comprised of census enumerations and registration statistics—birth, marriage, disease, and death.

Census data suffer from incomplete enumeration and inaccurate reporting of age. Age heaping occurs positively at preferred ages (zero, fives, and even numbers) and negatively at adjacent ages (Coale and Zelnik,

---

[3] For additional fertility rates, see Barclay (1958), pp. 171–80; Thompson (1953), pp. 146–70; and National Center for Health Statistics (1965), pp. 6–18.

TABLE 3–1

Birth rates in selected countries[a]

Country	Year	Crude birth rate[b] (per 1,000)	Fertility rate[c] (per 1,000)	Rate of natural increase[d] (per 1,000)	Annual rate of increase[e] 1958-64 (per 100)
Africa					
Congo (Brazzaville)	1960-61	41.1	129.7	16.7	1.6%
Ghana	1960	47-52	211	23-28	2.7
Southern Rhodesia	1961	48.1	207	34.1	3.3
Tunisia	1959	47	191.9	21	2.0
North America					
Canada	1965	21.4	75.6	13.9	2.0
Dominican Republic	1959-61	48-50	124.7	32-35	3.6
Mexico	1965	45.3	159.5	35.8	3.2
United States	1965	19.4	75.6	10.0	1.6
South America					
Argentina	1964	21.8	73.0	13.5	1.6
Brazil	1959-61	40-43	. . .	29-31	3.1
Venezuela	1959-61	47-50	155.6	35-41	3.4
Asia					
China (mainland)	1957	34	. . .	23.0	1.5
India	1963-64	38.4	136.7	25.5	2.3
Japan	1965	18.6	53.4	11.5	1.0
Europe					
Austria	1965	17.9	70.7	4.9	0.5
Belgium	1965	16.4	65.4	4.3	0.9
France	1965	17.6	68.6	6.5	1.3
Sweden	1965	15.9	54.7	5.8	0.6
Union of Soviet Socialist Republics					
USSR	1965	18.5	83.2	11.2	1.6
Ukrainian SSR	1965	15.3	. . .	7.7	1.3

a Statistical Office of the United Nations, Department of Economic and Social Affairs, *Demographic Yearbook, 1965* (United Nations, 1966), pp. 19, 103–21, 122–27.
b Crude birth rates are computed per 1,000 population.
c Fertility rates are computed per 1,000 female population, age segment 10–49.
d Rate of natural increase is the difference between crude birth and crude death rates, which is generally computed from registration statistics.
e The average annual percentage rate of population increase is quite a different figure and is generally computed as an annuity using census data for two points in time, as follows:

$$r = \left(\sqrt[t]{\frac{P_n}{P_0}} - 1 \right) \times (1000)$$

where P_0 = population in time $(_0)$; P_n = population in time (n); t = number of years between (t_0) and (t_n). This figure reflects rates of birth, death, and migration. In a closed society, with no migration, the rate of natural increase (per 100) will equal the average annual percentage rate of increase.

1963). Registration statistics suffer from quality differences among countries and the fact that they are not available for early years. In the United States, for example, not all states collected birth registration until 1933.

If the registration statistics were complete, it would be possible to estimate shortcomings of the census; and conversely, if the census were complete and accurate, gaps in registration statistics could be estimated. Because each published source has its shortcomings, errors in age distributions cannot be reconciled. To estimate the age distribution of a population, demographers have turned to the survey method. Using this technique, they estimate past birth rates by asking mothers to report on past births or the present ages of their children (Coale and Demeny, 1967). Survey data also provide information about the number of children expected, the perception of an ideal family size, impairments to reproduction, and methods of family limitation (National Center for Health Statistics, 1966; Freedman, Coombs, and Bumpass, 1965).

Demographers are attempting to understand the decision processes that alter birth rates. Each decision to have an additional child is based on present circumstances, including the present family size (Davis, 1959). The decision may have deep cultural and economic roots. For instance, in some countries large families are regarded as the only form of security for old age.

Research on fertility rates has identified new determinants which need to be measured before the extent of their influence can be estimated. These determinants include date of marriage, age at marriage, perception of ideal family size, spacing of children, socioeconomic background of parents, family income, religion, and degree of marital stability (Barclay, 1958, p. 177).

Multivariate statistical techniques have become important demographic tools for isolating and measuring the influence of the determinants of fertility. Simulations have been used to model the fertility process (Hyrenius et al., 1964–67) and to forecast the population by creating models of death, marriage, divorce, and birth rates (Orcutt et al., 1961). A system of differential equations has been developed to describe the effect of ecological contact on the growth of a population (Keyfitz, 1965).

DETERMINANTS OF CHANGES IN FERTILITY RATES

It is difficult to classify the broad forces that influence fertility rates. For the sake of exposition, they will be classified as economic development and social determinants.

Economic development

Industrialized nations share the characteristic of low fertility.[4] Evidence strongly suggests that this reduction has been a voluntary decision by the

---

[4] This discussion follows that of Ryder (1967); Whelpton (1964); and Peterson (1961).

couple and not the influence of government or church. Explanations center largely on changes in the role of the family during the shift from a rural to an urban life.

On the farm, a child was a contributor to family income. In the city, he ceased to be a contributor after the passage of child labor and compulsory education legislation. Many demographers also cite the improved status of women as a cause for a decline in fertility because of increased opportunities for seeking satisfaction outside motherhood.

Large families in the city are not economically desirable. The cost of training a child for an urban job is more expensive, and once trained, the income belongs to the child, not the parents, as was the case on the farm. City housing tends to be smaller than rural housing. Opportunities for social mobility are greater when families are small. This mobility tends to shift social involvement to organizations outside the family. Economic and educational functions have been shifted to the factory and the school. Personal goals have become individual, materialistic, and rational, in contrast to family or social goals.

In summary, with urbanization and industrialization, authority moved from the family to the individual and to formal organizations. These organizations seem to be necessary for the rational allocation of human resources in a technically oriented society. The family abdicated to society the functions of socialization, education, employment, and social security.

Two economic explanations which are independent of the changing role of the family must be noted. Improved public health and medical facilities tend to be associated with industrialization and urbanization. These facilities reduce mortality rates, which are not offset immediately by a reduction in birth rates. Second, mechanization on the farm has pushed labor from the farm to the city, where the influences noted above have tended to reduce fertility rates.

Social change

Differences in fertility (reproductive experience) among groups are not the results of differences in fecundity (physiological capacity to reproduce), but rather differences in customs, attitudes, and social practices (Thompson, 1953). The latter are identified by attributes such as place of birth, occupation, education, and psychological attitudes toward children.

The determinants of fertility have been examined using multiple regression techniques (Friedlander and Silver, 1967). Data from 18 developed countries, 20 of intermediate development, and 47 underdeveloped countries for the period from the late 1950s through the early 1960s, yielded the following relationships: (1) a positive and statistically significant relationship between fertility and illiteracy, child mortality, proportion of agricultural population, proportion of nonfarm self-employment and overcrowded housing; and (2) a negative significant relationship between fertility and communism and between fertility and education. No significant relationship was established between fertility and populaion density, social mobility, achievement motivation, protein in the diet, and religion.

Sociological, economic, and psychological forces modify fertility rates by varying the proportion of women who marry, their age at marriage, the desired family size, and the timing of births. The U.S. baby boom of the 1950s was not solely the result of more children per couple but also an increase in the proportion of women marrying (one of the highest in the West), a low average age at marriage (almost unique among modern nations), earlier childbearing, closer spacing of births, and making up of births postponed by the war (Westoff, 1964). The 1950–54 baby boom included 1.6 million births that had been postponed because of World War II, plus 900,000 births that were advanced from 1955 or later because of the tendency of women to marry earlier and to have children at an earlier age. The 1955–59 boom was inflated by 1.1 million postponed births and 2.1 million advanced from 1960 and beyond (Whelpton, 1963).

Closer spacing of births occurred in most of the socioeconomic groups. The relationship between socioeconomic forces and family size has been altered. The highest fertility is still among the low socioeconomic classes, but the lowest fertility is no longer in the highest class but somewhere in the middle (Westoff, 1964, p. 117).

There is evidence that timing in the United States reversed during the 1960s. "The trend toward earlier marriage and earlier childbearing has ceased for women under 25 years, but these young have not completed a sufficient proportion of their lifetime childbearing for a valid assessment of their eventual family size" (National Center for Health Statistics, 1965, p. 10).

MODELS FOR PROJECTING MIGRATION THROUGH SPACE

The location of the population in space is a primary input when developing a channels-of-distribution strategy and a media mix; therefore, migration models can contribute to long-range planning. Migration models may be classified as aggregate models (Markov models) and disaggregate models (multiple regression and simulation). These models may be classified also as explanatory (multiple regression), predictive (Markov), and optimizing (linear programming and simulation).

Explanatory models

Explanations of mobility among professional workers have been provided by multiple regression and factor analysis (Ladinsky, 1967). Multiple regression revealed that age accounted for most of the variance in mobility, followed by income, education, regional location, sex, family size, and marital status. Because only 21 percent of the variance was associated with these variables, we must conclude that these findings are only a beginning in the explanation of mobility among professional workers. Factor analysis identified two types of migration: occupational and family life cycle.

The U.S. Bureau of the Census (1966) used the survey method to identify the reasons for population mobility. These findings indicated that local moves are for reasons of housing and that longer moves are job-related. The latter finding brings us to the problem of predicting the mobility of labor.

Predictive models

The first industrial application of the Markov model predicted the movement of workers among industries (Blumen, Kogan, and McCarthy, 1955). The simple Markov model consistently underestimated the number of workers remaining in an industry because of the assumption that transition probabilities are statistically independent of previous years. To state it differently, "people in a common state do not always share the probabilities of a common fate because they are not necessarily homogeneous in their past histories" (Henry, McGinnis, and Tegtmeyer, 1968). A duration specific chain corrects this limitation by incorporating the axiom of cumulative inertia, which relates the likelihood of leaving a location to the duration of time in the location (ibid.).

The Markov model has been used to project population over time and through space, to compute the equilibrium distribution of population, and to measure nonwhite changes in population (Tarver and Gurley, 1965). These calculations were based on the assumptions that migration would continue at a constant rate, that migration rates were independent of prior rates, that the total population was constant, and that birth and death rates did not influence the distribution of population among census divisions.[5]

---

[5] The transition migration matrix (P) was developed from 1955–60 data and the initial population (m^0) was that of the 1960 census of population. The 1965 population (m^1) was estimated by matrix multiplication, $m^1 = m^0P^1$, and the 1970 projection would be $m^2 = m^0P^2$.

Some of these assumptions can be relaxed by introducing a matrix operator to reflect fertility, mortality, and geographic mobility (Rogers, 1966).

Optimizing models

The third type of migration model is concerned with the optimization of a distribution system. An example in marketing is the use of linear programming and simulation to select the optimum number and locations of warehouses. Behind the apparent neatness of a distribution simulator lies the need to plod through an inelegant morass of data. After developing distribution simulators for the H. J. Heinz and the Nestle companies, Gerson and Maffei (1963) observed that the difficult aspects of simulation were not the development of the logic of the system but the gathering of an adequate set of data and the organization of the computational procedures for implementing the model. To appreciate the magnitude of the measurement problem, the methods for implementing the Heinz and Nestle simulations will be considered briefly.[6]

Gerson and Maffei regard a typical system as one that includes 4,000 to 10,000 geographic market segments, 25 product categories, 5 to 10 size classes of shipments, 20 to 60 warehouses, 10 to 20 factories producing full or partial product lines, 30 to 50 freight tariff areas, and 5 to 10 tariff structures for each area. The characteristics of the customer that determine the cost of distributing a product to him include his location, annual volume, product mix, and order size. Warehouse costs are determined by whether the warehouse is public or private, by fixed costs (salaries and administrative costs), and by variable costs (storing, handling, stock rotation, and data processing). The factory contributes to the distribution costs through its location, the product mix, and the extent of warehousing performed. Transportation costs to the warehouse are a function of its location, the size of a shipment, and its commodity classification for freight tariffs. And finally, the delivery costs from the warehouse to the customer are the result of the size of the shipment, the location of the customer, and the commodity classification.

Not all locational measurements require mathematical sophistication. Direct-mail advertisers and mail-order companies have discovered some useful relationships between zip codes and consumer characteristics. The 39,550 five-digit residential zip codes frequently reflect the median family income of the area (Stone, 1967). The 552 sectional centers may be better economic and cultural units than politically determined units such as

---

[6] For a more detailed discussion of the measurement of the cost of marketing systems, see Sevin (1965).

counties (Baier, 1967). Once the direct-mail advertiser has identified the less profitable zip code segments, he may delete these from future mailings. While the zip code approach to market segmentation lacks the sophistication of simulation and Markov models, it is part of an attempt to better identify the spatial dimensions of consumer demand.

DEMOGRAPHIC AND ECONOMIC INTERACTION

"Ever since Keynes set forth his theory of income determination, demographic variables have been discussed as possible determinants of effective demand, and consequently of the level of unemployment" (Coale, 1957, p. 352). Demographic variables affect aggregate demand through the consumption function, net private investment, and government expenditures. Absolute changes in both population and age distribution must be considered: Absolute changes induce the private demand for housing, durable goods, clothing, transportation, communications, personal services, retailing, and the investments that produce these goods and services. They induce also the demand for public services such as education, roads, water, sewers, and the investments required to increase the capacities of these services. Age distribution, in contrast, determines the types of goods and services that will be demanded. For example, a crest of persons in the younger age classifications will stimulate a demand for primary education; as this crest passes through time, demand for high schools and colleges will emerge.

Questionable directions of causation

Many demographic events are closely related to economic ones. To understand demographic events, one must examine their effect on economic behavior and, in turn, the feedback to demographic behavior: population growth increases labor supply and aggregate demand; economic growth encourages immigration, marriage, and family formation; they, in turn, reinforce economic expansion, and the spiral continues. It is not clear whether population growth *causes* an economic boom; or an increase in investment and income *causes* changes in marriage, birth, death, and migration rates; or whether both are reacting to external political forces. One suspects that each scholar credits his discipline with having started the boom and, because of selective perception, starts with a point on the spiral which supports his biases.

Of the three variables in the population equation—birth, death, and migration—economic forces have been less influential on mortality rates than on birth rates and migration. Coale (1957) credits reduction in mortality to law and order, a regular food supply, pure water, environmental sanitation, the development of vaccines, serums, insecticides, chemotherapeutics, and antibiotics. But, the economists might counter, these developments could not exist without a favorable economic environment. Thus the argument continues. Causes of demographic behavior are not clear.

A comprehensive explanation of the relationship between economic and demographic behavior of a society has been provided by Easterlin (1966a), who has examined long swings in U.S. demographic and economic growth and their interaction. Long-run Kuznets economic cycles (of 15 to 25 years duration) according to Easterlin are the product of the interaction between immigration and fertility rates on the one hand and income and employment opportunities on the other. Prior to 1914, the most important demographic variable was migration—both foreign and domestic, the latter from the farm to the city. A business investment boom increased aggregate demand and economic growth which increased hourly wages and decreased unemployment. A tight labor supply increased immigration from the farm and abroad. The increase in employment, in turn, generated new demand and investment opportunities, thereby continuing the boom (Easterlin, 1965).

Restriction of free immigration (from outside the United States) in the late 1920s and the decline of farm population since 1940 removed a supply of labor that could react quickly to employment opportunities in the labor market. Therefore, the dominant position of foreign immigration has been replaced by rates of birth, labor-force participation (especially by older women), and household formation, with internal migration of continued importance (Easterlin, 1968, pp. 9–18). These demographic variables react less quickly than foreign immigration to employment opportunities. The new reservoir of labor is comprised largely of youths, females, and older persons, whose willingness to participate in the labor force is moderated by institutions such as compulsory education, family obligations, and social security.

An analysis of the baby boom

The demographic conditions of the economic boom beginning with World War II included (1) restricted immigration, (2) a reduced farm population, (3) a shortage of working-age population due to the effect of the 1930s depression on birth rates, and (4) young workers with an educational advantage over older workers because of an acceleration of secondary schooling since 1920. These conditions created a strong demand for younger men, which was reflected in their income. Their increase in income, in turn, had two demographic effects: a reduction in age at marriage, and a reduction in age of parents when the first child was born. Thus, the economic boom increased the total population, rather than shifting it through migration. (One might add that a labor shortage stimulates investment in laborsaving equipment, which further stimulates the economy through the effect of the multiplier and the accelerator.)

TABLE 3–2
Relative educational advantages

Age at specified date	Median school years completed					
	1920	*1930*	*1940*	*1950*	*1960*	*1970 (projected)*
1. 25–29	8.4	8.7	10.1	12.0	12.3	12.5
2. 45–54	8.1	8.2	8.4	8.7	10.0	12.0
Difference	0.3	0.5	1.7	3.3	2.3	0.5

Source: Easterlin (1961).

Birth rates during the 1950s were composed of births postponed because of World War II plus the accelerated births. The result was the well-publicized baby boom. By the late 1950s birth rates began to decline (see Figure 3–1). The postponed family formations were complete. New households were being formed at a later age and the birth of the first child was being delayed. The reason for the delay is not clear, and many explanations have been posited. Easterlin (1966b) suggests the following economic and demographic ones: (1) the young experienced high unemployment rates and their income grew only hesitantly; (2) home ownership in the 18–24 age group was less prevalent; (3) net worth in the 18–34 age group had declined; (4) veterans' benefits were exhausted; and (5) the younger cohorts had more expensive tastes than the previous generation, which was a product of the depression. Easterlin (1961) suggests that this newer generation does not enjoy the feeling of affluence enjoyed by its predecessor generation because its relative educational advantage is less great, as may be seen in the data of Table 3–2. If an educational advantage produces a feeling of relative affluence, there will be less of a feeling of affluence in the 1970s. Mayer (1967) notes that in the early 1970s there will be a flood of young engineers, scientists, and executives. Thus, we should not expect a return in the 1970s to the young marriages and family formations.

Economic booms and population cycles

The impact of an economic boom when limited immigration exists depends on the stage of the population cycle. If an economic boom occurs during a population ebb, the economic conditions of the young are favorable for household and family formation. If, however, the economic boom occurs during a population crest, economic conditions are not favorable to an increase in population. The latter seemed to be the condition of the late 1960s, which portends lower rates of family formation in the 1970s (Easterlin, 1968, p. 17).

The experience of the United States cannot be generalized to include developing countries where data are scarce and theoretical analysis is conflicting. As Easterlin (1967) notes, some analysts argue that high rates of population growth divert resources from capital formation to population maintenance, while others argue that large populations will support specialization and economies of scale.

Two findings have encouraging implications for developing countries (Adelman, 1963). The demographic effect of changes in per capita income is not dramatic, and there is a negative correlation between birth rates and education. A 25 percent improvement in per capita income would not increase the population more than 1 percent over a five-year period. If the economic increase were the result of an educational program, a decline in birth rate would be likely to follow.

SOME DEMOGRAPHIC LESSONS FOR MARKETERS

For the marketer there are many lessons to be learned from the demographics of long-range aggregate demand. First, the underlying forces that determine the size of a population determine the aggregate need for goods and services. For the government planner, these services might be related to health, education, and transportation. In industry, a planner needs to understand these forces when making a long-range plan for his operation in a specified country. If he is planning for a multinational firm, an understanding of demography is vital when analyzing conditions in countries that are in various stages of development. The planner will want to select that country whose development best meets the plans of his firm.

Second, marketers can learn from the experiences of demographers in their efforts to explain and predict changes in population. The initial success and then failure of models such as the logistic curve should serve as a warning when using aggregate models. The discussion of fertility rates, just one component of population change, reveals the naivety of the assumptions behind the application of the logistic to aggregate data. Marketers should be wary of models that predict but do not explain the underlying forces of change.

Finally, the magnitude of the marketing measurement problem is revealed when we see how complex measurement is for demographers, and then realize that demography is only one of several dimensions of demand.

The need for a demographic demand analysis is not limited to marketers of goods and services. A demand analysis is a prerequisite to planning for governmental, educational, and health-care institutions. There is growing evidence that public and private organizations have not made this analysis. For instance, the recent lower birth rate means that by the end of the 1970s tens of thousands of teachers, particularly in the lower grades, may be out of work or in nonteaching jobs. Toy manufacturers already feel the effects and may anticipate more dramatic losses; school construction, classroom equipment, and school supplies are likely to drop in demand; and manufacturers of baby foods and clothing will feel the effects. As this reduced number of children approaches young adulthood in the mid 1980s, the demand for youth products—clothing, records, cosmetics, motorcycles, and sports cars—will decline. This is the first drop in children under age 5 since the depression of the 1930s and the largest drop since the 1850s, when the records were first kept. The causes seem to be the availability of birth-control methods, legalized abortions, and changing American attitudes toward family size (Selover, 1971).

SUMMARY

As man has learned to control his environment, the demographic events of birth, illness, migration, and occupation have become less the product of chance and more the result of individual decisions. Methods of demographic analysis now include, therefore, measures of attitudes and expectations in an attempt to predict demographic decisions that lead to changes in the size of the population. Because of the importance of birth to population changes, much of demographic research has been directed toward improved measures of birth rates. Refinements have made measures less sensitive to variations in the age distribution of the female population.

Population changes influence economic events through aggregate demand and the supply of labor. An economic boom could begin with an increase in aggregate demand, an increase in investment or government expenditures, or some combination of these stimuli. This boom would increase the demand for labor. The effect of this demand on consumer income would depend on the labor supply. The quantity and quality of the labor supply would be determined by foreign immigration laws, unemployment levels, farm populations, educational systems, birth rates of the previous generation, retirement programs, and the percentage of women in the labor force. Favorable economic events, in turn, would have an effect on population through earlier marriages and family formations. Some analysts predict that not all the conditions producing the baby boom of the 1950s will be present in the 1970s when the postwar babies begin to marry. Thus, marketing forecasts of the 1970s should not anticipate a reprise of the 1950s.

Short-run applications of demographic variables to marketing management occur in the popular strategy of demographic market segmentation. Users of this strategy attempt to identify segments of the market that are relatively homogeneous in needs and tastes. Demographic variables such as age, education, location, and race are particularly useful because data are available from secondary sources. Distribution and media strategies require a knowledge of the demographic dimensions of demand.

This discussion of demographic variables is limited to long-range planning and the development of short-range strategies, thereby excluding the tactical decisions that focus on a time horizon of less than a year. The reason for this exclusion is simple. Most marketing decisions are concerned with change, and demographic variables do not change much within a year. Because they are relatively constant during the period when a tactical maneuver is planned and implemented, they do not contribute to the explanation, prediction, or control of marketing behavior and can be ignored. There is some danger, however, of a tactician's being promoted to a strategist or planner without having learned the importance of demographic variables.

READING QUESTIONS

1. What is the most important variable in models that project U.S. population? What have been the trends in this variable and why?
2. How does mobility generate the demand for goods and services? What social problems does it generate? What are the patterns of mobility in the United States?
3. What is the basic population model?
4. Why did the logistic curve first produce accurate population projections and then incorrect ones?
5. Why is the total fertility rate superior to the crude birth rate?
6. Discuss the economic and social determinants of fertility rates.
7. Discuss the several models of migration.

CLASS DISCUSSION QUESTIONS

1. Explain the economic and demographic forces that produced the baby boom in the late 1940s and early 1950s. Will there be an echo effect in the 1970s? Do you see these forces at work in other countries?
2. How does economic development lead to a reduction in birth rates?
3. Describe how demographic forces determine personal values which in turn shape consumer demand for goods and services.
4. What products and services does Figure 3–1 suggest for the 1970s?
5. Evaluate the teen-age market from the viewpoint of a conglomerate firm considering expansion into new fields.
6. For what products and services does mobility generate a demand? Do you anticipate similar patterns in other countries? What social problems does mobility create?
7. Consult the most recent U.S. Bureau of the Census population projections (P-25) to determine whether it has been necessary to revise projections upward or downward. Explain any revisions.
8. Discuss the advantages of the total fertility rate over the crude birth rate.
9. Develop a form to collect data that will be used to build a simulation of the physical distribution system of a consumer convenience product (to be selected by you).

SUGGESTED CASE

Locating bank branches*

The recent growth of branch banking offices has focused attention on the problem of evaluating the potential of various locations. With this problem in mind, the Branch Location Group of a major metropolitan commercial bank is interested in developing an analytical model to predict the deposit potential of possible sites. The population is concentrated, there is some mobility, and there are significant ethnic differences among neighborhoods. A very competitive retail banking environment is created by other commercial banks, savings banks, and savings and loan associations.

What variables and sources of information would you use to develop a model that would predict deposits? (*Deposits* include checking and savings accounts. They may be measured as the number of accounts and the dollar volume.)

---

* This case and the suggested solution, which appears in Appendix B, were written by Mr. Bertram H. Lowi, assistant vice-president and director of marketing research, Bankers Trust Company, New York, N.Y. This contribution is gratefully acknowledged.

SUGGESTED READINGS ━━━━━━━━━━━━━━━━━━━━━━━━━━━━

CHAMBERLAIN, N. W. *Beyond Malthus: Population and Power.* New York: Basic Books, Inc., Publishers, 1970.

EASTERLIN, R. A. "On the Relation of Economic Factors to Recent and Projected Fertility Changes," *Demography,* Vol. 3 (1966), pp. 131–53.

HEYMAN, T. R. "Use of Census Data in Interregional Marketing," *Sloan Management Review,* Vol. 12 (Winter 1971), pp. 17–31.

LINDEN, FABIAN. "Age by Income—1980," *The Conference Board RECORD,* June 1971, pp. 25–27.

PETERSEN, WILLIAM. *Population.* 2d. ed. New York: The Macmillan Co., 1969.

SIMON, J. L. "Some 'Marketing Correct' Recommendations for Family Planning Campaigns," *Demography,* Vol. 5 (1968), pp. 504–7.

4

Illustrative cases in economic demand analysis

Marketing decisions for product development, pricing, and the allocation of promotional effort require an economic analysis of demand.[1] The appropriate variables and models depend on the decision, which, in turn, depends on the life cycle of the product (Figure 4–1). Product development, which occurs in the first stage of a product's life cycle, requires an understanding of the favorability of economic conditions to the introduction of a new product. These conditions must be examined at three levels of aggregation—general business conditions, the economic outlook within the industry, and economic conditions at the consumer level (past and anticipated income and expenditures). As noted in Figure 4–1, historical analysis of comparable products is a method used frequently at this first stage. The economic analysis for the Mustang will be discussed as an example of a historical analysis of a comparable product during the development of a new product. The procedure for analyzing the demand for a new industrial product will be illustrated with the case of the National Lead Company.

Pricing strategies may be developed at the second stage in the product cycle. Market tests and experimental designs are used frequently to test the *price elasticity* of a product. The concept and models of price elasticity will be discussed in Chapter 5. During the rapid-growth stage of the cycle, market surveys are used to estimate buying intentions as a means for de-

---

[1] For a comparison of selected forecasting techniques see Chambers, Mullick, and Smith (1971). For a discussion of business forecasting techniques and available sources of data for the variables see Butler and Kavesh (1966); and Silk (1963 and 1970).

FIGURE 4–1

Types of decisions made over a product's life cycle, with related forecasting techniques

Stage of life cycle	Product development	Market testing and early introduction	Rapid growth	Steady state
Typical decisions	Amount of development effort Product design Business strategies	Optimum facility size Marketing strategies, including distribution and pricing	Facilities expansion Marketing strategies Production planning Sales	Promotions, specials Pricing Production planning Inventories
Forecasting techniques	Delphi method Historical analysis of comparable products Priority pattern analysis Input-output analysis Panel consensus	Consumer surveys Tracking and warning systems Market tests Experimental designs	Statistical techniques for identifying turning points Tracking and warning systems Market surveys Intention-to-buy surveys	Time-series analysis and projection Causal and econometric models Market surveys for tracking and warning Life-cycle analysis

Source: Chambers, Mullick, and Smith (1971).

tecting the turning point in the cycle from a state of rapid growth to the steady state of a mature product. Models and measures of buying intentions appear in Chapter 5.

When a product reaches maturity and sales approach a steady state, two important problems are the locating of new markets for the existing product and the most productive allocation of promotional budgets. An economic demand analysis can contribute to the solution of both problems. The problem of identifying new markets is illustrated in this chapter by the case of a manufacturer of corrugated boxes. Budgets are allocated productively when they are allocated in proportion to the market potential within a territory. Sales quotas are the means by which the effort of the sales force is allocated to the markets with the greatest potential. These quotas are developed by two procedures—the buildup and the breakdown method. The former will be illustrated by the case of a manufacturer of automobile batteries and the latter by a TV manufacturer.

The models in these illustrative cases are largely verbal ones. In two cases these verbal models are translated into mathematical models to illustrate how mathematical expression of demand models helps to clarify the assumptions.

Economic demand analysis, like all demand analyses, requires the identification of the relevant variables. A computerized procedure known as the Automatic Interaction Detection (AID) algorithm will be discussed and illustrated as it is applied to generic and brand demand analysis.

NEW PRODUCT PLANNING

The need for an economic analysis of the demand for a new product is proportional to the size of the expected loss if the product is a failure. There would be no need, for example, if excess productive capacity were used to make goods to order where the capacity could not be used for other alternatives. But this is the unusual case. The more typical case occurs when a new product demand analysis is needed, but none is made. An inadequate market analysis was cited as the primary cause of new product failure by 45 percent of the respondents in a Conference Board study (Hopkins and Bailey, 1971).

The precision of the estimate of demand will vary among firms, products, and the stage of the new product investigation. In the early stages a crude estimate may be sufficient to determine if the engineering department should proceed with cost estimates. The estimate can be refined as the engineering, production, and finance departments refine their estimates.

Estimates of industrial market demand can be very sensitive to change in technology. For instance, an equipment manufacturer developed a machine to assemble the components of printed circuit boards for TV sets. Its original estimate of market potential was reduced because technological obsolescence (due to miniaturization of components) occurred more rapidly than anticipated. Also reducing the original estimate was the slow adoption rate of color TV by consumers and the unexpected entry of competitive equipment (MacDonald, 1967, p. 76).

New products may be a product extension, such as the Ford Motor Company's adding the Mustang, or the product may take the company into a completely new product line for which it has no historical data available for analysis. The National Lead Company case illustrates the latter instance.

Product-line extension—the Mustang

In the product planning for the Mustang,[2] the demographic analysis revealed the potential for an automobile designed to meet the needs of the 18- to 24-year-old market segment (Chapter 2). But would the general business outlook, economic conditions within the industry, and the purchasing power of the segment support the introduction of such an automobile? The answer to this question required an analysis of general business variables, industry conditions, and the economic potential of the segment.

General business conditions. In the early 1960s, when Ford was considering the Mustang, the general business outlook was uncertain. Four commonly used indicators were favorable, and four were unfavorable. The favorable ones included a favorable balance of trade (exports exceeded imports), the public held adequate liquid assets, corporate profits were increasing, and commercial loans were showing greater strength. The unfavorable factors were slow retail sales, a slowed rate in capital outlays, a delay in a decision to reduce taxes, and a reduced rate in federal expenditures.

Auto industry conditions. An analysis of the outlook for the auto industry requires a time-series analysis of industry sales. Time-series data include four components: trend, cycle, seasonal, and irregular components such as war, floods, and strikes. Trend and cycle components for new car sales appear in Figure 4–2. The straight line indicates an increasing trend

[2] The cooperation of Robert J. Eggert, of the Ford Motor Company, is gratefully acknowledged. For a discussion of forecasting in the auto industry, see Eggert and McCracken (1966).

FIGURE 4–2
The 1963 Mustang analysis: Long-run growth in new car sales, 2.8 percent per year

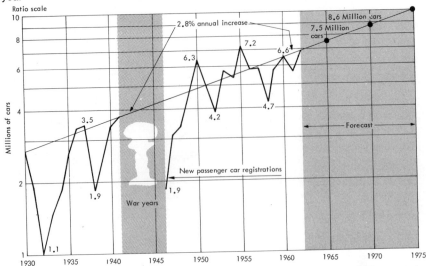

Source: Historical data—R. L. Polk & Company, new car registrations. Projections by Marketing Research (three-year averages centered), quoted in the 1963 research report of the Ford Motor Company.

of 2.8 percent per year. The effect of the cycle may be seen around the trend line.[3] Seasonality patterns appear in Figure 4–3. The horizontal line shows the average sales for each year. The seasonal pattern is the wavy line around this average. The timing and magnitude of seasons are predictable in many industries. In some retail sales, for instance, there are peaks in early September (the opening of school) and at Christmas. The patterns in Figure 4–3 suggest that seasonal patterns in auto sales are not always predictable. Sales declined at the year-end in 1955, 1957, 1959, 1960, 1961, and 1962, but they increased at the ends of 1954 and 1958, and were average during 1956.

The demand for new cars for consumer use comes from three sources: new owners of cars, present owners buying additional cars, and the replacement of cars presently owned. The latter depends on the scrappage rate. Purchase of automobiles, like all durables, may be postponed. Thus, scrappage rates decline during recessions. It appears that trends and cycles within the auto industry were favorable for the introduction of a new automobile during the mid 1960s.

---

[3] The fact that the trend line does not bisect the cycles suggests that the trend is based on data before 1930 or on the period from 1950 to 1960, where the trend appears to bisect the cycles.

FIGURE 4–3

The 1963 Mustang analysis: Seasonally adjusted annual rates of new car retail deliveries

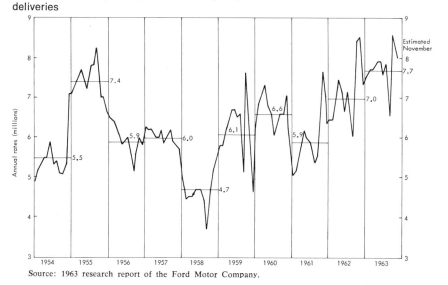

Source: 1963 research report of the Ford Motor Company.

The economic potential of the segment. The ability of prospects to buy a new car is reflected in data such as per capita disposable income, rates of automotive installment credit extension and repayment, and the net cash position of consumers. An examination of trends in these data supported the introduction of the Mustang.

A survey of consumer expenditures and income by age classifications is reproduced in Table 4–1 because it not only reflects the economic potential of the 18 to 24 segment but it also suggests the price of the car. In 1960 the under-25 segment spent an average of $760 per year on autos and their upkeep. If members of this segment bought a new car instead of buying and maintaining a used car, they would expend $2,280 in three years, the typical financing period. Perhaps this figure suggested the initial selling price of the Mustang, about $2,300.

The data in Table 4–1 illustrate another point. The segment that spends the largest share of its income on a product is not necessarily the segment that spends the largest amount in absolute terms. The under-25 segment spent the largest share (14.4 percent), but the 35 to 44 and 45 to 54 segments spent the most in absolute terms ($880).

Additional data, not shown, revealed the importance of segmentation by income classifications. About one fourth of the families with incomes over $10,000 buy a new car each year. The over-$10,000 families accounted for 37 percent of new car sales.

TABLE 4–1

The 1963 Mustang analysis: Young people are heavy spenders on autos and home furnishings

		1960 expenditures			
	1960	*Autos and upkeep*		*Home furnishings*	
Age of family head	*money income (before taxes)*	*Dollars*	*Percent of income*	*Dollars*	*Percent of income*
Under 25.	$5,270	760	14.4	300	5.7
25–34.	7,275	795	11.0	350	4.8
35–44.	8,105	880	10.9	370	4.6
45–54.	8,685	880	10.1	340	3.9
55–64.	7,470	595	8.0	230	3.1
65–74.	4,710	295	6.3	115	2.4
75 and over	3,550	110	4.3	110	3.1
All ages.	7,265	715	9.8	295	4.1

Source: 1960 Survey of Consumer Expenditures and Income, averages of following eight cities: Atlanta, Boston, Chicago, Detroit, New York, Philadelphia, San Francisco, and Washington, D.C., quoted in the 1963 research report of the Ford Motor Company.

Evaluating new ventures—The National Lead Company

The procedure used by The National Lead Company to analyze the demand for alternative ventures consisted of three steps, ending in a report to management (MacDonald, 1967, pp. 77–80). The first stage was a literature search to determine the marketing environment, which included potential product applications, principal markets, usage trends, present users, present competitors, and the patent situation. The second stage consisted of primary research to determine the usage factor of the new product per gallon of paint, per ton of plastic or paper, etc. The marketing research department conducted personal interviews with the technical, marketing, and purchasing directors of major users. A mail questionnaire was used for small users, distributors, dealers, and jobbers too numerous to visit. A personalized letter and a follow-up letter yielded a 70 percent response to the mail survey. Purchasing departments provided additional information such as the names of major suppliers, pricing structures, and delivery requirements.

The final report to management classified these data as follows: (1) past and expected trends in usage rates per end product, (2) trends in the sales of end products, (3) profiles of major users, (4) profiles of major competitors, and (5) special requirements—technical, delivery, and packaging requirements, order size, and price structures. The most attractive market segments were identified. Share of the market and the time required to achieve the potential were estimated. Four alternatives were evaluated—invest, enter into a joint venture, acquire a going producer, or drop the product idea. Recommendations were given following the evaluation of the pros and cons of each alternative.

IDENTIFYING NEW MARKETS FOR EXISTING PRODUCTS

As a mature product reaches its stable sales level, one means for expanding sales is to locate untapped markets. The demand analysis may consist of applying existing measures and models to new market segments to locate those with the highest potential. In industrial marketing these segments are frequently defined in terms of the Standard Industrial Classification (SIC) numbers used in the Censuses of Business.[4]

Discovering new markets for an industrial product—corrugated boxes

A regional manufacturer of corrugated boxes thought that Phoenix, Arizona (Maricopa County), might have untapped potential for his products in industries not regularly approached by his salesmen (U.S. Department of Commerce, 1966, pp. 40–51). Of the $250,000 of sales in Phoenix, $200,000 went to firms in the food and kindred products industry; the remainder went to firms manufacturing electrical machinery.

The procedure for measuring the market potential is summarized in Table 4–2. The first task was to estimate the corrugated box consumption (in dollars) per employee in each industry (columns 1, 2, and 3). These rates were multiplied by the employment in each industry (column 4) to yield an industry potential in Phoenix (column 5). The manufacturer was reaching only 5.4 percent of his potential market ($250,000/$4,616,000). While he realized 10.8 percent of the potential in SIC 20 and 9 percent in SIC 36, the second largest market, SIC 32, was untapped. To tap this market he should assign sales quotas in SIC 32.

This demand analysis may be expressed in terms of the equation for generic demand introduced in Chapter 1, which is as follows:

$$G_{kt} = N_{kt} R_{kt}. \tag{4-1}$$

In the present case G_{kt} is the generic demand for corrugated boxes for selected industries in Phoenix, Arizona, in 1962; N_{kt} is the number of em-

---

[4] SICs are the Standard Industrial Classifications used by the U.S. federal government to classify manufacturing industries. Definitions of classifications may be found in U.S. Bureau of the Budget (1967). Revisions of these definitions are discussed in The Institute for Inter-Industry Data (1968).

TABLE 4–2

Estimated market for corrugated and solid fibre box by industry groups, Phoenix, Arizona, standard metropolitan statistical area, 1962

SIC major group code	Using industry	Value of box shipments by end use ($000)*† (1)	Employment by industry groups‡ (2)	Consumption per employee by industry groups (1 ÷ 2) (dollars) (3)	Maricopa County	
					Employment by industry groups‡ (4)	Estimated potential share-of-the market (3 × 4) ($000) (5)
20	Food and kindred products	586,164	1,578,305	371	4,973	1,845
21	Tobacco	17,432	74,557	233	⋯	⋯
22	Textile mill products	91,520	874,677	104	⋯	⋯
23	Apparel	34,865	1,252,443	27	1,974	53
24	Lumber and products (except furniture)	19,611	526,622	37	690	26
25	Furniture and fixtures	89,341	364,166	245	616	151
26	Paper and allied products	211,368	587,882	359	190	68
27	Printing; publishing, and allied industries	32,686	904,208	36	2,876	104
28	Chemicals and allied products	128,564	772,169	166	488	81
29	Petroleum refining and related industries	28,328	161,367	175	⋯	⋯
30	Rubber and misc. plastic products	67,551	387,997	174	190	33
31	Leather and leather products	8,716	352,919	24	⋯	⋯
32	Stone, clay, and glass products	226,621	548,058	413	1,612	666
33	Primary metal industries	19,611	1,168,110	16	2,889	46
34	Fabricated metal products	130,743	1,062,096	123	2,422	298
35	Machinery; except electrical	58,834	1,445,558	40	5,568	223
36	Electrical machinery, equipment and supplies	119,848	1,405,382	85	6,502	553
37	Transportation equipment	82,804	1,541,618	53	5,005	265
38	Professional, scientific instruments, etc.	13,074	341,796	38	⋯	⋯
39	Misc. manufacturing industries	200,473	369,071	543	376	204
90	Government	10,895	⋯	⋯	⋯	⋯
	Total	2,179,049†				4,616

* Based on data reported in *Fibre Box Industry Statistics 1963*, Fibre Box Association.
† U.S. Bureau of the Census, *1962 Annual Survey of Manufacturers: General Statistics for Industry Groups and Industries* (M62(AS)-1 Revised) Table 1—General Statistics for Industry Groups and Industries: 1962, 1961, and 1958, p. 10.
‡ U.S. Bureau of the Census, *County Business Patterns, First Quarter 1962*, Parts 1 and 9.
Source: U.S. Department of Commerce (1966), p. 51.

ployees in these industries; and R_{kt} is the box usage rate per employee, expressed as the value of box shipments per employee in each industry (national value of box shipments in the industry/national industry employment).

Expressing the analysis procedures in algebraic terms highlights assumptions that may limit the validity of the procedure. First, there is no attempt to project the data over future time periods; thus, the analysis is a static one. Furthermore, it is not clear that all data have been projected to a common time period. The second, and perhaps the most limiting, assumption is the use of a national usage rate in a segment as small as a single county. Furthermore, calculating the rate in this manner assumes that all firms within an industry are at the same level of technology. This method provides a useful first approximation of demand, but its assumptions and limitations should be clearly understood.

Limitations of the SIC method

The SIC method for measuring market potential has several limitations. One limitation is that many applications of the SIC approach use only one independent variable, generally the number of employees, because this is the most available figure. Sales, value added, and total wages are also used when they are available. Single variable demand models are very sensitive to errors in the independent variable. Using a single-variable model, a study of the percentage distribution of errors in SIC estimates for 10 products revealed that the potential was seriously overestimated (Piersol, 1968). Additional variables are used by many industrial marketers. Allis-Chalmers, an industrial and farm equipment manufacturer, uses three variables—number of employees, past sales, and future sales estimated by district managers (Heinecke, 1957).

Other limitations of the SIC method are more difficult to correct. The key variable, average usage per employee, makes two critical assumptions. Technology is assumed to be constant over time and among firms. In many rapidly changing industries, such as the electronic and space-age industries, such an assumption is unwarranted. Second, the use of an "average" assumes that the production function is linear with regard to the product in question. This assumption may overlook economies of scale, which would result in an overestimation of potential. Conversely, diminishing returns would result in an underestimation of potential.

One limitation of the data is the failure of the primary or secondary Standard Industrial Classification number to represent all the activities of the firm. Conglomerates, multiproduct firms, and integrated firms complicate classifications. The number of employees per SIC number may not accurately portray the firm's activities within that classification. Second, data for large firms must be excluded from *County Business Patterns* when reporting would result in disclosure of confidential information. Thus, important data are missing for some counties. The availability of commercial sources not subject to disclosure laws is correcting this limitation. Third, data are collected at the county of production, not the county in which buying decisions are made. When these are not in the same county, the SIC method could assign a quota to the wrong salesman. A final limitation is the speed with which the data become obsolete. This problem is being corrected by more frequent reporting and the availability of commercial sources. *County Business Patterns* is now published annually. The increased competition among commercial data suppliers tends to force them to revise their data banks continuously.

The SIC method can be applied to a variety of industrial products, which include capital equipment, raw materials, semifinished materials and subassemblies, and operating and administrative supplies. In addition to analyzing the demand by manufacturers, the method is used to study the demand of institutional buyers (hotels, restaurants, hospitals, schools, universities, etc.) and industrial demand by buyers in agricultural industries, extractive industries (lumbering, mining, oil pumping, and fishing), construction, and manufacturing. Thus, the illustration in this section, which is concerned with manufacturing, represents only a fraction of nonconsumer demand.

ALLOCATING PROMOTIONAL EFFORT ACCORDING TO POTENTIAL DEMAND

When a product reaches maturity, marketing decisions turn toward more efficient allocation of promotional budgets. Ideally, promotional effort should be proportional to the potential demand in a market segment. The effort of salesmen is generally allocated by assigning quotas, with the highest quotas assigned to segments with the greatest potential. The procedures for establishing sales quotas may be described as the buildup or the breakdown methods. The buildup method starts with disaggregate data and builds quotas for sales territories. The company annual quota is the sum of territory quotas. The breakdown method starts with a company forecast and breaks it down into territory quotas. In practice both methods are frequently used, with the final quota being a reconciliation of the two quotas. The two cases in this section illustrate the buildup and the breakdown methods.

Building a sales quota—automobile batteries

The A.B.C. Battery Company, a manufacturer of automobile replacement batteries, received complaints from sales managers that present quotas were not fair (U.S. Department of Commerce, 1966, pp. 54–55). As a result of these complaints, new quotas were developed using the measurement procedures outlined in Table 4–3. The method made the following assumptions: (1) replacement rate would continue at 31 percent of automobile registrations, (2) the average sale value at the manufacturing level was $10, (3) the company would retain its 10.9 percent market share, and (4) auto registrations would continue to increase at the annual rate of 4.1 percent.

The number of registrations (column 1) for states and counties was determined from the secondary sources noted in Table 4–3. An annual industry forecast, in units, was computed for each county by multiplying data in column 1 by 0.31, the replacement rate. This unit forecast was converted to a dollar forecast (column 3) by multiplying column 2 by the average value of a battery, $10. The company's share of this potential is computed by multiplying column 3 by 0.109, its national average market share. The county sales quotas (column 5) were established by multiplying column 4 by $(1.041)^2$, the growth rate for two years (1963 to 1965). The company and industry forecasts were built up by adding state and county estimates.

The demand analysis procedure for the A.B.C. Battery Company may be summarized with the following equation:

$$B_{\text{ABC},1965} = \sum_{k=1}^{n} M_{\text{ABC},k,1965} N_{k,1965} R_{k,1965} S_{k,1965} \qquad (4\text{–}2)$$

where

$B_{\text{ABC},1965}$ = the estimated dollar sales of the ABC battery brand for 1965;

$M_{\text{ABC},k,1965}$ = the market share of the brand in segment k;

$N_{k,1965}$ = the number of automobiles registered in segment k;

$R_{k,1965}$ = the probability of a battery being replaced during 1965 in segment k; and

$S_{k,1965}$ = the sales value per battery at the manufacturing level.

Market segments k are defined in terms of counties. Future registrations were estimated by extrapolation, thus

$$N_{t+n} = N_t A^n \qquad (4\text{–}3)$$

where A is the annual growth rate.

TABLE 4–3

Automobile registration and company sales quotas by state and county, 1963, and projections for 1965 (in thousands)

Specimen states and counties	Automobile registrations, 1963* (1)	Estimated automobile replacement batteries in 1963 (2) × 0.31	Estimated value of replacement batteries, 1963 ($) (3) (2) × $10	A.B.C. Battery Co. replacement quota, 1963 ($) (4) (3) × 0.109	A.B.C. Battery Co. estimated replacement sales quota for 1965 ($) (5) (4) × (1.041)²
Alabama	1,184	367	3,670	400	433
Arizona	580	180	1,800	196	212
Arkansas	588	182	1,820	199	215
California	7,712	2,391	23,910	2,606	2,823
Colorado	817	254	2,540	276	299
Illinois	3,594	1,114	11,140	1,214	1,316
Missouri	1,536	476	4,760	519	562
New Jersey	2,431	754	7,540	821	889
North Carolina	1,536	476	4,760	519	562
Ohio	3,970	1,231	12,310	1,342	1,454
Pennsylvania	4,020 ††	1,246	12,460	1,358	1,472
Allegheny	564	175	1,750	191	207
Berks	117	36	360	39	43
Erie	106	33	330	36	39
Jefferson	21	6	60	7	8
Montgomery	206	64	640	70	77
Philadelphia	595	184	1,840	201	218
Somerset	33	10	100	11	12
Westmoreland	131	41	410	45	49
All other counties	2,247	697	6,970	760	823
Total United States	68,730	21,306	213,060	23,224	25,188

* U.S. Bureau of Public Roads, *Highway Statistics, 1963*, Table MV–1, State Motor Vehicle Registrations 1963, p. 14.
† Pennsylvania Bureau of Publications, *Pennsylvania Statistical Abstract, 1964–1965*, Table 204, Number of Motor Vehicle Registrations by County 1963, p. 306.
‡ Columns may not add due to rounding.
Source: U.S. Department of Commerce (1966), p. 55.

Expressing the procedure in mathematical terms reveals assumptions which should be questioned. First, the national levels of M, R, and S are assumed to be appropriate at the county level. This assumption ignores the fact that market share in each county will vary according to the quality of local dealers. Clearly, the probability of replacing a battery would be higher in colder climates. Price competition may vary the sales value among counties. Secondly, one may question the projections over time. To assume that the probability of replacement in 1965 is the same as the probability in 1963 is to ignore possible changes in the average age of automobiles. A large number of new automobiles in 1964 would lower the replacement probability. Similarly, extrapolation of registrations at an average growth rate fails to consider the fact that automobile sales vary annually according to economic conditions. The forecast's sensitivity to these assumptions should be tested as they were in the case of the Port of New York Authority. The battery manufacturer should consider Equation 4–2 as a first approximation of a demand model that may require refinement.

Breaking down a company quota—TV sets

In contrast to the battery manufacturer, a TV manufacturer who fore-casted sales at $15 million faced the problem of allocating this corporate goal to territories (U.S. Department of Commerce, 1966, p. 53). A multiple-factor index was used. The five variables—population, number of housing units, income, appliance sales, and TV sets in place—were weighted 1, 2, 3, 4, and 5 respectively to reflect the differences in their importance. Examples of this weighting procedure are illustrated in Table 4–4. These weighted variables were summed (column 12), and these sums were converted to a percent of the U.S. total (column 13). The market potential for each territory was computed by multiplying this percent times the total company forecast of $15 million (column 14).

The weighting factors may be determined by executive judgment or by the statistical procedure of multiple regression. Multiple regression would probably reveal a high correlation between population and housing units, so that one of these variables could be eliminated when constructing the index.

IDENTIFYING IMPORTANT VARIABLES—AID ANALYSIS

Intuition is frequently used to identify the important demographic variables. Identification of important economic variables and their interrelationship with demographic variables requires more formal procedures, such

TABLE 4–4

The combined-factor method in establishing market potential index for television sets

Company's sales territory (1)	Population, 1960 Per cent of U.S.* (2)	Weighted by 1 (3)	Housing units, 1960 Per cent of U.S.† (4)	Weighted by 2 (5)	Aggregate income in 1959 of the population, 1960 Per cent of U.S.† (6)	Weighted by 3 (7)	Appliance, radio, television store sales Per cent of U.S.‡ (8)	Weighted by 4 (9)	TV sets in place Per cent of U.S.† (10)	Weighted by 5 (11)	Sum of weighted factors, columns 3, 5, 7, 9, and 11 (12)	Market index col. 12 is per cent of U.S. total (col. 12 ÷ 15) (13)	Company market potential (col. 13 × co.'s sales forecasts of $15 million) (dollars) (14)
Alabama	1.8	1.8	1.7	3.4	1.2	3.6	0.7	2.8	1.5	7.5	19.1	1.3	195,000
Arizona.	0.7	0.7	0.7	1.4	0.7	2.1	0.8	3.2	0.6	3.0	10.4	0.7	105,000
California . . .	8.8	8.8	9.4	18.8	10.9	32.7	14.0	56.0	9.2	46.0	162.3	10.8	1,620,000
Colorado. . . .	1.0	1.0	1.0	2.0	1.0	3.0	0.8	3.2	1.0	5.0	14.2	0.9	135,000
Illinois	5.6	5.6	5.6	11.2	6.6	19.8	5.7	22.8	5.8	29.0	88.4	5.9	885,000
Missouri. . . .	2.4	2.4	2.6	5.2	2.3	6.9	1.7	6.8	2.6	13.0	34.3	2.3	345,000
Wyoming. . . .	0.2	0.2	0.2	0.4	0.2	0.6	0.2	0.8	0.2	1.0	3.0	0.2	30,000
U.S. total	100.0	100.0	100.0	200.0	100.0	300.0	100.0	400.0	100.0	500.0	1500.0	100.0	15,000,000

* Percentages based on U.S. Bureau of the Census: U.S. Census of Population, 1960. Vol. I, Characteristics of the Population, Part I, United States Summary.
† Percentages based on U.S. Bureau of the Census: U.S. Census of Housing, 1960. Vol. I.
‡ Percentages based on U.S. Bureau of the Census: U.S. Census of Business, 1958, Vol. I, Summary Statistics.
Source: U.S. Department of Commerce, 1966. p. 53.

as multivariate statistical techniques. One technique, the Automatic Interaction Detection (AID) algorithm, is illustrated below. The marketing applications of additional techniques, such as factor analysis, cluster analysis, and multiple regression may be found in Gatty (1966), Kotler (1971), and Sheth (1971).

The AID analysis identifies the characteristics of those market segments with the highest probability of buying a product or brand.[5] This analysis readily handles the difficult data that are so common in a demand analysis, such as variables that are discontinuous, intercorrelated, and nonlinear (Sonquist, 1970).

While the AID technique is a recent development (Sonquist and Morgan, 1964), it is being used by an increasing number of market researchers. Two common applications are the identification of the determinants of generic demand and of brand demand.

Generic demand

Demographic and economic determinants of the generic demand for a car, as identified by the AID method, are summarized in Figure 4–4. The data were generated by surveying a panel of consumers at several points in time (Snowbarger and Suits, 1967). The problem facing the researcher was the identification of consumer characteristics that would predict the purchase of an automobile. Many demographic and economic dimensions, such as length of marriage, debt ratio, and expectations for buying a car, were measured during an initial interview. A subsequent interview revealed that 25 percent of the respondents had purchased a car since the initial interview. The AID analysis identified respondents' characteristics that accounted for the most variation in purchase rates.

Each step in the AID analysis divided the sample into two groups. The variable that accounted for the greatest amount of variation in buying rates was buying expectations. In Figure 4–4 it will be noted that 358 respondents stated that they definitely or probably would buy a car or that they were undecided. Fifty-one percent of this group bought a car before the second interview. Twenty percent of the 1,756 respondents who stated that they would not buy did purchase a car before the second interview.

The next split that accounted for the most variance in buying rates was the debt ratio of the "will not buy" respondents. These subsets of "will not buy" are designated in Figure 4–4 as groups 4 and 5. The data

---

[5] The AID algorithm may be described technically as a step-wise one-way analysis of variance that partitions the sample into nonoverlapping dichotomized subgroups whose means account for more variation in the dependent variable than any other combination of dichotomized groups (Sonquist, 1970).

FIGURE 4-4

AID analysis: Demographic and economic determinants of demand for a car

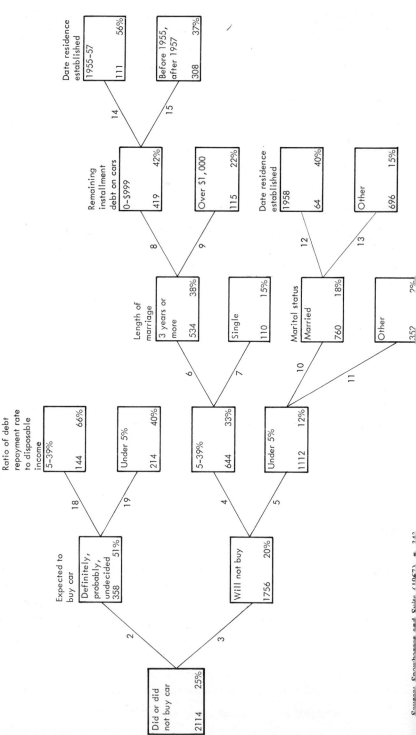

Source: Snowbarger and Spitz (1967), p. 343

in box No. 4 may be read as follows: 33 percent of the 644 respondents who initially said that they would not buy a car and who had a debt ratio from 5 to 39 percent purchased a car before the second interview. These percentages are frequently interpreted as probabilities. Thus, referring to box No. 18, there is a 0.66 probability that a person will buy a car if he states that he expects to buy and if his debt ratio is from 5 to 39 percent.

Because only 28 percent of the variance in the car purchase rates was associated with these variables, we must conclude that many of the determinants of the demand for automobiles were not in this analysis.

Brand demand

Segmentation of the market for brand X of a consumer nondurable product along demographic and economic dimensions is shown in Figure 4–5. The top branch of this AID tree diagram is interpreted as follows: 16.5 percent of the sample purchased the brand, 61.9 percent of the women who lived in the north central part of the United States, who were heavy users of the generic product, and whose income was under $12,500, used the brand. The percentages along the lines indicate the part of the sample that is in the next box; thus this segment, whose probability of purchase is 0.619, represents only 5.2 percent of the total sample. The decision to develop a strategy for this segment would depend on the absolute number of persons in the segment and the availability of media and messages that would reach the segment. The figures in parentheses at the end of each branch are the percent of the sample that was in the segment and bought the brand. These percentages total only 16.0 percent because 0.5 percent of the sample was not within the segments shown in Figure 4–5.

SUMMARY

Economic demand analysis contributes to the marketing activities of product planning, the identification of new markets for existing products, and the allocation of promotional effort. Product planning, which marks the beginning of a product's life cycle, requires an analysis of the economic conditions at three levels—general business conditions, industry conditions, and the economic outlook for the buyer—to determine if the economic climate is favorable to the introduction of a new product. The Mustang, a product-line extension for a consumer good, illustrated the type of analysis required. The National Lead Company case illustrated how an industrial firm evaluates the potential for new products.

FIGURE 4–5
AID analysis: Demographic and economic segmentation of the market for brand X

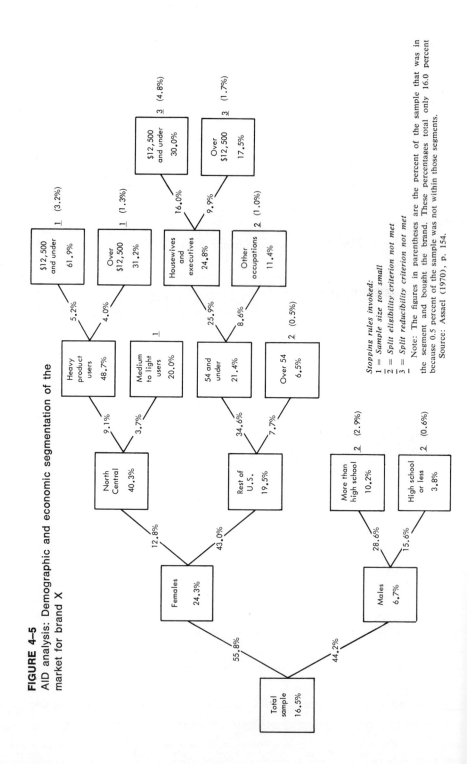

Stopping rules invoked:
1 = *Sample size too small*
2 = *Split eligibility criterion not met*
3 = *Split reducibility criterion not met*

Note: The figures in parentheses are the percent of the sample that was in the segment and bought the brand. These percentages total only 16.0 percent because 0.5 percent of the sample was not within those segments.
Source: Assael (1970), p. 154.

When a product reaches a stable level of sales, one means for expanding sales is to locate new markets for the product. Industrial demand analyses are frequently built using Censuses of Business which classify firms according to a Standard Industrial Classification (SIC). An example of such an analysis illustrates the method and highlights its limitations. The reliability of many of these models is limited because they include only one independent variable—sales or number of employees per company within an SIC. Validity is in doubt because it is assumed that technology is constant among firms and over time and because economies of scale are ignored. Because only the major activities of a firm are classified, a firm's activity in a classification is overstated, which inflates estimates of potential.

Ideally, advertising budgets and salesmen's time should be allocated in proportion to the potential demand within a market segment. Two procedures for developing sales quotas are known as the buildup and breakdown methods. The former develops a company quota by summing the quotas for each territory, while the latter breaks down an aggregate company quota into territory quotas by developing a territory index of potential demand. In practice the final quota is frequently the result of reconciling the quotas generated by the two methods.

The identification of relevant variables—demographic, economic, social, and social-psychological—is simplified by the availability of multivariate statistical techniques. One technique, the Automatic Interaction Detection (AID) algorithm, illustrated one means for identifying demographic and economic variables for generic and brand demand analyses.

READING QUESTIONS

1. What kinds of marketing decisions require an economic demand analysis? How do these decisions vary over the product life cycle?
2. What are the time components of historical data?
3. Distinguish between the two methods of developing quotas for sales territories.
4. What function does the AID algorithm perform in an economic demand analysis?
5. What are the limitations of SIC models in industrial demand analyses?

CLASS DISCUSSION QUESTIONS

1. Using *Industrial Outlook* and *Predicast* (see Appendix A for a description of these sources of information), select three industries with bright futures. Evaluate these industries for possible employment or investment.

2. Select a consumer durable good and conduct an economic demand analysis similar to the Mustang analysis. (Sources of information noted in Appendix A should be consulted.)

3. Develop a generalized plan for estimating the potential demand for an industrial product of your choice. Note clearly the assumptions that your method makes.

SUGGESTED CASES

Fanta Chemical Company. Bursk and Greyser (1968), pp. 112–22.

The decision whether to increase plant capacity for ethylene glycol will be based on the potential demand for automotive antifreeze. A previous forecast was lucky because it had offsetting errors—an underestimate of cars on the road and an overestimate of usage per automobile. The latter error was the result of a decline in use of ethylene glycol as an antifreeze and the smaller radiators of compact cars.

1. Does the potential demand justify increasing the plant capacity?

2. Would your decision change if you could get better information? If yes, what information do you need, where would you get it, and how much would it cost?

New Era Specialty Paper Company. Bursk and Greyser (1968), pp. 27–30.

The company was considering producing and marketing a new fiber reinforced film to be used as a moisture vapor barrier for building foundations.

1. Based on present information, what product would you produce, for which market segment, and what attributes would you promote?

2. Before making the final decisions, what additional information would you want?

Seaberg Machine Tool Company. Bursk and Greyser (1968), pp. 18–21.

A mail survey was used to identify seven types of information about metal working plants. SIC numbers were assigned to present and potential customers.

1. Evaluate the strengths and weaknesses of this method of industrial demand analysis.

2. What changes would you recommend?

Standard Electronic Development, Inc.: Commercial microwave operation (A). Boyd and Davis (1971), pp. 157–71.

In 1966 the company was exploring industrial microwave heating applications. Some of the applications included drying adhesives during the manufacture of corrugated board, drying paper during pressing operations, drying foundry cores, and food and pharmaceutical drying.

1. Using data in the case and secondary sources such as *Industrial Outlook, predicasts,* and other sources noted in Appendix A, rank the applications according to market potential.
2. Compare your demand analyses with the actual experience of the company in 1968 and 1970, as reported by Boyd and Davis (1971), Standard Electronic Development (B) and (C), pp. 172–84.
3. Would your demand analysis have led to a more or less favorable outcome in 1970?

SUGGESTED READINGS

BUTLER, W. F., and KAVESH, R. A. *How Business Economists Forecast.* Englewood Cliffs, N.J.: Prentice-Hall, Inc., 1966.

CHAMBERS, J. C.; MULLICK, S. K.; and SMITH, D. D. "How to Choose the Right Forecasting Technique," *Harvard Business Review,* Vol. 49 (July–August 1971), pp. 45–74.

FARLEY, JOHN U., and HINICH, MELVIN J. "Spectral Analysis," *Journal of Advertising Research,* Vol. 9, No. 4 (December 1969), pp. 47–50.

PETERS, WILLIAM H. "Relative Occupational Class Income: A Significant Variable in the Marketing of Automobiles," *Journal of Marketing,* Vol. 34, No. 2 (April 1970), pp. 74–77.

SILK, LEONARD SOLOMON. *A Primer on Business Forecasting, with a Guide to Sources of Business Data.* New York: Random House, Inc., 1970.

5

Economic models
of demand

While demographic variables reflect physiological needs, economic variables reflect buyers' abilities to meet these needs. This distinction can be seen clearly in Figure 5–1, which is a marketing adaption of a social-psychological model of behavior (Pollak, 1948). *Motivation,* it will be noted, is the perception of *needs* and *goals,* which are the means available for meeting needs. The economic variables of price, income, savings, and credit reflect an individual's economic *capacity* for attaining these goals. The *opportunity* to acquire a product is made possible by promotion and channels of distribution. The final *purchase* and *use* of the product lead to a state of *satisfaction* or *dissatisfaction* which, through a feedback loop, will modify future goals. Economic models of demand make observations at only two points in this demand system—economic capacity and purchase. Thus, buyers' perceptions of needs, goals, opportunities, and states of satisfaction are not considered directly but are at best implied through these economic relationships. Despite this limitation, economic models perform an important role in describing generic and brand demand, which lead to strategies for products, price, and promotion.

ECONOMIC MODELS OF GENERIC DEMAND[1]

Economic models of generic demand describe the sales of an industry or of a firm which is the only producer of a product—a monopoly. The

[1] For additional discussions of the models of consumer behavior, see Ferber (1962); Nicosia (1966), chap. 3; and Suits (1963). For a discussion of the limitations of economic analysis of consumer behavior, see Martin (1964).

FIGURE 5–1

A social-psychological model of demand

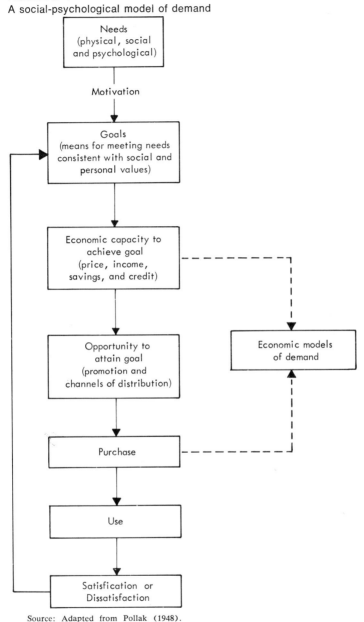

Source: Adapted from Pollak (1948).

most basic economic demand model is one that relates the quantities (Q) of a good sold at various prices (P). Assume that the following price-quantity relationships have been observed:

Price	Quantity sold
$4.	130
6.	90
8.	50

These relationships are described graphically in Figure 5–2. The observed demand curve is AC, but the dotted lines assume that the linear relation-

FIGURE 5–2
Two demand curves

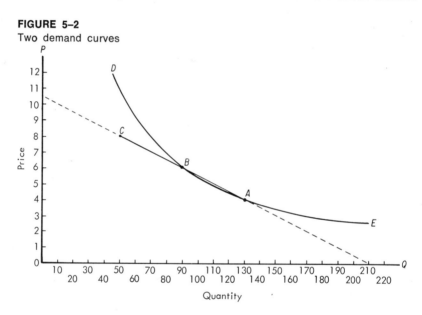

ship would exist beyond the observations. This line may be described by the following equation:

$$Q = 210 - 20P \qquad (5\text{–}1)$$

where Q is the quantity sold, P is the selling price, and 210 is the quantity that would be sold if the price were zero. The maximum sales of 210 may be read directly from Figure 5–2 by observing the point at which the demand curve CA intersects line OQ. The right-hand element in this equation states that every dollar increase in price will reduce sales by 20 units. (In practice, equations such as 5–1 are estimated using the statistical technique known as *regression*.)

Price elasticities[2]

When developing a pricing strategy a marketing manager generally thinks in terms of percentage changes in sales that would be stimulated by percentage changes in prices. The ratio of these percentages is known as the *price elasticity* of the product and is expressed as follows:

$$e_{qp} = \frac{\dfrac{\Delta Q}{Q}}{\dfrac{\Delta P}{P}} = \frac{\Delta Q}{Q} \cdot \frac{P}{\Delta P} = \frac{\Delta Q}{\Delta P} \cdot \frac{P}{Q} \tag{5-2}$$

where e_{qp} is the elasticity and ΔQ and ΔP are the changes in quantity and price. The value of e_{qp} expresses the percentage change in quantity that is associated with a 1 percent change in price. To illustrate the calculation of elasticities and a property of linear demand curves, we may compute the elasticities at points *A, B,* and *C* as follows:

$$A \quad e_{pq} = \frac{40}{-2} \cdot \frac{4}{130} = -0.62$$

$$B \quad e_{qp} = \frac{40}{-2} \cdot \frac{6}{90} = -1.33 \tag{5-3}$$

$$C \quad e_{qp} = \frac{40}{-2} \cdot \frac{8}{50} = -3.20$$

The elasticity of -3.20 at point *C* means that a 1.0 percent reduction in price at this point on the demand curve will yield a 3.2 percent increase in sales. The elasticity for point *A* is *inelastic* because it is less than 1.0, and the curve is *elastic* at points *B* and *C* because the elasticities are more than 1.0, a phenomenon known as *unit* elasticity. Elasticities for a linear curve, such as *AC* in Figure 5–2, will always be higher at the higher price.

Elasticities can be very useful when making a pricing decision. To maximize dollar sales, the decision rule is simple: change price to that point where elasticity is -1.0. In practice this rule is constrained by the cost of a price change (e.g., reprinting catalogs), competitive reaction, corporate policies, and antitrust legislation.

When a demand curve is nonlinear, such as *DE* in Figure 5–2, elasticity could be computed by drawing an arc between two points on the curve, such as *AB*. *Arc* elasticity would be computed at the midpoint, a quantity of 110, using Equation 5–2. This elasticity, which turns out to be -0.91, is only an approximation of the elasticity along the curve *DE*. To compute

---

[2] For additional discussion of elasticities see Johnston (1963); and Kotler (1971), pp. 24–31.

the precise price elasticity we must use *point* elasticity by replacing $\Delta Q/\Delta P$ in Equation 5–2 with dQ/dP, thus

$$e_{qp} = \frac{dQ}{dP} \cdot \frac{P}{Q}, \tag{5-4}$$

where dQ/dP is derived by differentiating the demand equation with respect to price. The equation for curve DE in Figure 5–2 is

$$Q = \frac{540}{P} \tag{5-5}$$

so dQ/dP equals $-540/P^2$. Point elasticity at a quantity of 110 is -1.00, which illustrates that arc elasticity is only an approximation.

Equation 5–5 is a hyperbolic function which appears as follows in general terms:

$$Q = AP^{-\beta}. \tag{5-6}$$

This curve has the convenient property that a percentage change in price will be offset by an equal percentage change in quantity so that price elasticity is constant over the entire demand curve. The elasticity at every point on Equation 5–5 is -1.0. The coefficient of *constant* elasticity in Equation 5–6 is $-\beta$ which may be demonstrated as follows:

$$e_{qp} = \frac{dQ}{dP} \cdot \frac{P}{Q} = (-\beta AP^{-\beta-1}) \frac{P}{AP^{-\beta}} = \frac{-\beta AP^{-\beta}}{AP^{-\beta}} = -\beta. \tag{5-7}$$

Constant elasticity may be estimated directly by regressing the logarithm of quantity on the logarithm of price, which appears as follows:

$$\log Q = \log A - \beta \log P \tag{5-8}$$

with $-\beta$ the estimate of constant elasticity. Two examples in this chapter used this double-log transformation to estimate constant elasticity. (Estimates of elasticities for personal consumption goods and services may be found in Houthakker and Taylor [1970].)

Coefficients of constant elasticities simplify computation, but in practice it can be dangerous to assume a hyperbolic function if the true function is linear or some other function. For example, in Figure 5–2, the elasticity at a quantity of 50 on the hyperbolic function is -1.0 while it is -3.2 on the linear curve. The former would suggest no change in price while the latter would recommend a substantial price decrease.

Another form of price elasticity is *cross elasticity,* which relates a percentage change in the quantity of product A to a percentage change in the price of product B. These two products may be complements (e.g., gasoline and automobiles) or substitute products (e.g., Ford and Chevrolet).

Before proceeding to additional economic variables, two distinctions must be made between generic demand in economic models, generally represented by Q, and generic demand in marketing models, introduced in Chapter 1 as G. Economic data acknowledge demand only after a purchase is made. Marketers, in contrast, regard demand and motivation as synonyms, and therefore record activities such as shopping for information even though the effort may never result in a sale. Marketers are also concerned with events after a sale, such as consumption rates and satisfaction.

The second distinction is concerned with the units in which demand is expressed. Generic demand was expressed in Chapter 1 as follows:

$$G_{kt} = N_{kt}R_{kt},\qquad(5\text{--}9)$$

where G_{kt} is the generic demand in segment k in period t, N is the number of people in the segment, and R is their usage rate. In the short run, when there is no change in N, and R is measured in historical terms, the concepts of economic demand Q and G are identical. In the long run, when population changes, these rates should be expressed in per capita terms, so that Q/N is identical to R, which is G/N.

Income elasticities

Income elasticities may be computed using the price elasticity procedures. Income elasticities will vary among products. Convenience foods, for instance, are income elastic because they represent the addition of a service to the basic food product and the income elasticity for services is greater than the elasticity for food (Harp and Miller, 1965).

The problem in computing income elasticity is the manner in which income should be expresed. Economic theory suggests that expressing income in absolute terms does not reflect consumer behavior. Relative income theory uses a ratio of present income to average income (Dussenberry, 1949). Permanent income theory divides income and consumption into two components, transitory and permanent. The permanent component is viewed as the discounted present value of a stream of future receipts. Permanent consumption, therefore, is a function of the anticipated returns from the resources of a consumer over his lifetime.[3]

Examples of economic models of generic demand

Refinements in economic models of generic demand include additional independent variables of an individual's savings, credit terms, present

---

[3] For a discussion of income models see Ferber (1962).

stocks of durable goods, the price of competing goods, attitudes toward business conditions, attitudes toward product attributes, and subjective probabilities of buying. The following examples will illustrate the contribution of some of these variables to explanations of generic demand. Conspicuously absent from these models is any variable which reflects the promotional effort by the industry of the product class being examined. Perhaps the absence of promotional variables reflects the prevailing opinion among economists that marketing effort does not increase generic demand but only changes market shares.

Demand for a stock of durable goods. Consumers acquire new goods according to priorities that reflect their personal life styles. McFall (1969) has demonstrated that the order of acquisition forms an unidimensional scale, so that knowledge of the durable good purchased last permits estimates of other goods owned and enables predictions of the durable good to be purchased next. Predictions of the next purchase, however, are subject to maintaining the present stock in working order. Thus, replacement of an old washing machine may delay the purchase of a new color TV.

The demand for automobiles at the industry level of aggregation has been studied extensively. The Chow (1960) model is of interest because it viewed the demand for automobiles as an attempt to maintain a stock of automobiles and because it used the concept of permanent income.

Chow viewed buyer behavior as an attempt to fill the gap between the quantity of a stock desired and the quantity of old stock available for consumption. Therefore, the dependent variable (X_t) in the Chow model is the stock of automobiles per capita at the end of time period (t). Estimates for the years 1921–53, excluding 1942–46, yielded the following equation:

$$X_t = -0.7247 - 0.048802P_t + 0.025487I_{et}$$
$$R^2 = 0.895 \qquad\qquad\qquad (5\text{--}10)$$

where P_t represents a price index of automobiles and I_{et} signifies expected or constant incomes.[4]

Estimating the annual demand for automobiles. The Dyckman (1965) model for estimating the demand for automobiles represents an extension of the classic price and income models because it includes measures of auto credit terms and consumer liquid asset holdings, both of which reflect consumers' ability to buy. It differed from the Chow model in three ways. First, it estimated annual sales of automobiles, not the desired stock of automobiles. Second, it used the double-log transformation to estimate constant elasticity. And finally, it examined the relationships between an-

---

[4] For the computation of the point elasticities of price and income, see Problem 1 at the end of the chapter and the solutions in Appendix B.

nual changes (Δ) in the log of sales and changes in the logs of the independent variable. The model was as follows:

$$\Delta \log X_t = -0.001 + 3.951\Delta \log Y_t - 0.792\Delta \log P_t$$
$$+ 0.051\Delta C_t - 1.934\Delta \log S_t + 0.062\Delta L_t \quad (5\text{-}11)$$
$$R^2 = 0.939$$

where

X_t = demand for new cars per capita
Y_t = real disposable personal income
P_t = price index for cars
C_t = auto credit terms
S_t = present stock of autos
L_t = liquid asset holdings
Δ = first difference

Income price elasticities may be read directly. A 1.0 percent increase in income is associated with a 3.951 percent increase in the demand for automobiles; thus autos are income-elastic. A 1.0 percent decline in price is associated with a 0.792 percent increase in demand; thus, automobiles were price-inelastic in this model.

Estimating the potential demand for a new convenience food. A model of the demand for convenience foods (Harp and Miller, 1965) illustrates the use of economic models to estimate the demand for a product that is still being developed, the concepts of cross elasticity for substitute goods, and the concept of distribution elasticity. The incentive for the study is found in the fact that food manufacturers introduce approximately 5,000 new products or innovations per year but only 500 survive the first year (ibid., p. 1). The unique attribute claimed for these products is new convenience.

The model for estimating the sales of a new convenience product is as follows:

$$\log Y = -0.60 - 0.60(\log X_1)^2 - 0.85 \log X_2 + 0.28(\log X_3)^2$$
$$+ 0.31 \log X_4 + 0.65 \log X_5 - 0.16(\log X_5)^2 + 0.44 \log X_6$$
$$+ 0.23 \log X_7 - 0.58X_8 + 0.33X_9$$
$$R^2 = 0.87$$
$$(5\text{-}12)$$

where

Y = sales (in units of 100 million servings), for example, brown-and-serve yeast rolls sold annually in supermarkets
X_1 = cents per serving of convenience foods (excluding labor and fuel)
X_2 = market share of competitive convenience foods as a percent of sales of the entire product group, for example, rolls

X_3 = cents per serving of fresh or home-prepared foods

X_4 = cents per serving of highest volume-competitive convenience food, for example, frozen and chilled rolls

X_5 = importance of food group in the consumer purchase pattern, measured as sales of product group, for example, all convenience forms of yeast rolls

X_6 = an index of availability in supermarkets

X_7 = success of similar convenience products, measured as the sales of the highest volume-competing convenience product

X_8, X_9 = dummy variables to adjust for unusually high or low predicted sales

Because the logarithm of sales was regressed on the logarithm of some of the independent variables, the coefficients of these variables are estimates of constant elasticity. Cross elasticity of demand between yeast rolls and frozen rolls is estimated by the coefficient of variable X_4, the cost per serving of a competitive convenience food. Thus, a 1.0 percent increase in the serving cost of a competitive product will increase the sales of the new convenience food by 0.31 percent. A 1.0 percent improvement in the index of availability, variable X_6, will increase sales 0.44 percent. (The coefficient of determination, R^2, indicates that 87 percent of the variance in sales was associated with the variance in the nine independent variables.)

The major limitation of this model is the exclusion of three important variables—product quality, brand promotion, and the life cycle of the product—owing to lack of data.

Variations in elasticities over the product life cycle

The **S**-shaped curve, computed as a logistic or Gompertz function,[5] makes many appearances in discussions of demand. In Chapter 3 it appeared as a model for projecting total population. In Chapter 4 it described the decisions and forecasting techniques that are appropriate at each stage in a product's life cycle. In Chapter 7 it will describe the diffusion of innovations through a population. In this chapter changes in price and promotional elasticities over the life cycle of a product will be discussed. Thus, the **S**-shaped curve should be considered when computing elasticities.

Mickwitz (1959) ranked the elements of the marketing mix at each life cycle stage from the most elastic to the least elastic element. The stages and rankings are summarized in Table 5-1. Mickwitz views a product's life cycle as moving from generic demand in the early stages, to brand

---

[5] For a discussion of the differences between logistic and Gompertz curves, see Kotler (1971), pp. 35–37.

TABLE 5–1
The rank importance of the elasticities of the marketing mix at each stage in the product life cycle

| Generic 1 | Specific | | | Generic 5 |
	2	3	4	
1. Product quality	1. Advertising	1. Price	1. Quasi-quality (e.g., package)	1. Advertising
2. Advertising	2. Quality	2. Advertising	2. Advertising	2. Service– quasi-quality
3. Price	3. Price	3. Quality	3. Quality service	3. Quality
4. Service	4. Service	4. Service	4. Price	4. Price

Source: Adapted from Mickwitz (1959).

demand in the middle stages, and finally back to generic demand at the final stage in the cycle. This sequence highlights a marketer's motivation for branding his product—to remove his product from the uncertainties of marketing a commodity. If he can establish brand loyalty, he can predict his sales and develop more economical production runs and inventories.

Observations of competition in Finland and Sweden led Mickwitz to identify the following five marketing mix elements whose elasticities changed during a product's life cycle: product quality, advertising, price, service, and quasi-quality, which he defined as package changes and other forms of differentiation that do not improve the quality of the product. Reading across the highest elasticities in Table 5–1, one concludes that the sequence of strategies throughout the cycle should be product quality, advertising, price, quasi-quality, and advertising. This table should serve only as a guide for marketers because generalizations across a wide range of products and markets are not available, but it does emphasize the danger of assuming that elasticities remain constant over time.

Elasticities and time-series analysis

Estimates of elasticities and the timing of the implementation of marketing strategies should consider general business conditions and industry trends, cycles, and seasonal factors, as was noted in the Mustang case in Chapter 4.[6] An estimate of a price elasticity, for instance, may be inflated

---

[6] Methods for forecasting general business conditions, Gross National Product, industry sales, financial conditions, and sources of statistical data may be found in Butler and Kavesh (1966) and Silk (1970). A nontechnical discussion of forecasting with input-output analysis may be found in Leontief (1965); Blackett (1971); Elliott-Jones (1971); and U.S. Department of Commerce (1966), pp. 75–83. Statistical techniques and computer programs for processing time-series data are discussed by Salzman (1968).

or deflated simply by the timing of the observations along the upswing or the downswing of a cycle. Recently developed computer techniques simplify the task of identifying these temporal influences in historical data (Chambers, Mullick, and Smith, 1971; and Salzman, 1968).

Attribute models

Attribute models, a new economic approach to studying consumer behavior, consider a product as a bundle of attributes. Buying behavior is determined by the ability of each attribute to meet a buyer's need and his perception of the importance of the need. These models provide descriptions that are closer to observed consumer behavior than many other models. For example, a consumer does not buy a car but a bundle of attributes including style and transportation. Style decays faster than the ability of the car to provide transportation. A consumer who considers style very important will replace an automobile while it still can perform adequately the function of transportation.

Attribute models are used to place brands in multidimensional psychological space (Chapter 8). An economic attribute theory has been provided by Lancaster (1966). The Lancaster model may be described as the inverse of a production model. In production several inputs are combined in a ratio fixed by the state of technology to yield an output of goods. Lancaster suggests that consumption starts with goods as inputs that yield an output of attributes that are demanded by consumers in accordance with a function called consumption technology. Most of the analytical power of the model is based on an examination of the structure of consumption technology. The model has some interesting implications for marketing economists. Instead of computing price and income elasticities for a quantity of products, this model suggests that we should compute elasticities for the characteristics of the products.

One advantage of the Lancaster model is the analytical tools that it brings from operations research. Lancaster uses linear programming, for example, to define the consumer as attempting to maximize utility (as a function of product characteristics) subject to budget constraints.

Economic-attitudinal models

Consumers' attitudes toward their economic situation and their income levels determine to a large extent their discretionary spending. For example, attitude surveys conducted by the Survey Research Center, University of Michigan, from 1952 through 1961 (Mueller, 1963), yielded the following equation of consumer durable goods expenditures (D):

$$D = 0.18Y_{t-1} + 0.40A - 48.00 \qquad (5\text{--}13)$$

where Y_{t-1} equals the deflated disposable personal income during the six-month period preceding the survey, A is the Index of Consumer Attitudes developed by the Survey Research Center, both coefficients were significant, and R^2 increased from 0.29 to 0.76 with the addition of the index of attitudes. Thus, attitudes were an important component of consumer behavior. Recent support for this point has been reported also by Katona (1971) and Murray (1969).

The U.S. Bureau of the Census conducts quarterly surveys among a sample of households regarding their expectations of buying specific durable goods. Since July, 1966, these expectations have been measured with the following scale of subjective probabilities (McNeil and Stoterau, 1968; U.S. Bureau of the Census, 1967):

100	Absolutely certain
90	
80	Strong possibility
70	
60	
50	
40	
30	
20	Slight possibility
10	
0	Absolutely no chance

A comparison of these probabilities with automobile purchases reported in later interviews revealed that respondents tended to underestimate their six-month buying rates. Despite this downward bias, 76 percent of the variance in subsequent automobile purchases was associated with the variance in purchase probability and a dummy variable used to reflect supply shortages caused by strikes (U.S. Bureau of the Census, 1969). Clawson (1971) found that three-month purchase probabilities resulted in a consistent overestimation of actual buying rates. The accuracy of the estimates varied among products and services, which may be a reflection of differences in planning periods prior to purchase. Clearly, more must be known about the relationship between time intervals and the validity of estimates (Byrnes, 1965). Since subjective probabilities may be defined as weighted attitudes (Chapter 9), these findings give additional evidence of the importance of attitudes to economic behavior.

BRAND DEMAND

In Chapter 1 it was noted that the demand for brand j in time $t(B_{jt})$ may be expressed as follows:

$$B_{jt} = M_{jt}G_t \tag{5-14}$$

where M_{jt} is the market share of brand j in time t. We turn now to the problem of developing models that describe the determinants of M_{jt}. The elasticity models described above cannot be applied directly because they do not account for competitive promotional effort and they do not measure the cumulative effect of past advertising.

Cumulative effect models

The present sales of a company may be influenced by its previous and present marketing effort. Models of previous effects must solve two problems—the number of prior periods to be considered in the model and the shape of the decay function. The Koyck (1954) model of distributed lags may be used if one assumes that the effectiveness of advertising decays at a geometric rate.[7] Thus, if effectiveness in time period t is 1.00 and effectiveness in $t - 1$ is 0.90, effectiveness in $t - 2$ is 0.81, and $t - 3$ is 0.729. The effectiveness rates for periods $t - 2$ and $t - 3$ were computed by raising 0.90 to the second and third powers.

How far back should effectiveness rates be computed? Koyck demonstrated that all of the cumulative effects are accounted for by estimating the influence of only the previous time period, $t - 1$. His model, as applied to advertising by Palda (1964), is derived as follows:

Let

S_t = sales in time t
b = the effectiveness of advertising in period t
λ = the effectiveness of advertising in $t - 1$ relative to period t, thus λ is the first lagged period decay rate
A = advertising expenditures
u = error term

then

$$S_t = bA_t + b\lambda A_{t-1} + b\lambda^2 A_{t-2} + \cdots + u_t. \tag{5-15}$$

By lagging Equation 5–15 one period and multiplying it by λ we have

$$\lambda S_{t-1} = b\lambda A_{t-1} + b\lambda^2 A_{t-2} + \cdots + \lambda u_{t-1}. \tag{5-16}$$

[7] Che (1971) has demonstrated that it is not necessary to assume a geometric decay function. He used the binomial distribution to create advertising effectiveness functions that peaked at various points along the lagged periods.

By subtracting Equation 5–16 from Equation 5–15 we derive an equation that will account for all of the previous effects of advertising, thus

$$S_t = \lambda S_{t-1} + bA_t + (u_t - \lambda u_{t-1}).$$ (5–17)

When Equation 5–17 is fitted by regression analysis to historical sales and advertising expenditures data, λ is interpreted as an estimate of the cumulative effect of advertising. When other variables such as personal selling expenditures are included in 5–17, λ is an estimate of the cumulative effects of all of the previous marketing strategies of the firm. There is no way that the individual cumulative effects of each marketing element can be separated from λ.

While equations such as 5–17 can be very useful in understanding the effects of promotional effort on demand, it should be noted that single equation models lead to problems in estimating parameters when there are two-way influences. A two-way influence exists in marketing when advertising influences sales and when advertising budgets are established according to levels of sales. Simultaneous equations can reflect this two-way influence. They have been used successfully by Bass (1969a) and Bass and Beckwith (1971) to describe advertising-sales relationships.

Modeling competitive effort

Many marketing economists consider the effectiveness of advertising to be determined not by a firm's absolute advertising expenditures but by its share of expenditures relative to its industry. Market share, therefore, is determined by a firm's share of promotional effort. If the cumulative effects are considered, the basic model is as follows:

$$M_{jt} = \lambda M_{j(t-1)} + b\,\frac{ME_{jt}}{ME_{It}}$$ (5–18)

where ME_j is the marketing effort of firm j and ME_I is the total marketing effort of its industry.

Lambin (1970) estimated the following model for the manufacturer of a small electrical appliance sold in Europe:

$$M_{jt} = 1.12 + 0.35M_{j(t-1)} + \frac{0.43A_{jt}}{A_{It}} - \frac{0.26P_{jt}}{P_{It}}$$
$$+ \frac{0.44D_{jt}}{D_{It}} + \frac{0.74Q_{jt}}{Q_{It}}$$ (5–19)
$$R^2 = 0.75$$

where A is advertising expenditures, P is price, D is distribution, and Q is quality. The $R^2 = 0.75$ indicates that 75 percent of the variance in the market share of this product is associated with the variance in the independent variables of this model.[8]

One limitation of market share models, such as 5–19, is the assumption that demographic, economic, social, and psychological variables affect all brands equally and that the influence of these variables is eliminated by expressing all data in market share terms. This assumption seems to ignore the popular strategy of market segmentation where products and promotion are designed specifically for segments defined along demographic, economic, social, and psychological variables. If successful, this strategy assures that brands are not influenced equally by these variables.

A limitation of the share and industry models is the assumption that promotional effort influences only the share of the market and does not increase the size of the market. Industry models such as 5–10 and 5–11 should include industry promotional expenditures so that the promotional elasticity of primary demand may be estimated. During the early stages of introducing a new product, promotion will be more effective than a price reduction in increasing the primary demand. An example is provided by a study conducted in 1962 by the U.S. Department of Agriculture (1965) and 22 cooperating producers of Florida frozen concentrated orange juice. The study concluded that a promotional campaign increased sales at a cost to the industry of $3.5 million, while a reduction in price to attain the same increase would have resulted in a revenue loss of $16.8 million at retail.

MIXED GENERIC-BRAND STRATEGIES

Marketers may want to consider a strategy that attempts to expand generic and brand demand at the same time. An example of such a strategy is a bank that aggressively promotes its services among new residents of a community. Perhaps it has only 10 percent of the present residents, but

---

[8] Lambin (1970) adapted the Dorfman-Steiner (1954) theorem to his model so that the brand share optimality occurs when a brand's selling price divided by its market-share elasticity with respect to its relative price equals its advertising dollars per unit divided by its market share elasticity with respect to its relative advertising, which, in turn, equals its marginal cost of quality change times its relative quality index divided by its market share elasticity with respect to its relative quality. This rather complex optimization rule is simply an extension of the well-known rule for optimizing the profit of a firm: operate at that level of output that equates marginal revenue and marginal cost. The market share rule can be applied directly to Equation 5–19 because all variables were expressed in logarithms. Therefore the coefficients are estimates of constant elasticities.

through aggressive promotion it gains an average of 20 percent of new residents. In the long run it will expand its market share.

PROBLEMS IN IMPLEMENTING REGRESSION MODELS

Because economic models are frequently estimated by using multiple regression models, some consideration should be given to the problems of implementing regression models. Quandt (1964) notes that these problems include: (1) the identification of relevant variables; (2) the identification of the structure of the equation (absolute, first difference, lagged variables, diminishing or increasing functions, etc.); and (3) the failure of all data (company data, census, media, subscription rating services, etc.) to conform to compatible geographic areas.

When using regression models the marketing planner must remember that correlation may not mean causation. The use of historical sales and advertising expenditure data always raises the question of the direction of causality. Does advertising cause sales or do sales cause advertising? There are two common practices in which sales cause advertising expenditures. Advertising budgets are sometimes determined by spending a fixed percentage of sales, rather than building to a budget after determining the communication tasks to be accomplished. Increased advertising expenditures may be ordered after a sales decline is noted. In this case, sales determine advertising expenditures and a single equation model will yield a negative sign. An analyst who is not aware of this advertising practice may come to the erroneous conclusion that advertising lowers sales.

Implementation of market share models introduces the problem of collecting data about competitors. In a publicly regulated industry, such as banking, data for market share models are available from the regulatory agency (e.g., Hughes, 1970). Data from nonregulated firms must be collected from industry associations, advertising media, and marketing research firms which collect these data regularly.

SOURCES OF DATA

Data for implementing economic models of consumer behavior come from three sources—historical data, experiments, or surveys. Historical data may be internal to the firm, such as accounting records; industry data compiled by trade associations or a financial analyst; or data reported by governmental agencies such as the Department of Agriculture or the Department of Commerce. Experiments may be conducted in either the field or the laboratory (Cox and Enis, 1969; and Sevin, 1965). An in-store experimental design may be used to study the effect of price levels on sales and the effect of the interaction of price and promotional variables. Elasticities may be estimated from data generated in laboratory experiments (Pessemeir, 1966). Individual and group interviews are used to estimate price elasticities when the product is only a concept (Wells, 1970), when historical data do not exist, or when field experimentation would reveal plans to competitors.

The use of accounting data introduces the problem of joint costs and joint revenues because most companies sell many products. Dividing the salesmen's costs, for instance, requires an estimate of their allocation of time to various products and customers. These estimates may require a time and duty study similar to those used in production (Minor, 1965). Problems in joint revenue are common. Customers frequently buy standard assortments of goods so that the seller must carry a complete line even when some of the items are unprofitable. The laboratory glass industry provides an example. Small manufacturers must specialize, so to carry a full line they buy infrequently sold items from their competitors.

SUMMARY

Economic models reflect a buyer's ability to buy a product or service and reflect his buying motivations only indirectly. Early economic models of generic demand considered only the influence of price. Later models consider the effects of personal income, savings, and credit terms. The relationships between sales and these independent variables are frequently expressed as elasticities—percentage changes in sales that are related to percentage changes in price, income, savings, or credit terms. Elasticities are computed as arc, point, or constant elasticity. Economic models may be used to estimate the demand for products in existence, as was illustrated by two models of automobile sales, or the model may provide an estimate of demand for a new product, such as the model for a new convenience food. Because elasticities are sensitive to the product life cycle, and to trend, cycle, and seasonal effects, marketers should try to account for these influences when computing elasticities and when building marketing strategies upon them.

The most recent economic models of generic demand have included product attributes, attitudes, and buying intentions. Thus, there is some convergence between economic and psychological models of demand.

Economic models of brand demand estimate the influence of the elements of the marketing mix on sales. These models introduce the problems of accounting for competitive influence and measuring the cumulative effects of marketing effort.

The use of regression models creates specific measurement problems. These include: the identification of variables; the identification of the structure of the model; adjustment of the data to conform to common classifications, such as geographic areas; the identification of the direction of causality, particularly with the advertising-sales relationship; and the collection of competitive data for market share models.

The generation of data for economic models can be an expensive process. There are three sources of these data—historical sources (company accounting records, trade association records, and data collected by government agencies), experiments (e.g., laboratory and field), and surveys (individual and group interviews).

READING QUESTIONS

1. What are the advantages and disadvantages of arc, point, and constant elasticities of price or income for analysis of demand?
2. What decision rule should a firm follow if its goal is to maximize sales?
3. Distinguish between economists' and marketers' concepts of demand.
4. Select a consumer product and estimate what you think the elasticities of price, product development, promotion, and distribution would be at each stage of that product's life cycle. How will these elasticities affect the marketing strategy for that product?
5. What is an attribute model of demand and why is it useful?
6. What are the applications, limitations, and assumptions necessary for the cumulative effect models?
7. What are some of the practical problems associated with using regression models in demand analyses?

PROBLEMS AND DISCUSSION QUESTIONS

(Suggested answers to the first six questions may be found in Appendix B.)

1. Compute the elasticity of price and the elasticity of income for the Chow equation of the demand for a stock of automobiles, Equation 5–10, given $\bar{X}_t$, in hundredths of a unit, $= 8.081$, $\bar{P}_t = 122.8$, and $\bar{I}_{et} = 580.6$. What do these coefficients of elasticity mean?
2. Determine the price and income elasticities associated with the change in sales, price, and income using the Dyckman model, Equation 5–11.
3. A food manufacturer is considering introducing a new convenience food and needs an estimate of sales potential of his territory. He estimated that his product will cost 2.01 cents per serving (X_1), the percent of convenience food sales in the product group (X_2) is 0.44, cost per serving

at home (X_3) is 2.99, cost per serving of the nearest competitor (X_4) is 2.82, sales of the entire product group (X_5) is 10.19. He thinks that he can achieve the same percentage of distribution as his present products (X_6) which is 0.70; sales of the highest volume convenience product in this product group (X_7) have been reported as 1.68 (100 million servings); and unusually high or low sales are not anticipated. What annual sales (in units of 100 million servings) would you predict for sales through supermarkets?

4. Why is promotional elasticity greater than price elasticity during the early stages of a product's life cycle while the reverse is the case during the late stages of the cycle?

5. When promotional elasticity is greater than price elasticity and a marketer advertises instead of lowering price, is his behavior counter to the best interest of society?

6. What would be the results of fitting a regression model to sales and advertising expenditures when the advertising strategy was that of increasing sales and reacting to a sales decline?

7. Develop an example that shows how the coefficient of elasticity for a 10 percent price increase differs from the coefficient for a 10 percent decrease in price.

8. Assume that data are available for product quality, brand promotion, and product life cycle. What functional form would these variables take in Equation 5–12?

9. What assumptions are necessary to apply Equation 5–19 to a branded grocery product?

10. Identify the variables and functional forms for an economic model of consumer demand for houses, refrigerators, and tractors. Check your hypothetical models with those reported by Harberger (1960).

SUGGESTED CASES

American Telephone and Telegraph—Princess Telephone (A). Bursk and Greyser (1968), pp. 21–27.

Market tests were conducted to estimate the potential for the Princess telephone under different rate plans.

1. Which rate plan do you recommend?
2. Which economic models are appropriate to this analysis?

Concorn Kitchens. Boyd and Davis (1971), pp. 125–36.

The packaged foods division of Concorn Kitchens has decided to use a computer model for developing its marketing plan. To test the new system, product managers for instant puddings and instant breakfasts were instructed to provide historical data and elasticity coefficients for their products.

1. Evaluate the economic variables used in the model. What changes do you recommend?
2. Do you agree with the method for computing response coefficients?
3. What noneconomic variables do you think should be included in such a model?

SUGGESTED READINGS

ANDERSON, W. T., JR. "Identifying the Convenience-Oriented Consumer," *Journal of Marketing Research,* Vol. 8 (May 1971), pp. 179–83.

BASS, FRANK M. "A Simultaneous Equation Regression Study of Advertising and Sales of Cigarettes," *Journal of Marketing Research,* Vol. 6, No. 3 (August 1969), pp. 291–300.

BURCH, S. W., and STEKLER, H. O. "The Forecasting Accuracy of Consumer Attitude Data," *Journal of the American Statistical Association,* Vol. 64, No. 328 (December 1969), 1225–33.

HOUTHAKKER, H. S., and TAYLOR, L. D. *Consumer Demand in the United States: Analyses and Projections.* 2d ed. Cambridge, Mass.: Harvard University Press, 1970.

KISH, LESLIE: "Variances for Indexes from Complex Samples," *Proceedings: American Statistical Association, Social Statistics Section* (1962), pp. 190–99.

STOUT, ROY G. "Developing Data to Estimate Price-Quantity Relationships," *Journal of Marketing,* Vol. 33, No. 2 (April 1969), pp. 34–36.

THIEL, HENRI. *Principles of Econometrics.* New York: John Wiley & Sons, Inc., 1971.

6

Social variables that influence management decisions

Three marketing decisions that may be greatly influenced by social variables are product development, promotion, and multinational marketing. Identifying the relevant social forces and assessing their influence are extremely difficult tasks that frequently lead to conflicting results, as some of the studies reported below indicate. Examples of marketing applications of social concepts leave the reader with a sense of vagueness in comparison to the illustrative cases from demography and economics. This review of social variables produces few generalizations, but it will help marketers to generate hypotheses that should be considered when evaluating the impact of social forces on demand, and it will help them to avoid previous errors.

Methods, such as multivariate statistics, which were used to identify market segments (N_k) using demographic and economic variables can be used with social variables (Frank, Massy, and Wind, 1972), but the very nature of social variables introduces complications. For instance, the direction of cause and effect may not be clear. Does a group determine an individual's values or do his values determine his selection of groups? Another difficulty arises in distinguishing between socially acceptable means for meeting a need, such as foods that are acceptable to religious teachings, and needs which can be fulfilled only by social interaction, such as the need for belongingness and love (Maslow, 1954). A person who dines with friends in a fine restaurant is fulfilling three needs—physiological, social, and aesthetic—all of which are influenced by social forces. In the discussion that follows there will be no attempt to distinguish between social needs and social constraints on the fulfillment of nonsocial needs. Our present level of knowledge about the influence of social variables on consumer and buyer behavior is sufficiently confused without making this subtle distinction. Therefore, the discussion will be limited to market segmentation by social variables, the influence of social communications on buying decisions, and cultural differences that should be considered when marketing multinationally.

MARKET SEGMENTATION WITH SOCIAL VARIABLES

Social variables for segmenting markets have ranged from broad variables, such as culture and social class, through small group concepts such as role (which includes the family life cycle), to individual variables, which include values, beliefs, and personality. In the following discussion it will be noted that the trend is toward individual variables because the broad variables have not been good predictors of buyer and consumer behavior.

Culture

A complex culture may be divided into homogeneous segments with similar social needs. In the United States ethnic segments have received considerable attention among marketers. Two ethnic segments that have been studied extensively are the Spanish-speaking and black cultures. The few generalizations that can be derived from studies of the black culture should be noted.

Marketing studies of the black culture tend to focus on a comparison of black and white expenditure patterns. After reviewing eight studies of the consumption patterns of blacks and whites with the same incomes, Alexis (1962) came to the following conclusions: blacks save more; they spend more for clothing and nonautomobile transportation (because more live in the city); they spend less for food, housing, medical care, and automobile transportation; and there is no racial difference in expenditures for recreation, leisure, or home furnishings. Bauer, Cunningham, and Wortzel (1965) reanalyzed over a dozen surveys and concluded that the basic dilemma of black consumers is whether to strive to attain middle-class values or to live without them. They found also that the black experiences anxiety in making a buying decision because he wants to avoid a mistake when spending scarce resources. The reliance on branded products tends to reduce his economic and social risk. Because of this sense of high risk, blacks tend to seek more information when making a buying decision. Bauer and Cunningham (1970) compared the expenditures of blacks and whites of the same income level and concluded that blacks spend more on goods and services for the immediate; less on items such as medical care, education, appliances, and homes. These differences are a reflection of the deprived status of blacks in American life (ibid., p. 179).

Is there a market segment that uniquely reflects black value systems? Generalized answers are dangerous because this cultural segment is changing rapidly. The black segment can be divided further into segments guided by white culture and those guided by black culture (ibid.). Differences in spending patterns reflect differences in life styles. Marketers will probably find activity or psychographic variables (Chapter 7) more useful than race in identifying buying behavior.

Social class

Social classes represent attempts to group persons judged to possess equal social status. The judgment is along dimensions such as education, income, and dwelling.[1]

Studies indicate that buying patterns differ among classes. Upper class tastes tend to be subtle and symbolic while the lower classes prefer the bold and functional. Preferences in furniture in the upper middle class, for example, may be determined by aesthetics, while the lower middle class is concerned with being right and respectable (Levy, 1958). A lower class family may enjoy a larger than average income because the wife is working. This family is classified by R. P. Coleman (1960) as overprivileged while he classifies a professor whose tastes exceed his income as underprivileged. The former will buy a medium luxury car while the latter may buy a "sensible" compact car.

Martineau (1958) generalized that middle-class persons tend to point toward the future, have an urban identification, be rational, possess a well-structured sense of the universe, enjoy perceptions of vast horizons and a greater sense of choice making, be self-confident and take risks, think in immaterial and abstract terms, and see themselves related to the national scene. In contrast, the lower status psychological framework is pointed toward the present and past, has a short-range viewpoint, has a rural identification, is nonrational, views the world in vague and unstructured terms, perceives a limited but sharp horizon, senses only limited choices, is concerned with security, thinks concretely, and perceives the world as being his family and his body. Thus, social class variations are variations in life style (Levy, 1958). Life style determines much more than buying behavior. For instance, it determines birth rates, family training, education, religion, and leisure activities (Engel et al., 1968, p. 267).

---

[1] For a detailed discussion, see Robertson (1970); and Engel, Kollat, and Blackwell (1968).

One may question the utility of combining variables such as education and income into a social class index. The distinctions made by Martineau could be explained largely by differences in education. The refined tastes of the upper class may be the result of education's lowering the thresholds of perception (Myers and Reynolds, 1967). The aggregation of a class index reduces our ability to identify the specific causes of behavior.

The techniques of mass promotion are eroding class-determined buying behavior, so the findings of early studies should be used as hypotheses, not laws.

Life cycles

The vast majority of consumer purchases are made for family consumption. Families may consist of one person (e.g., a bachelor or solitary survivor) or even several generations (e.g., dependent parents living with a child and his family). Buying behavior is determined by the needs of the family, the role of each member, and the memberships of family members in other groups.

The needs of the family are expressed best in terms of the family life cycle. Ranging from bachelorhood, through family formation, to solitary retired survivor, stages in the life cycle show marked differences in consumption patterns and financial well-being. These stages are summarized in Table 6–1 along with the typical consumption patterns at each stage. Life cycle is a special case of the concept of role. The stages could be described as bachelor, husband, father, etc.

Wells and Gubar (1966) found that the life cycle variable was a better predictor of buying behavior than age for products such as household durables, toys, vitamins, food products, and services which relate to children and their activities. Conversely, age was a more discriminating variable than life cycle for age-related health care, luxuries such as furs, men's jewelry, slenderizing treatments, and repairs by contractors. Age was also a better predictor of sales of products for the under-25 market—coin-operated washing machines, portable TV sets, sterling silver, kitchen wares, and bedroom suites. Expenditures for 50 percent of the products examined by Wells and Gubar were equally sensitive to age and life cycle variables, 10 percent were sensitive to age, and 40 percent were sensitive to life cycle. Therefore, the life cycle variable would be appropriate in 90 percent of their cases.

Work, social, neighborhood, and youth groups influence family buying patterns. For example, the presence of a teen-ager in the family increases the probability of the family's buying a new car. The teen-ager, in turn, is influenced by groups which change according to his stage of develop-

TABLE 6-1
An overview of the life cycle

Bachelor stage; young single people not living at home	*Newly married couples; young, no children*	*Full nest I; youngest child under six*	*Full nest II; youngest child six or over six*	*Full nest III; older married couples with dependent children*
Few financial burdens	Better off financially than they will be in near future	Home purchasing at peak	Financial position better	Financial position still better
Fashion opinion leaders		Liquid assets low	Some wives work	More wives work
Recreation oriented	Highest purchase rate and highest average purchase of durables	Dissatisfied with financial position and amount of money saved	Less influenced by advertising	Some children get jobs
Buy: Basic kitchen equipment, basic furniture, cars, equipment for the mating game, vacations	Buy: Cars, refrigerators, stoves, sensible and durable furniture, vacations	Interested in new products	Buy larger sized packages, multiple-unit deals	Hard to influence with advertising
		Like advertised products	Buy: Many foods, cleaning materials, bicycles, music lessons, pianos	High average purchase of durables
		Buy: Washers, dryers, TV, baby food, chest rubs and cough medicine, vitamins, dolls, wagons, sleds, skates		Buy: New, more tasteful furniture, auto travel, nonnecessary appliances, boats, dental services, magazines

Source: W. D. Wells and G. Gubar (1966).

ment. The early influence is the small in-group or clique, then he associates with the crowd, and finally he participates in competitive dating. Myers and Reynolds (1967) report that Ford advertising was ineffective when it showed crowds of teen-agers at beach parties playing volleyball and other crowd activities. Surveys revealed that the advertisements were considered too juvenile. Later ads for Mustangs showed couples, not crowds.

Role conflicts

A company's assistant treasurer who is striving to be treasurer spends his day on matters of cost, economy, and efficiency—a paradigm of the economic man. He lunches at the Civic Club where the conversation is dominated by the topic of the need to hire minority groups despite their inadequate training. He agrees, in part, because he thinks that this is a short-run problem that will be solved by better education, and concludes that it is better to employ them for some work than to give them a dole. Returning to work with his economic values intact, he is jarred by the news that the treasurer has traded his intermediate class car for one clearly

Empty nest I; older married couples, no children living with them, head in labor force	Empty nest II; older married couples, no children living at home, head retired	Solitary survivor, in labor force	Solitary survivor, retired
Home owner- ship at peak Most satisfied with financial position and money saved Interested in travel, recrea- tion, self- education Make gifts and contributions Not interested in new products Buy: Vacations, luxuries, home improvements	Drastic cut in income Keep home Buy: Medical appliances, medical care, products which aid health, sleep, and digestion	Income still good but likely to sell home	Same medical and product needs as other retired group; drastic cut in income Special need for attention, affection, and security

in the luxury class. Is economy no longer a virtue? Perhaps it is wiser to "invest" in a better car. Does this purchase support the rumor that the treasurer is about to become president of a subsidiary company? While driving home from work, he is conscious of the limitations of the four-door economy car that he purchased four years ago, following the recommenda- tions of a consumer rating magazine.

Upon arriving home, the assistant treasurer learns that a washing ma- chine, now almost 20 years old, needs $75 worth of repairs. Furthermore, there is a local sale on a washer and a dryer for $375. At dinner, the eldest child, a teen-age boy, expresses his embarrassment at picking up his date in the family four-door economy car. The evening paper features an article on automobile safety.

The decisions are many. As assistant treasurer he may decide to make the car last another year and buy the washer and dryer while it is on sale, or trade the car for another four-door economy model. As a candidate for the role of treasurer, he might trade it for an intermediate luxury car, recognizing that a new role may require revising old values. This heavier car would be safer for his family. As father of a teen-age boy, he might want to trade for a family sports car, or keep the economy car and buy a second car, perhaps a little foreign sports car. What decisions will he make and what reason will he give when asked by friends or a survey interviewer why he chose the alternative he did? The choice depends on the centrality of each of these group values to his personal value system and his perception of his role in each of these groups.

Role differentiation occurs within the family as with any group. Myers and Reynolds (1967) note that the wife tends to perform the roles that are related to expressive values (love, religion, and art) while the husband performs those roles that are instrumental in values (largely economic). This role differentiation appears in the purchase of an automobile where the wife selects the color, trim, and upholstery and the husband chooses the engineering options. Similarly, while the husband inspects the construction of furniture, his wife selects the style and fabric.

There are also roles within roles. In examining role performance in shopping for autos, appliances, convenience foods, toiletries, and household items, Jaffe and Senft (1966) identified behavioral roles that were assumed by husbands and wives during different phases of the purchase decision. For instance, at the purchase phase there were the roles of suggester of product class and brand, the budgeter, the shopper, and the purchaser. The participation of husbands and wives varied among these roles and across products.

Values and beliefs

The society in which an individual is a member prescribes general values of what is good and bad. These values determine acceptable goals and acceptable behavior in meeting individual needs. Individuals are subject to social punishment for aspiring to other goals or acting outside the behavioral patterns prescribed by social values. The need for food and religious sanctions provide familiar examples. Meat is forbidden by some religions, it is forbidden on certain days by other religions, some religions forbid meats from specified animals, and methods of preparation are prescribed by some religions. Failure to comply may range from temporary to permanent banishment from society either in the present or the hereafter.

An individual develops his personal set of values within the limits of society. This development is the product of his environment, education, experience, reference groups, and social and commercial communication networks. Individual values represent one link that an individual has with society. (Role is another link.) Because values are a component of attitude, discussion of their relevance to marketing must begin in this chapter and be continued in the discussion of psychological variables (Chapters 8 and 9). Lunn (1968) provides an example of the use of measures of values to explain behavior in the marketplace. One of his findings is presented in Figure 6–1 where it will be noted that as housewives' preference

FIGURE 6–1
Relating product and buyer characteristics: Labor required and buyer traditionalism

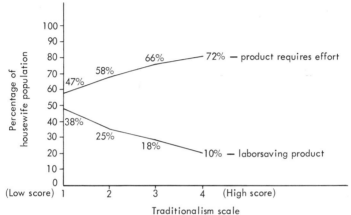

Source: Adapted from J. A. Lunn (1968).

for traditionalism increased, their preference for a laborsaving product decreased. Thus, a laborsaving product that was highly acceptable to one market segment was unacceptable to another segment. Developing a product to conform to a given value is a long-run strategy because values are slow to change.

Beliefs, like values, are determined by groups. A belief is simply the likelihood that something exists. They include uncontroversial beliefs, such as the sun rises in the east, and inconsequential beliefs, such as that one brand of mouth wash is more effective than another (Rokeach, 1964). In marketing, they are measured as probabilities or the states of awareness and unawareness (Chapter 9). Haley (1972) has found that measures of beliefs and perceived benefits segment consumer markets more clearly than measures of life style, demographics, or economic variables.

Personality

Personality is a social-psychological concept that either could be discussed in later chapters that consider psychological variables or could be examined as one of the social variables that influence behavior in the marketplace. It will be considered as a social variable because recent research (Alker, 1972; Frank, Massy, and Wind, 1972; and Mischel, 1968) indicates that variables are situation specific; that is, an individual's personality varies as his decision environment varies. Since environment is a social concept, it seems appropriate to discuss personality along with other social concepts, leaving to Chapters 8 and 9 the discussion of the psychological concepts of cognition.

Within the constraints of social values an individual develops his own style of behavior for meeting his needs. These personal patterns of behavior are called personalities and classify him as sociable, dominant, responsible, active, impulsive, and risk taker. Studies relating personality to product use have yielded interesting results. Summarizing Robertson's (1970) review of the literature we may note that owners of convertible cars were more active, impulsive, and sociable; acceptance of new male fashions was positively related to ascendency and sociability; use of headache remedies was negatively related to emotional stability; compulsive persons used more antacid-analgesic products; smokers were higher than average in expressed needs for sex, aggression, achievement, and dominance but lower on compliance, order, self-depreciation, and association; high-compliant persons were heavier users of mouthwash, soap, wine; and high-aggressive persons were heavy users of men's cologne and manual razors. While findings such as these are colorful, general personality scales have not been good predictors of buying behavior. A review of studies attempting to link personality to consumer behavior led Kassarjian (1971) to conclude that the results were "equivocal." The most promising findings have come from studies that used theory and experimental designs to test definite hypotheses about specific personality traits, rather than search through many personality traits with multivariate statistical techniques to find significant relationships. Using the more precise approach, Jacoby (1971) found that low dogmatic individuals tended to be innovators and Wilson (1971) found that purchasing agents' need for certainty was a good predictor of their decision style (normative or conservative).

The contribution of personality variables to marketing decision making has been limited for several reasons. First, results have not replicated despite the attempts by researchers using identical or comparable personality scales. Secondly, personality does not predict well the rates of product use. Activity and psychographic variables (Chapter 7), recent developments in marketing, show promise of being better predictors of product use. Third, the selection of media to match a desired personality profile is difficult because the media report their circulations by demographic characteristics, not personality classifications. The marketer must conduct additional research to establish the media habits of persons with given personalities.

Life style

Because broad personality measures have contributed only slightly to explanations of buyer behavior (Frank, 1968; and Massy, Frank, and Lodahl, 1968), there have been many recent attempts to use more refined measures which are specific to a buying situation. These early refinements focused on an individual's *life style*. Life style may be defined as an individual's response patterns for solving specific problems and interacting with his immediate environment. Thus, life style is a more precise, and therefore more limited, concept than personality. Marketers should note that making personality measures more precise improves their explanatory powers but reduces their generality across products and buying situations.

Recent refinements in the concept of life style have led to measurements of activities, interests, and opinions (AIO), psychographics, and activities and attitudes. The distinctions between these concepts have been explored by Hustad and Pessemier (1971), and instruments for measuring them will appear in Chapter 7. At this point in the discussion it would be useful to see how life-style variables contribute to the development of marketing strategies.

Tigert (1971) used AIO statements in a mail survey of 1,200 married men and 1,000 married women who represented a cross section of the U.S. population. Each respondent used a six-point scale to report his level of agreement with statements such as the following:

—I like to play poker.
—You can't have any respect for a girl who gets pregnant before marriage.
—There is too much violence on TV today.
—Communism is the greatest peril in the world today.
—Investing in the stock market is too risky for most families.
—We often serve wine at dinner.
—Liquor is a curse on American life.
—I often read the Bible.

Tigert (p. 224) described the heavy beer drinker as follows:

The life-style findings suggest that the male heavy user of beer is a total hedonist: he exerts effort only when it results in his personal pleasure, or when it in some way furthers his fantasy-view of himself as the hard-drinking, swinging he-man. Being extremely self-indulgent (heavy eating, heavy smoking), he gives no indication that he is concerned with the everyday responsibilities of job, wife or family. In fact, he prefers to live dangerously, playing poker, betting at the races, taking chances, etc.

Indeed, he seems to think that, "you only go around once in life, so you have to grab with all the gusto you can."

Tigert (p. 225) found that the female heavy user of mouthwash had a life style that was in marked contrast to the heavy beer drinker.

The female heavy mouthwash user is all hung up about dirty dishes, messy garbage, odors in the home, her family's and her own health, invisible dirt, and her personal appearance.

A little reflection on these findings suggests numerous copy strategies for these products. Measures of life style are becoming important for product development and promotion, especially in consumer package goods companies.

In addition to these attempts to segment markets with measures of personality, these measures have been used also when studying the communication networks that are used during the diffusion of a new product or service through a group. In the latter case the search was for a generalized personality that could identify innovators and opinion leaders.

SOCIAL COMMUNICATIONS AND PROMOTIONAL STRATEGIES

In many consumer decisions social communications dominate over all sources of information. The influence of these sources varies across products and through the life cycle of products. In planning his promotion the marketing strategist must consider these influences along with other sources over which he has control, such as advertising media and personal selling. Important concepts to be considered by the strategist are reference groups, personal influence, and variations in the influence of mass media throughout the diffusion process.

Reference groups

Reference groups are most influential on the individual's buying of goods that are consumed within public view, such as automobiles, furniture, clothing, food served at parties, etc. Group pressure to conform can be strong, as was observed during the introduction of television. Only the

very hearty could withstand the near epidemic spread of television an-
tennae among closely knit communities.

Reference groups can influence the decision to buy the generic product
and the selection of a specific brand. The relative influences suggested by
Bourne (1957) are summarized in Table 6–2 for specific products. This
table aids in the development of an advertising strategy.

TABLE 6–2
Reference group influence on the decision to buy a product
and a brand

		Reference group influence on the decision to buy a *product*	
		Weak influence on *product*	*Strong* influence on *product*
Reference group influence on the decision to buy a *brand*	*Strong* influence on *brand*	Clothing Furniture Magazines Toilet soap (Promote brand)	Cars Cigarettes Drugs (Promote product or brand, depending on saturation levels)
	Weak influence on *brand*	Laundry soap Radios Canned peaches (Promote product attributes)	Air conditioners Instant coffee TV (black and white) (Promote the product through industry advertising)

Suggested promotional strategy appears in parentheses.
Source: Adapted from F. S. Bourne (1957).

Starting in the upper, left-hand cell, we see that advertising copy should
emphasize brand so as to reinforce the existing group pressures with regard
to clothing, furniture, etc. When reference groups influence product and
brand selection, as with cars, cigarettes, and drugs, promotional strategy
becomes more complicated. The advertiser must select his theme after considering the saturation level of the market, his share of the market, and
promotional elasticities. If only 20 percent of the market is using the product and if he dominates the market, then the proper strategy would be
product promotion. Conversely, if the market is saturated so that sales
are largely repeat purchases and if the advertiser has only a small share
of the market, brand promotion would be the best strategy. Decisions to
buy products such as laundry soap, radios, and canned peaches are relatively uninfluenced by reference groups; therefore, product attributes must

be stressed. A strategy that is used frequently by laundry soap manufacturers is a theme that attempts to move the product to the upper left, the brand influential cell. This strategy uses ads in which housewives are comparing laundries as they hang them out to dry. The lower right-hand cell represents products that are in early stages of adoption and are relatively unknown to the mass market. As the product is adopted by the market, its classification moves to the upper right-hand cell. Instant coffee is an example of such a movement. At the time Bourne developed this matrix, instant coffee was not socially acceptable, so that effort was required to correct the negative influence of group pressure. Now that improved product quality and promotion have made it acceptable, consumers distinguish among brands. Thus, to make the matrix current, instant coffee should be moved to the upper, right-hand cell.

How will consumers react to conflicting evidence, for example, when a reference group recommends a product that a person perceives as having negative attributes—for example, fattening? Bourne presents evidence that a person is more likely to conform to reference group perceptions than to his own perceptions. Cohen and Golden (1971) found that subjects' evaluation of the taste of coffee was modified by the perceived evaluation of other subjects. It would appear, therefore, that consumers buy some products to meet their social rather than their physical needs. Bourne suggests that some products should be promoted to "whole social groups rather than primarily to individuals."

Personal influence

One of the earliest and most extensive studies of personal influence was by Katz and Lazarsfeld (1955). Patterns of communications were observed among family, friendship, and work groups. An index of opinion leadership was derived which measured the influence of persons in several life-cycle and social classes on opinions held by other persons toward marketing, fashion, public affairs, and movie-going. Some findings may be summarized as shown in Table 6–3.

TABLE 6–3
Index of opinion leadership

Variable	Marketing	Fashion	Public affairs	Movie-going
Life cycle	0.203	0.276	0.089	0.326
Social status	0.055	0.113	0.161	0.040

Source: Katz and Lazarsfeld (1955).

An index of zero means the variable has no influence on the subject in his forming an opinion, and 1.0 means total influence. Reading vertically, life cycle is more important than social status in forming opinions about marketing, which in this case means product preferences. Reading horizontally, life-cycle variables influence opinions on movie-going more than opinions on public affairs.

Another famous sociometric study of marketing behavior was conducted by Coleman, Katz, and Menzel (1957) who researched the following question: "What were the social processes which intervened between the initial trials of the drug by a few local innovators and its final use by virtually the whole medical community?" Each doctor was asked to whom he turned for advice, with whom he discussed cases, with whom he associated professionally, and who were his social friends. Answers to these questions made it possible to trace out communication links in the medical community. As would be expected, the professional network was important during the initial diffusion of the new drug.

Media effectiveness throughout the adoption process

The importance of sources of information about a new product varies with the stage of the adoption process, as may be seen in Table 6–4, which summarizes the adoption process for agricultural innovations. The mass media perform the functions of informing and creating interest. During

TABLE 6–4
Rank order of information sources by stages in the adoption of agricultural innovations

Awareness (learns about a new idea or practice) →	Interest (gets more information about it) →	Evaluation (tries it out mentally) →	Trial (uses or tries a little) →	Adoption (accepts it for full-scale and continued use)
1. Mass media: radio, TV, newspapers, magazines		1. Friends and neighbors		1. Personal experience is the most important factor in continued use of an idea
2. Friends and neighbors: mostly other farmers		2. Agricultural agencies		2. Friends and neighbors
3. Agricultural extension agencies		3. Dealers and salesmen		3. Agricultural agencies
4. Dealers and salesmen		4. Mass media		4. Mass media
				5. Dealers and salesmen

Source: Adapted from H. F. Lionberger (1960).

the evaluation of the innovation peers (friends and neighbors) are the most influential source of information. At the adoption stage personal experience ranks above all other sources.

The adoption of Nylon, Orlon, and Dacron by housewives in a small midwestern community (Beal and Rogers, 1957) replicated the findings of agricultural innovation: the mass media were important during early stages, then personal influences, and finally experience; but personal influences dominated the trial stage in the form of in-store personnel. Lazer and Bell (1966) found contradictory evidence when they studied the adoption of color television, stereo equipment, dishwashers, and air conditioners in Detroit. During the awareness stage only 14 percent of the respondents referred to mass media, and 39 percent mentioned friends as the source of initial information about the innovation. At the interest and evaluation stages the mass media were mentioned by 97 percent of the respondents.

A review of 708 diffusion studies led Rogers and Stanfield (1968) to the following generalizations. Innovativeness is related positively to the demographic variables of education and literacy, but there is no relationship with age. Positively related psychological variables include attitudes toward change, achievement motivation, and aspirations toward education. Sociological variables comprise the most numerous positive correlates with innovativeness. These include: cosmopolitanism, mass-media exposure, contact with change agencies, deviation from social norms, group participation, exposure to interpersonal communication, and opinion leadership. These authors found also that the rate of adoption was related positively to the relative advantage of the innovation, its compatability with existing values, and its ability to fulfill felt needs.

The adoption process in industrial marketing

Studies of diffusion are not limited to consumer products. Mansfield (1963) built an economic model of the rate of diffusion of diesel locomotives among U.S. railroads. The consumer adoption model was generally appropriate for the acceptance of automatic machine tools with the exception that personal selling was the most important source during the early stages and impersonal sources were important during the evaluation stage (Ozanne and Churchill, 1968). The diffusion model was used to examine the adoption of promotional games by food chains (Allvine, 1968).

Innovator personalities

Are there innovative and opinion leadership personalities? Marketers of new products would like to identify these personalities if they exist. The results of research attempting to answer this question have been fragmentary and sometimes conflicting. Robertson and Myers (1969) found the relationship between personality and adoption so low that they doubted that personality variables would be useful in the marketing of appliances, clothing, and food. Boone (1970) used the same instrument as Robertson and Myers (the California Psychological Inventory) and concluded that there were personality differences between innovators and followers in subscribing to Community Antenna Television (CATV) services.

In studies of the relationship between conservatism and liberalism, and the adoption of television, canasta, supermarkets, and two forms of health insurance Graham (1956) concluded that acceptance of a single innovation was not an index of the acceptance of others. This finding rejects the concept of a generalized innovator. Readiness to learn was identified as a trait leading to early adoption (Foote, 1965). Findings in the search for generalized opinion leadership are unclear. Some evidence supports the concept of generalized opinion leadership (Montgomery and Silk, 1969), some findings support the concept of leadership for clusters of related products (King and Summers, 1969), while other research has rejected generalized opinion leadership (Silk, 1966). Summers (1969) concluded that psychological variables were better than personality variables in predicting opinion leadership in women's fashion. Summers also identified demographic and sociological characteristics of opinion leaders. Too frequently studies using personality measures fail to include demographic and sociological variables, thereby foregoing the opportunity of determining whether personality variables are superior to the more easily measured demographic and sociological variables.

The potential and limitations of personality variables in studies of buyer information processing will be discussed in Chapter 8 where it will be noted that measures of perceived risk and risk-taking propensity in studies of information processing yielded generalizable results. These results suggest that personality is more influential on the processing of information than on buying behavior.

MULTINATIONAL MARKETING

The needs of men are basically the same, but acceptable patterns of behavior for meeting these needs make cultures distinctive. An understanding of these patterns is especially important when a multinational firm is developing promotional campaigns and selecting channels of distribution in other cultures.

Cultural constraints on product and promotional strategies

Culture may be defined as institutionalized behavioral patterns adopted by a society to meet the needs of its members (Krech, Crutchfield, and Ballachey, 1962, p. 380). These patterns prescribe acceptable and unacceptable behavior and the rewards and punishments associated with each. Behavioral patterns are communicated to and stored by individuals in the form of cultural beliefs and values. Several examples will illustrate the contributions that cultural anthropologists can make to the development of multinational marketing strategies.[2]

Product designs for furniture, appliances, clothing, and the location of controls in automobiles have benefited from the advice of physical anthropologists. Cultural anthropologists contribute to the identification of appeals, the avoidance of taboos, and an understanding of the art of negotiation, including labor negotiations. In one case labor peace followed the adjustment of factory work schedules to the patterns that the culture prescribed for child care, clan, and household behavior.

Swett (1967) reports that a soft-drink firm attempted to sell in a country where wine was the traditional beverage. Sales lagged until a folk belief was discovered. It was generally believed that nonalcoholic carbonated beverages reduced male sexual potency. Sales zoomed when the advertising showed strong, handsome men drinking the product while surrounded by admiring women.

There are many taboos in communications that can ensnare advertisers. Meanings associated with symbols and colors vary among cultures, thereby complicating trademark selection, package design, and advertising layouts. For example, the colors for mourning in North America, Japan, Latin America, and Iran are black, white, purple, and blue, respectively. Pairs of anything must be avoided in advertisements in the Gold Coast of Africa, and feet should never be shown in advertisements in Thailand. Winich (1961) reports one advertisement that violated three French Canadian taboos—a wife wearing shorts, playing golf with her husband, and serving a certain kind of fish as an entree.

Some cultural errors are simply inadequate translations. A chemical manufacturer translated a brand name into Spanish for the South American market. Only after the product was put on the market did the company learn that the translation was a profane word in one South American country. In Japanese, the General Motors slogan "Body by Fisher" translates into "Corpse by Fisher," and 3M's "Sticks like Crazy" becomes "Sticks Foolishly."

---

[2] The examples are derived from Scanlan (1965); and Swett (1967).

Negotiations among businessmen must reflect cultural differences. Hall (1960) emphasizes the importance of differences in the perception of time. In Ethiopia the time required to make a decision is directly proportional to its importance. To hurry a decision is to downgrade its importance. In the Arab East speed of response is determined by family relationships, with nonrelatives placed after all relatives. In the Middle East a deadline is rude and may terminate negotiations. Hall reports that the Japanese use time to improve the terms of an agreement, delaying for years so as to get better terms because they have observed that North Americans detest long waits.

Cultural influences on channel strategies

Existing patterns of social behavior can limit channel strategy and make channel management difficult. Until recently, the daily shopping behavior of many European housewives limited the scale of retailing to small shops. In Spanish markets Sears found channel management difficult because the Spanish suppliers are proud of their own brand and will not use the Sears label (Goldstucker, 1968). In some countries health is considered the responsibility of society. As a result, the government becomes a large consumer of drug products, thereby establishing some control over channels of distribution and prices of drugs.

An early study by Martineau (1958) related social class to shopping behavior. Shoppers avoided stores whose images were a threat or whose sales clerks "make you feel like a crumb." Architecture, furnishings, and color schemes also convey a class image. Bank branches are frequently designed to fit the class of the neighborhood they serve so customers will feel at ease. Lower status persons prefer the local, face-to-face stores because they get friendly reception and easy credit (Levy, 1966).

Shopping patterns differ among classes. Upper middle-class women are knowledgeable and organized shoppers. Lower middle-class women are anxious and uncertain about purchases and place considerable effort on locating the best buy. Lower class women are the least organized, using shopping as an excuse to get out of the house (ibid.).

SUMMARY

Society influences demand in three ways. First, it meets the social needs of individuals—belonging and love. Secondly, it prescribes goals and behavioral patterns for attaining all individual needs—physical, social, and psychological. Finally, it provides communication networks that perform important roles in controlling and changing behavioral patterns.

Value differences among cultures become important to the multinational firm as it plans its marketing effort. The color of a product, package, or advertisement may be acceptable in one market and offensive in another. Advertisements are particularly vulnerable to violations in taboos and beliefs. Studies of ethnic segments of the U.S. market have revealed differences in buying patterns, but these differences might be explored better by measures of differences in life style than by ethnic or racial classifications. Similarly, differences in buying patterns among social classes may be predicted better by the variables composing social class (income, education, and dwelling) than by an index of class because an index confounds the influences, making explanation and prediction impossible.

Reference groups are especially influential when a product is consumed publicly. Perceived social pressure to use a product may overcome perceived negative product attributes and result in the purchase of a product. An individual may be influenced by a group in which he holds membership or to which he aspires.

The concept of role in a group is identical with the concept of role in a play. In both instances a person's role determines his patterns of behavior, his language, his costume, and the rewards associated with the role. Family roles are identified with child rearing and are known as life cycles. Large purchase decisions are frequently difficult because of conflicts in group values and roles.

In most societies an individual can develop his own values, beliefs, and personality within the broad constraints prescribed by society. Measures of values have not been used widely in marketing, and personality variables lack the ability to predict buying behavior. Measures of life style show more promise in explaining marketing behavior than broad measures of personality. Beliefs have been used widely in marketing, generally measured simply as awareness and unawareness (Chapters 8 and 9).

Social communication networks influence demand through personal influence and variations in media effectiveness during the adoption process. Innovativeness is associated positively with education, favorable attitudes toward change, achievement motivation, and exposure to mass media, group, and personal sources of information. The adoption model has been applied successfully to industrial products as well as agricultural and consumer innovations.

Social patterns may influence strategies of distribution and pricing. Cultural differences in negotiation will determine whether the price will be fixed or negotiated, and if negotiated, the length of negotiation.

READING QUESTIONS

1. What marketing management decisions do social forces influence?
2. How are family life cycles and role theory related?
3. Distinguish between values, beliefs, and life styles.
4. How do reference groups alter promotional strategies for a new product?

CLASS DISCUSSION QUESTIONS

1. Ask two international students from one country to participate in the following experiment. Have the first student translate an advertising slogan or copy theme into his language. Have the second student translate the first student's translation into English. Compare the original English version with the double-translated version. Discuss with these students the language and cultural problems of using U.S. promotional campaigns in their country.
2. Request permission from the owner of a local furniture store to observe the behavior of couples as they buy furniture. Discuss the behavior with the furniture salesmen. Do you confirm Levy's (1958) hypothesis of furniture buying?
3. Where would the following products fit into Table 6–2, the matrix of reference group influences on products and brands: electric razors (male, 18–25 segment), washing machines, subscriptions to the symphony, and caffeine-free coffee?
4. What sociological variables would you consider when building a demand model for the products in question 3?

SUGGESTED CASES

Griffith Insurance Agency: Social class influences on planning. Blackwell, Engel, and Kollat (1969), pp. 126–33.

Social class was used to segment the market for insurance and develop a promotional strategy.

1. Was social class the appropriate social dimension for the marketing plan? What other social variables would you consider?
2. What demographic and economic dimensions would you use to segment the market for life insurance?

Medwick Carpet Company (A): Investigating information-seeking behavior. Blackwell, Engel, and Kollat (1969), pp. 196–204.

A survey was conducted to determine the sources of information used when buying carpet.

1. Did the information-seeking behavior of Medwick buyers differ from other buyers?
2. How does your answer to the above question determine the advertising budget?

Wolff Drug Company. Bursk and Greyser (1968), pp. 43–45.

Recent market research findings were examined to evaluate the relative importance of various sources of information used by doctors when prescribing drugs.

1. Do the sampling procedures permit generalizations?
2. What type of behavior does each study explain?
3. Relate these findings to the diffusion process.

SUGGESTED READINGS

ALPERT, LEWIS, and GATTY, RONALD. "Product Positioning by Behavioral Life-Styles," *Journal of Marketing,* Vol. 33, No. 2 (April 1969), pp. 65–69.

BLISS, PERRY (ed.). *Marketing and the Behavioral Sciences.* 2d ed. Boston: Allyn & Bacon, Inc., 1967.

DAVIS, HARRY L. "Dimensions of Marital Roles in Consumer Decision Making," *Journal of Marketing Research,* Vol. 7, No. 2 (May 1970), pp. 168–77.

————. "Measurement of Husband-Wife Influence in Consumer Purchase Decisions," *Journal of Marketing Research,* Vol. 8 (August 1971), pp. 305–12.

MANSFIELD, EDWIN. *Industrial Research and Technological Innovation.* New York: W. W. Norton & Co., Inc., 1968.

MYERS, JOHN G. "Patterns of Interpersonal Influence in Adoption of New Products," in *Science Technology and Marketing* (ed. Raymond M. Haas), Proceedings of the Fall Conference. Chicago: American Marketing Association, 1966.

ROBERTSON, T. S. *Innovation and the Consumer.* New York: Holt, Rinehart & Winston, Inc., in press.

7

Social models and
measures of demand

Market segmentation and promotional strategies frequently use social variables, as was seen in Chapter 6. In terms of the model for generic demand, $G_t = N_{kt}R_{kt}$, segmentation with social variables attempts to identify N_{kt}, the number of persons who share a common social variable, and promotional strategies are built on the influence that social communication systems have on usage rates, R_{kt}. In this chapter we explore the models and measures of social influences on demand.

GROUP INFLUENCES ON INDIVIDUAL BEHAVIOR

Perhaps the most succinct model of a group may be found in Boulding's (1956) definition of an organization: ". . . a structure of roles tied together with lines of communication." The degree of influence that a group has on an individual's behavior depends on his commitment to the values of the group. His commitment, in turn, is reflected in the role that he performs in the group.

Role centrality and values

A role is a task to which the group has assigned expected patterns of behavior and rewards and punishment for conforming to these expectations. The more central roles require larger commitments to group values and provide greater rewards. The term role as used in social psychology is equivalent to that used in the theater. In both cases role determines behavior, responsibilities, rewards, props, costumes, and languages. In a firm, for instance, the behavior expected by the mailboy, the newly arrived college student, the sales manager, and the president are quite different. Myers and Reynolds (1967) provide a colorful example of role behavior. A member of a motorcycle club must have the props (a motorcycle), a costume (a black leather jacket), a setting (the rally), and he must learn the lines or language of the group.

Organizational functions and values

The structure of a social system is formed by series of related events that move the group toward its goal. By rearranging events the group can perform numerous functions. Four types of organizational functions have been identified by Katz and Kahn (1965): (1) production (e.g., mining, farming, manufacturing, transportation and communication); (2) maintenance of society (e.g., schools and churches); (3) adaption (e.g., change agents, including research laboratories, advanced forms in art and music, and the marketing activities of promotion and market research); and (4) management ("the coordination and control of people and resources, and the adjudicating among competing groups"). Marketing systems perform productive, adaptive, and managerial functions by communicating between buyers and sellers, by diffusing innovations, and by coordinating supply and demand.

Separate criteria exist for evaluating each of these functions. Production functions are judged according to their efficiency, maintenance functions are evaluated in terms of group stability and predictability, adaptive functions are evaluated by their degree of external control and internal flexibility, and management functions are judged by their ability to compromise, control, and survive (ibid.).

The criteria for evaluating performance in each of these organizations determine the values of an organization. For instance, production systems value efficiency, low cost, and speed. The systems will allocate rewards to individuals who share these values and act accordingly. A creative person who does not share these values would be uncomfortable in a production-oriented organization. There is considerable doubt about the cause-and-effect relationship between an individual's values and those of a group. Do individual values determine group membership, do groups change individual values, is there conformity to group values only when the individual is with the group, or is the relationship some combination of these conditions? Research to answer these questions is lacking.

SOCIAL MEASURES FOR PREDICTING DEMAND

Social variables have been used frequently by marketers to describe and predict behavior in the marketplace. One of the early social variables was social class, which implied values that may explain buying behavior. Later approaches used instruments to measure values directly. Recent approaches have examined specific patterns of behavior that reflect an individual's values. These patterns are known as life styles or activities.

Social class

Social class captured the hopes of many marketers in their attempts to predict and understand consumer behavior. Social class has been used in attempts to explain three types of marketing behavior—shopping behavior, buying behavior, and the communication of innovations.

An understanding of the applications and limitations of social class as a determinant of marketing behavior has been made difficult by the lack of a common definition and the lack of agreement among researchers on the means for measuring class. A citizen of any town can describe who in town is upper, middle, and lower class in his view. If pressed for his criteria, he would use some of the same ones used by sociologists, which include occupation, source of income, residential area, type of dwelling, education, roles in the community, father's occupation, memberships in location organizations, and values. But how are these dimensions weighted to form social classes—clusters of persons whose behavior is on an equal status with other members of the cluster? Are the resulting clusters exhaustive and mutually exclusive?[1]

There are three procedures for measuring social class—the objective, the subjective, and the reputational (Krech, Crutchfield, and Ballachey, 1962). The objective method uses variables such as income, education, and occupation, for which data are available from secondary sources like the U.S. Bureau of the Census. Persons are placed along these dimensions, and their class score is a sum of these measures or an index, with the important variables weighted more heavily. The class scores are then divided into discrete classifications such as upper upper, lower middle, etc., to suit the needs of the researchers.

---

[1] For a more complete discussion of social class, see Robertson (1970); and Engel, Kollat, and Blackwell (1968). For a review of the technical problems, see Carman (1965); and *Social Class Definition* (1963).

The subjective method uses a survey to determine where members of a community place themselves in the status hierarchy. Respondents are asked to classify themselves as upper, middle, working, or lower class, etc. This method tends to produce large groupings in the middle classes.

The reputational method uses a survey but requires selected informants to rate other members of the community. The validity of the reputational method depends on the objectivity of the informants and their knowledge of community members. As the size of the community increases, anonymity increases and knowledgeable informants are more difficult to locate. The reliability of the method has been questioned because results have not been replicated.

Social class variables have several limitations. The number and content of classifications differ among researchers. A comparison of classification schemes by Engle, Kollat, and Blackwell (1968) revealed that five studies of social class used five different schemes with from five to nine classes in each scheme. This lack of agreement among researchers prevents generalizations on the effects of social class on behavior.

For marketers the most important limitation is the inability of social class to predict buying behavior. Perhaps differences in shopping and buying patterns among social classes are eroding due to increased income, increased education, and the rapid diffusion of innovation through the commercial mass media. New fashion does not start with the upper class and trickle down to the masses. The mass media bring new ideas to all classes simultaneously (Rich and Jain, 1968; and King, 1963). The most serious limitation of social class indices is that they confound the effects of individual variables such as education, income, and social values. Once these variables are combined into an index there is no way of identifying the effect of each element of the index and the relationships among them. A better approach would be to use these variables in a multiple regression model so that the influence of each variable could be estimated for each market segment. Such a model may appear as follows:

$$R_{kt} = b_1 E + b_2 I + b_3 V \qquad (7-1)$$

where the coefficients b_1, b_2, and b_3 reflect the importance of education, income, and values on rates of consumption (R_{kt}).

Values

The concept of value has a broad range of meanings. In its broadest usage it includes patterns of attitudes and behavior that could be described by adjectives such as those used by Allport and Vernon—theoretical, economic, esthetic, social, political, and religious.[2] Slightly more specific are the values identified by Rokeach (1968), which include terminal values (e.g., equality, freedom, and a sense of accomplishment) and instrumental values (e.g., honest, responsible, and broadminded). These concepts are too broad, however, to predict generic and brand demand, which are very specific forms of behavior.

In marketing the concept of value takes on a specific meaning—the importance of the attributes or benefits of a product. There are numerous instruments for measuring importance (Chapter 9). One useful instrument is the constant-sum scale, which is as follows:

Indicate the importance of the following attributes when
buying a new car by allocating 100 points:

Style	_____
Economy	_____
Safety	_____
Total	100

Fishbein (1967, pp. 477–92, and 1971) reflects the influence of group values on the individual in his model of behavioral intentions, which is as follows:

$$BI = b_1 A_{act} + b_2(NB \cdot Mc). \qquad (7\text{--}2)$$

BI represents the intention of behaving in a specified way, b_1 and b_2 are the coefficients to be estimated, A_{act} is the attitude toward the act, *NB* is a normative belief (what he and others think he should do in this situation), and *Mc* is the motivation to comply with these norms. Thus, instead of attempting to relate attitudes to behavior, Fishbein analyzes the components of behavior and shows that an attitude is only one of many variables that determine behavior. In Equation 7–2 the attitude toward the object enters indirectly through the attitude toward an act, such as buying or using a product. Fishbein (1971) reported that correlations between *BI* and later behavior ranged from 0.30 to 0.97.

Specific patterns of behavior

Man is a creature of habit. To predict what he will do tomorrow, observe him today or ask him what he did yesterday. The measurement of

---

[2] For a discussion of these values see Brogden (1952). See White (1951) for a scheme for identifying values by content-analyzing written material.

past or expected behavior is central to techniques known variously as psychographics (Ziff, 1971); activity, interest, and opinions (Wells and Tigert, 1969); attitudes and activities (Hustad and Pessemier, 1971); and life style (Lazer, 1963). These concepts and techniques were developed because demographic and economic variables failed to explain buyer behavior for many products.

The newness of these techniques and the personal preferences of the researchers explain why it is difficult to distinguish the similarities and differences among the methods. A review of the techniques by Hustad and Pessemier (1971) led them to conclude that *life-style* measures emphasized behavioral patterns without considering attitudes adequately and that *psychographic* implied general traits that may be too broad to be useful in marketing. *Activity, interest,* and *opinion* (AIO) measures fall within the measures of *attitudes* and *activities* that are suggested by Hustad and Pessemier. One author defines psychographics as multivariate statistical analysis (Demby, 1971); other authors think of them in terms of product benefits (Garfinkle, 1971; Nelson, 1971); and at least one author deplores the lack of a standard definition but makes no attempt to provide one (Ziff, 1971).

An *activity* is defined as "a manifest action such as viewing media, shopping a specific store, buying a given brand, or telling a neighbor about a new service" (Hustad and Pessemier, 1971). Wells and Tigert (1969) focus on more generalized marketing activities by measuring behavior with respect to price, fashion, children, housekeeping, and art. Examples of their scales for measuring these activities are presented in Table 7–1. These scales provide coarse measures of the probability of specified behavior in given situations.

This definition of an activity and the scales in Table 7–1 enable us to place the concept of marketing activities in the context of social-psychological theory. *Activities* are simply personalities referring to specific behavior, in this case the behavior of buying and consuming. At the risk of further proliferation of terms, *marketing personalities* may be a more accurate term than *activities*. Personality, it will be recalled (Chapter 6), is a consistent personal pattern of behavior for meeting needs and interacting with the environment. Scales for measuring these patterns classify persons as sociable, dominant, responsible, etc. Measures of activities were developed because personalities were too general to predict behavior as specific as buying a product or brand. Thus, marketers are moving toward an established psychological concept, that of situation specific personalities (Alker, 1972; Mischel, 1968).

TABLE 7–1
Examples of generalized scales for measuring activities

Price conscious
  I shop a lot for "specials."
  I find myself checking the prices in the grocery store even for small items.
  I usually watch the advertisements for announcements of sales.
  A person can save a lot of money by shopping around for bargains.
Compulsive housekeeper
  I don't like to see children's toys lying about.
  I usually keep my house very neat and clean.
  I am uncomfortable when my house is not completely clean.
  Our days seem to follow a definite routine such as eating meals at a regular time, etc.
Community minded
  I am an active member of more than one service organization.
  I do volunteer work for a hospital or service organization on a fairly regular basis.
  I like to work on community projects.
  I have personally worked in a political campaign or for a candidate or an issue.
Self-confident
  I think I have more self-confidence than most people.
  I am more independent than most people.
  I think I have a lot of personal ability.
  I like to be considered a leader.

Source: Wells and Tigert (1969).

Early results with activity measures suggest that the loss in generality has been offset by a gain in the ability to predict behavior. Predictions could be improved further by being even more specific, for instance, by asking the probability of buying a brand, but such a measure is devoid of any explanatory power. Is it better to have an explanatory or predictive measure of activities? It depends on the problem to be solved. If the problem is inventory control or an efficient system of logistics, then predictive power is the most desirable characteristic. If the problem is the development of a product and a promotional strategy, then the measure should help to explain as well as predict behavior in the marketplace. The management task determines whether the goal of measurement and modeling is the description, prediction, or control of the marketing system (Chapter 10).

The concept of life style may be seen in Table 7–1. Patterns of marketing and nonmarketing activities such as these yield what is commonly called a style of living, or life style. Life style should not be confused with the concept of life cycle. Life cycle, it will be recalled (Chapter 6), represents a series of roles that are performed in the family (e.g., husband, father of one child, and father of several children). These roles determine specific needs for household and family formation. Life style represents patterns of behavior for meeting these needs.

MODELS OF THE DIFFUSION OF INNOVATIONS

The social processes that diffuse information through groups can be modeled with greater precision than was illustrated during the discussion of the adoption process (Chapter 6). The discussion here goes beyond these verbal models to include analytical models using matrices, directed graphs, algebra, and calculus.

Network models

The influence of a group will be determined in part by the individual's frequency of exposure to the group. Table 7–2 presents one method for summarizing the probability of interclass contact. Persons in the row classes refer to the classes in the columns.

TABLE 7–2
Probability of interclass contact

		Reference class		
		Upper	*Middle*	*Lower*
Seeking class	Upper	0.80	0.10	0.10
	Middle	0.30	0.70	0.0
	Lower	0.50	0.35	0.50

Data are hypothetical.

This matrix may be interpreted as follows: Contacts of upper social class members are largely within the class (0.80), but it is *avant garde* to accept some values of the lower classes (e.g., the use of slang) so that there is a 0.10 probability of contact with middle and lower classes as reference groups. Middle-class contacts are largely in the middle class (0.70) with an effort toward upward mobility through the seeking of contacts in the upper class (0.30) and zero probability of reference to lower classes. Half of the lower class contacts in this hypothetical matrix are within this class, with considerable reference to the middle class (0.35) as well as reference to the upper class (0.15).

Provision must be made for estimating the degree of influence of each social class with regard to a specific product or product class. Following the example of Katz and Lazarsfeld (1955; illustrated in Chapter 6) we could form a vector of influence which, when multiplied by the matrix of probabilities of interclass contacts, would yield a vector of social influence in buying behavior. This would appear as follows:

$$\begin{pmatrix} \text{Probability of} \\ \text{interclass contact} \end{pmatrix} \times \begin{pmatrix} \text{Influence of opinion} \\ \text{leaders' class when} \\ \text{buying an automobile} \end{pmatrix} = \begin{pmatrix} \text{Social influence} \\ \text{in automobile} \\ \text{buying behavior} \end{pmatrix}$$

$$\begin{array}{c} \\ Upper \\ Middle \\ Lower \end{array} \begin{array}{ccc} Upper & Middle & Lower \\ \begin{pmatrix} 0.80 & 0.10 & 0.10 \\ 0.30 & 0.70 & 0.0 \\ 0.15 & 0.35 & 0.50 \end{pmatrix} \end{array} \times \begin{pmatrix} 0.30 \\ 0.15 \\ 0.01 \end{pmatrix} = \begin{pmatrix} 0.26 \\ 0.20 \\ 0.11 \end{pmatrix} \quad (7\text{--}3)$$

Matrices such as these can summarize reference group and social class theories and enable the marketing strategist to include estimates of social influences in his promotional plan. The matrix of interclass contact reflects enduring social networks, thereby eliminating the need for frequent estimates of cell entries. Once this matrix is established, plans for a new product require only the cell entries for the vector of group influence.

It is possible to build models of communications networks by using directed graphs. A directed graph indicates the transmitters and receivers of information. A directed graph can be expressed as a matrix and manipulated to reveal complex communication patterns over time that could not be shown graphically.[3]

Kernan (1966) provides an example of a directed graph and its accompanying matrix for a hypothetical network of housewives. The graph is reproduced in Figure 7–1 and the matrix in Table 7–3. All of the information in the graph is expressed in the matrix. For example, the matrix shows that housewife B talks only to A but listens to A, D, and F. The main diagonal contains zeros, indicating that no housewife talks to herself. Mrs. E is a talker, Mrs. B is a listener, and Mrs. G is practically incommunicado.

The advantage of the communication matrix is the ease with which the dynamics of the network can be traced over time. For example, suppose that the above matrix represents a weekly interaction and Mrs. A has some new-product experience to communicate. How many weeks will be required for everyone to hear of this experience? In week one B and C hear of the experience. In week two C tells E. Talkative Mrs. E tells D, F, and G in week three. Thus, by the end of week three, everyone has the news.

---

[3] For a more detailed discussion, see Coleman (1964), pp. 430–68.

FIGURE 7–1
A directed graph of a housewife
communication network

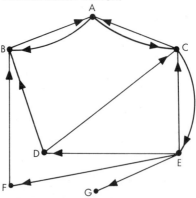

Source: Adapted from Kernan (1966).

By adding to the matrix rows and columns for commercial communication we could build a communications matrix that would represent marketing networks. It would include promotion (rows), marketing research
(columns), and channel intermediaries who talk and listen. Mass communications would try to talk to everyone. Messages would be diffused quickly
to all listeners in the network, which would preclude the need for the
three-week trickle down in the above example. The fact that fashion is
diffused across persons and classes largely by the mass media, and to a
lesser extent by fashion leaders, could be presented easily in matrix form.
Internal information processing by the individual would be represented by
the main diagonal.

TABLE 7–3
A matrix of a housewife communication network

Who talks	Who listens							Total talking
	A	B	C	D	E	F	G	
A	0	1	1	0	0	0	0	2
B	1	0	0	0	0	0	0	1
C	1	0	0	0	1	0	0	2
D	0	1	1	0	0	0	0	2
E	0	0	1	1	0	1	1	4
F	0	1	0	0	0	0	0	1
G	0	0	0	0	0	0	0	0
Total listening	2	3	3	1	1	1	1	12

Source: Adapted from Kernan (1966).

Modeling the rate of adoption

Studies of the diffusion of medical innovation led Coleman, Katz, and Menzel (1966) to conclude that the rate of adoption could be expressed as follows:

$$\frac{dy}{dt} = k(1 - y) \qquad (7\text{--}4)$$

where dy/dt is the rate of adoption, y is the cumulative proportion of individuals who have adopted the innovation, t is time, and k is a constant that represents the rate of receptivity of the group. High integration within a group will produce a snowballing or epidemic effect. New adopters in one period of time exert an influence in subsequent periods. These authors model the snowballing effect as follows:

$$\frac{dy}{dt} = ky(1 - y) \qquad (7\text{--}5)$$

The additional y reflects the fact that the rate of adoption increases as the cumulative proportion of adopters increases, thereby increasing the pressure on those who have not accepted the innovation.[4]

Modeling the product life cycle

The life cycle of a new product is determined by buyers' rates of adoption. Thus, product planning requires consideration of the concept of social communication networks.

The concept of the product life cycle is basic to marketing planning because it describes well the stages through which a product passes and the appropriate marketing mix at each stage. In the early stages (Figure 7–2) the product is unknown, so the mix is weighted heavily toward the communication task with large expenditures for promotion. During the second stage the rate of sales accelerates, so emphasis must be placed on channel strategy and logistics systems. At the third stage the product has competitors, comparative advantages are less distinct, and price dominates the marketing strategy. At the last stage the strategy is largely one of price and reducing the costs of promotion and distribution to keep the product profitable. When the product becomes unprofitable, two possible strategies are to drop the product or to improve the product and repeat the cycle.[5]

---

[4] For a diffusion model that considers message decay and advertising schedules, see Myers and Yen (1969).

[5] For a discussion of marketing strategies related to the life cycle, see Kotler (1965); Levitt (1965); and Wasson (1971). For empirical evidence supporting the life cycle, see Polli and Cook (1969). For a theory of market behavior after innovation, see Haines (1964).

FIGURE 7–2
Product life cycle and the marketing mix

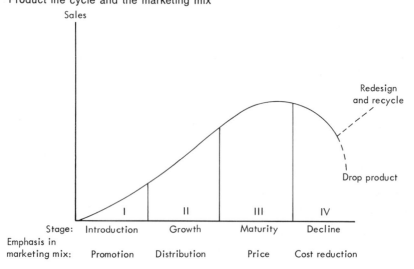

The curve in Figure 7–2 has received many applications in the be-havioral sciences. The shape of this curve is similar to the logistic curve which was popular in demography for the prediction of population (Chapter 3). It will be recalled that long-term prediction with the logistic curve was dangerous because the model aggregates birth, death, and migration rates, thereby disguising the causes for changes in population. Marketing planners should reflect on this limitation when using the concept of the product life cycle. The concept aggregates the rates of switching into the brand, out of the brand, and migrating to or from the product class. These rates should be known when developing a marketing plan.

Persons who adopt an innovation are classified according to how soon after introduction they adopted the innovation. They are known as innova-tors, early adopters, early majority, late majority, and laggards.[6] Bass (1969) used the behavioral rationale in this descriptive model to develop a model that will predict the timing of adoption (initial purchases) of con-sumer durable goods. He combined the above classes into innovators and imitators. The timing of initial purchases by innovators is independent of social influences, while imitators are influenced by the number of previous buyers. The influence of innovators diminishes monotonically with time. This relationship may be expressed in the following model:

$$P(T) = p + \left(\frac{q}{m}\right) Y(T) \qquad (7\text{–}6)$$

---

[6] For a summary of the diffusion literature, see Rogers and Stanfield (1968).

where $P(T)$ is the probability that an initial purchase will be made at time T, p is the probability of an initial purchase when $T = 0$ (thus p is the coefficient of innovation), q is the coefficient of imitation, m is the number of initial purchases of the product throughout its life, and $Y(T)$ is the number of previous buyers. The social pressure on imitators who have not adopted the product is reflected in the quantity $(q/m)Y(T)$.[7]

Bass derived the following model of sales at T (using a continuous model, a density function of time to initial purchase, and calculus):

$$S(T) = pm + (q - p)Y(T) - \frac{q}{m} Y^2(T) \qquad (7\text{--}7)$$

where $S(T)$ is sales at T.

TABLE 7–4

A comparison of predicted and observed time and magnitude of peaks in the initial sales of selected durables

Product	Time (years) since introduction		Sales peak (units) (000,000)	
	Predicted	Actual	Predicted	Actual
Home freezers.	11.6	13	1.2	1.2
Television				
(black and white).	7.8	7	7.5	7.8
Water softeners	8.9	9	0.5	0.5
Power lawnmowers	10.3	11	4.0	4.2
Automatic coffee makers	9.0	10	4.8	4.9

Source: Adapted from Bass (1969).

Bass used regression to fit Equation 7–7 to time-series data for 11 different consumer durables (e.g., refrigerators, black and white television sets, power lawnmowers, and record players). The model fitted the data well, explaining over 88 percent of the variance in initial sales in 8 of the 11 cases. The model was tested further by comparing the times that were predicted with those that were observed. The predicted and observed peaks were also compared. The predictions were quite close to the observed times and magnitudes, as is shown in Table 7–4. Data such as these could be very important when planning the budget for a product over its life cycle.

The final test of the model was a prediction of color television sets. A prediction made in 1966 identified 1968 as the peak year with 6.7 million sets the magnitude of the peak. Industry leaders did not reach the same prediction until 1967. Sales from 1968, 1969, and 1970 were 6.21,

---

[7] By rearranging terms and differentiating Equation 7–5, the model becomes a model of the rate of adoption like Equation 7–4.

6.19, and 5.3 millions respectively (*Merchandising Week,* 1970; 1971). Thus, the peak year was predicted correctly, but the volume was incorrect.

If the product is not on the market, prediction requires estimates of p, q, and m. Estimates of p and q may be calculated using data from a related product (black and white television in this case). The total number of initial purchases during the product's life cycle, m, is the result of a demand analysis. The model has been applied to nondurable goods by Bass and King (1968) and therefore is not limited to the planning for durable goods. Thus, Bass has shown that the concept of social communication networks helps to explain the concept of product life cycle.

Measuring exposure to information

Social organizations provide an opportunity for the individual to be exposed to formal and informal sources of information. Education, religion, television, newspapers, and magazines are formal sources while the opinions of relatives and friends are informal sources. Exposure to information does not mean that the information has been influential. A person tends to selectively perceive and process information according to his need for the information (Chapters 8 and 9).

Instruments for measuring media exposure and frequency are generally very direct questions. The media may be classified according to their content, for example, cultural, light reading, fashion, or homemaking (Pessemier, Burger, and Tigert, 1967). Survey questionnaires frequently include unguided or guided questions about media habits. An example of an unguided question is as follows:

List the magazines to which you subscribe:

_____ _____
_____ _____
_____ _____
_____

A guided question might be as follows:

Check the magazines to which you subscribe:

_____ *Readers' Digest*　　_____ *McCall's*
_____ *Harper's*　　_____ *Time*
_____ *Playboy*　　_____ *Business Week*

Guided questions tend to be more fun for respondents, but there is a tendency for them to inflate the number of responses and to bias responses toward the intellectual media.

Commercial market research services are available that measure regularly the reading of magazines and specific advertisements in magazines (e.g., Starch Reports and Gallup-Robinson). Similarly, services are available for the measurement of radio listening and television viewing habits (for details see Robinson et al., 1968).

SUMMARY

Market segmentation and promotional strategies that use social variables require an understanding of the concepts of role and values. These concepts determine the influence that groups will have on an individual's demand for goods and services. Social class implies values that may influence demand, but class variables have not proven to be good predictors of buying behavior. Direct measures of value, such as the Allport-Vernon and Rokeach scales, are too general to describe behavior as specific as generic and brand demand. More precise measures of value in marketing focus on attribute importance. The latest development in measuring values has been to measure specific patterns of behavior that reflect values. These patterns are known by various terms, such as life style and activities.

Networks of social communications may be modeled using directed graphs. Theories of reference groups, social class, diffusion networks, and information processing are summarized efficiently using matrices and matrix algebra. Algebra and calculus have been used effectively to model the rate of adoption, the timing of initial purchases, the magnitude of peaks, and the duration of periods of innovation. Models such as these aid in planning the marketing mix and budgets over the life cycle of a new product.

READING QUESTIONS

1. How does the group influence individual behavior?
2. Evaluate social measures for predicting demands. Which would you recommend to market a prepaid health-care service?
3. How does matrix algebra aid in the analysis of group influence on buying decisions?
4. What is the relationship between diffusion rates and product life cycles?

CLASS DISCUSSION QUESTIONS

1. Debate the following statement: Marketing's contribution to society is the breaking down of social class barriers.

2. What criteria are used to evaluate the performance of the following departments of a fully integrated oil company: accounting, advertising, production, research and development, and top management? Explain how these different criteria may lead to organizational conflict.

3. Illustrate how models of communication networks could be used to market a prepaid health-care service.

4. What social influences do you think would be the most important when estimating the demand for the following products and services: mass transportation, ski touring equipment, winter vacations, video tape cameras and recorders, and phonovision educational systems?

5. What are the differences and similarities among the concepts of values, psychographics, activities, and personalities?

SUGGESTED CASES

Bender Mattress Company. Bursk (1965), pp. 8–11.

The media plan was being revised. A survey of families revealed the contribution of husbands and wives to the decision, the relationship between prepurchase brand preferences and brand purchased, the relationship between brand recall and media, and the influence of personal experience, social, and commercial sources of information on brand selection.

1. How could existing social theories and models help you organize these findings?

2. From your knowledge of social theories, what additional information would you like?

3. Describe a new media plan for Bender.

Topic Publishing Company, Inc. (A)—"Topic" magazine. Bursk and Greyser (1968), pp. 122–40.

The company faces basic policy, strategy, and organizational decisions with regard to magazine content, pricing, circulation, and advertising.

1. How do changes in individual values affect the decisions to be made by Topic?

2. What potential opportunities do these changes in values create?

Topic Publishing Company, Inc. (B). Bursk and Greyser (1968), pp. 141–55.

Topic Publishing Company is considering the introduction of a new publication that will appeal to a market segment defined as upper income, higher education, and thoughtful persons.

1. What other market segments should the company consider?
2. How do changes in personal values influence the decision to introduce a new publication?
3. Evaluate the instruments used to measure beliefs, values, and attitudes.

The Touch-Tone Telephone: Diffusion of an innovation. Blackwell, Engel, and Kollat (1969), pp. 274–97.

The characteristics of innovators and noninnovators were studied.

1. How would you use these findings to develop a communication campaign?

SUGGESTED READINGS

BLAKE, B.; PERLOFF, R.; and HESLIN, R. "Dogmatism and Acceptance of New Products," *Journal of Marketing Research,* Vol. 7, No. 4 (November 1970), pp. 483–86.

KING, C. W., and RYAN, G. E. "Identifying the Innovator as a Consumer Change Agent," in Gardner (1971), pp. 446–51.

PESSEMIER, E. A., and BRUNO, A. "An Empirical Investigation of the Reliability and Stability of Selected Activity and Attitude Measures," in Gardner (1971), pp. 389–403.

POLLAK, OTTO. "The Family for the Future," *Wharton Quarterly,* Spring 1971, pp. 25–29.

ROBERTSON, T. S. *Innovation to the Consumer.* New York: Holt, Rinehart & Winston, Inc., in press.

TIGERT, D. J. "A Research Project in Creative Advertising through Life Style Analysis," in King and Tigert (1971), pp. 223–27.

———, and ARNOLD, S. J. "Profiling Self-Designated Opinion Leaders and Self-Designated Innovators through Life Style Research," in Gardner (1971), pp. 425–45.

ZALTMAN, G., and DUBOIS, B. "New Conceptual Approaches in the Study of Innovation," in Gardner (1971), pp. 417–24.

8

Illustrative cases in
psychological demand
analysis

THE NEED FOR PSYCHOLOGICAL VARIABLES

The demand for buying a product or service in an affluent economy is not limited to an individual's physical needs (food, shelter, etc.) or his ability to buy the product (income). Demand also includes social-psychological needs. Segmentation of the market according to psychological dimensions follows logically from segmentation according to demographic, economic, and sociological variables. But for many generic products, and especially for brands, demographic, economic, and sociological variables do not distinguish between buyers and nonbuyers, or heavy and light buyers of a brand.

Psychological variables, it will be recalled from Chapter 1, influence generic demand by influencing consumption rates (R_t), thus

$$R_t = f(D_t, E_t, S_t, P_t) \qquad (8\text{--}1)$$

where D, E, S, and P are demographic, economic, sociological, and psychological variables respectively. Market share (M_{jt}) for brand J is a function of the preference rank of brand j in time t (P_{jt}), thus

$$M_{jt} \approx f(P_{jt}) \qquad (8\text{--}2)$$

where P_{jt} is a function of the Euclidean distance between a buyer's perception of brand j and the ideal brand in n-dimensional psychological space.

POSITIONING A BRAND IN PSYCHOLOGICAL SPACE

When a marketing manager refers to the *positioning* of his brand he basically means moving his brand away from his competitor and toward the ideal brand, as perceived by buyers. This movement in psychological space is accomplished through product development and promotion. Psychological space is known as *product-attribute space* when the dimensions are product characteristics; it may be called *consumer-benefit space* when the dimensions are measured in terms of consumer needs. Frequently these perceptions of attributes and benefits correctly reflect the actual characteristics of a product and identify means for improving the product. When perceptions do not correspond to actual product characteristics, there is a need for a promotional effort to correct the beliefs about the product. In a later example we will see that General Motors used this approach when developing advertising strategies.

Marketers should not forget that a buyer does not buy a product for its intrinsic value but for its ability to meet his needs. A marketing strategy to position a new brand or to reposition an old brand requires first the identification of dimensions that are important to the buying decision and second the measurement of buyers' perceptions of each brand along these dimensions. These two steps amount to measuring buyers' attitudes toward brands.

A person does not buy a frozen food product. He buys a bundle of attributes such as taste, sustenance, quality, social acceptability, and convenience. Each of these attributes meets a different need, which may be physical, social, or psychological. The goal of the marketer is to meet these needs. This goal is accomplished by developing products or services with attributes to meet needs and promoting the attributes to potential buyers. Psychological variables are central to all promotional strategies because the goal of promotion is to change attitudes by changing their components—beliefs and values.

The importance of psychological variables to the development of a promotional strategy may be seen by examining the six steps in creating this strategy. These steps include: (1) identifying the marketing goals, (2) determining the motivation for buying, (3) developing a message, (4) determining the most efficient media for communicating the message (including package design), (5) measuring the effectiveness of the campaign, and (6) modifying the message and media when the goals have not been met or have been exceeded. (Colley, 1961; and Hughes, 1971). An understanding of the psychological variables is necessary to translate the marketing goals into promotional goals (step 1 to step 3), when controlling the promotional budget (step 5), and when reallocating the budget (step 6).[1]

ATTITUDES DEFINED

The marketing concept of a brand's position in n-dimensional psychological space is identical to the psychological concept of an attitude toward a brand. Most of the measuring instruments and models that are used by marketers have been developed by psychologists. To understand the applications and limitations of these measures and models it is necessary to define briefly the concept of an attitude.

Psychologists' use of the term *attitude* for over a century has produced numerous definitions and comparisons of definitions (e.g., Allport, 1935; Insko, 1967; Shaw and Wright, 1967). Most definitions agree that an *attitude* is a learned mental state that reflects an individual's attraction toward or repulsion from an object, person, or concept. Authors disagree, however, on the number of components in an attitude. Krech, Crutchfield, and Ballachey (1962) consider three components—beliefs, feelings, and response tendencies—while Shaw and Wright (1967) restrict their definition of an attitude to the feeling (evaluative) component. The current trend in marketing is to define an attitude in terms of two components—beliefs and values. The product of a belief times a value yields an attitude toward a product attribute. An overall attitude toward an object (A_o) is the sum of the attitudes toward each attribute, which is expressed in the Fishbein (1967) model as follows:

$$A_o = \sum_{i=1}^{n} B_i a_i \qquad (8\text{–}3)$$

where B_i is the individual's belief that the object has attribute i and a_i is the value or importance that he places on this attribute.

The appropriateness of Equation 8–3 to marketing may be illustrated with a toothpaste brand. Brand selection may be determined by four product attributes—decay prevention, brightness, flavor, and cost. If all attributes are of equal importance and if a brand is rated favorably along the first three attributes and unfavorably on cost, then the overall attitude toward the brand will be favorable. If, however, cost is more important than all other attributes combined, then the buyer's overall attitude toward the brand will be negative. Promotional strategies attempt to change beliefs and attribute saliences. (Attribute salience is the value component in the Fishbein model.)

---

[1] For an example of a complete strategy see Hughes (1971), chap. 2.

Attitudes are learned mental states because their components (beliefs and values) are learned. Because attitudes are learned they are subject to change through new information, foregetting, and rationalization (internal processing of stored information).

APPLICATIONS OF PSYCHOLOGICAL VARIABLES

Five examples will illustrate how attitudes are used to plan for new products and promotional campaigns. The first example uses Irish housewives' beliefs about the attributes possessed by margarine brands. The second case maps clusters of voters into candidate space during the 1968 U.S. presidential election. The third case is an example of nonmetric mapping of toothpaste brands. The fourth case illustrates how measures of beliefs, attitudes, and probabilities are used by General Motors to develop promotional campaigns. The final case is most unusual. It shows how measures of attitudes may be used to improve governmental services, in this instance the postal service.

Attribute beliefs about margarine brands

The problem was the development and promotion of a brand of margarine for the Irish market where there was a strong social stigma against margarine, especially as a spread (Downing, 1960). The influence of this stigma was reflected in the fact that margarine had only 12 percent of the butter-margarine market in Eire against 48 percent in the United Kingdom, despite the fact that margarine was cheaper in Eire than in the United Kingdom. Irish housewives were unaware of the composition and varieties of margarine but they were aware of the price differential between butter and margarine, which reinforced their poor attitude toward the latter. Thus, an appeal to thrift may be counter productive because it would be rejected by the working class "who saw themselves as fulfilling the stereotype of the stage Irishman, lazy, feckless, self-indulgent, easy-come, easy-go and enjoying the good things of life (such as butter) without thought for the morrow" (ibid., p. 59). The solution was the development of a new product—a margarine containing 10 percent butter, sold at a premium, wrapped in gold foil—advertised to create butter associations by emphasizing spreading qualities.

The success of this marketing plan is revealed in Figure 8–1 which compares the attribute beliefs of users and nonusers of margarine (brand A) and the new product with 10 percent butter (brand B). The 19 product attributes were identified in housewife discussion groups. The respondent

FIGURE 8-1
Attribute beliefs toward margarine brands

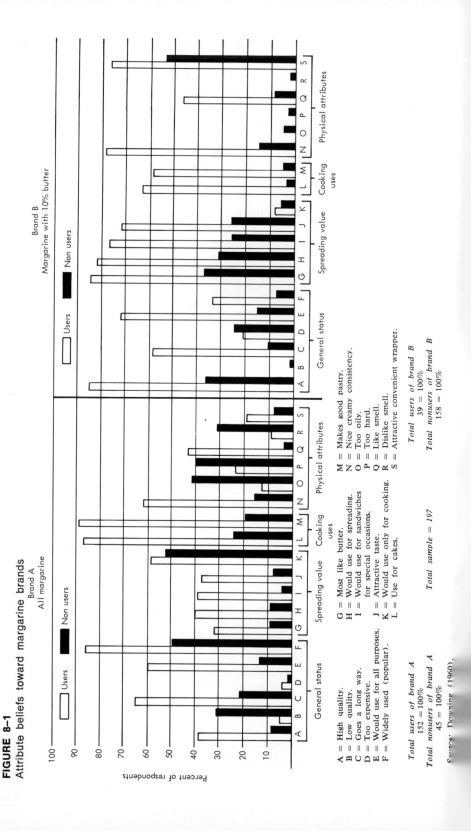

A = High quality.
B = Low quality.
C = Goes a long way.
D = Too expensive.
E = Would use for all purposes.
F = Widely used (popular).

G = Most like butter.
H = Would use for spreading.
I = Would use for sandwiches for special occasions.
J = Attractive taste.
K = Would use only for cooking.
L = Use for cakes.

M = Makes good pastry.
N = Nice creamy consistency.
O = Too oily.
P = Too hard.
Q = Like smell.
R = Dislike smell.
S = Attractive convenient wrapper.

Total users of brand A
152 = 100%

Total nonusers of brand A
45 = 100%

Total sample = 197

Total users of brand B
39 = 100%

Total nonusers of brand B
158 = 100%

Source: Downing (1960).

was asked to report which of six brands was described best by the attribute. These attributes were classified according to general status, spreading value, cooking uses, and physical attributes. A comparison of beliefs of the nonusers toward status, spreading, and physical attributes revealed that larger percentages of housewives believed that brand B possessed favorable attributes (A, F, G through K, Q, and S) and fewer percentages believed it possessed unfavorable attributes (B, O, P, and R). Thus, the product and promotional strategy succeeded in its initial goal—improving the beliefs about a new brand of margarine. These more favorable beliefs should increase the probability of nonusers becoming users of brand B.

A map of voters and presidential candidates

Prior to the 1968 U.S. presidential election, 1,000 consumers were asked to agree or disagree with 35 political statements using a four-point scale (Johnson, 1971).[2] The current political topics were the war in Vietnam, welfare, and law and order. Respondents also reported their perceptions of political figures' stands on issues. A map of voter clusters in candidate space is shown in Figure 8–2. The dimensions of this political space are liberal/conservative and reduce/increase government involvement. To test the model the responses of a class of sociology students in a western state university were plotted on the map as S. It will be noted that this group is close to McCarthy, the candidate who was popular with the students at that time. A political planner can use a map such as this to reposition his candidate in space so he is close to the ideal points of large clusters of voters, clearly different from other candidates, and along dimensions that are important.

A mapping of the British electorate placed the Conservative, the Labour, and the Liberal parties in two-dimensional space where the dimensions were egalitarian and populist (Morgan and Purnell, 1969). The populist favored more state welfare, Britain first, and less taxation. The egalitarian opposed elitism and automation and he favored foreign aid. A computerized search routine designed to locate new brands in product space was used to identify the characteristics of a new political party. The point identified for this party was high on the populist dimension and at the lowest point on the egalitarian dimension. This point was interpreted as close to the traditional Fascist position. Further analysis indicated that initial support for the party whould be 24 percent of the voters, drawn evenly from all parties. Later, the present parties would be forced to take

---

[2] Scaling devices are discussed in Chapter 9. The one used in this survey seems to be a Likert scale.

FIGURE 8–2
A map of voters in candidate space in the 1968 presidential election

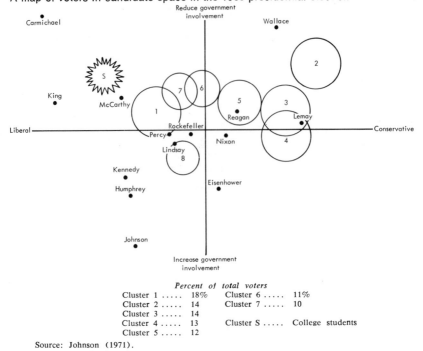

Percent of *total voters*

Cluster 1	18%	Cluster 6	11%
Cluster 2	14	Cluster 7	10
Cluster 3	14		
Cluster 4	13	Cluster S	College students
Cluster 5	12		

Source: Johnson (1971).

more extreme positions, which would result in further shifts in support. The repositioning of the parties would increase the support for the New and the Conservative parties and decrease the support for the Labour and Liberal parties.

Nonmetric mapping of toothpaste brands

Recently developed techniques make it possible to map brands in space when the data are only ranks of brands.[3] A map of toothpaste brands and an ideal point that was developed with nonmetric methods are shown in Figure 8–3 (Neidell and Teach, 1969). To test the model the rank order of the market share of each brand was compared with the rank order of the Euclidean distance of each brand from the ideal point. The distance was found to be a good predictor of the ranks of market share.[4] Inspection of the position of Cue, the newest brand, leads to the conclusion that it

---

[3] For a discussion of nonmetric methods, see Green and Carmone (1969 and 1970); and Green and Rao (1971).

[4] The similarity of this unfolding model (Coombs, 1964) to the St. James model has been noted by Marchant (1971).

FIGURE 8–3
An ideal point and brand space for toothpastes

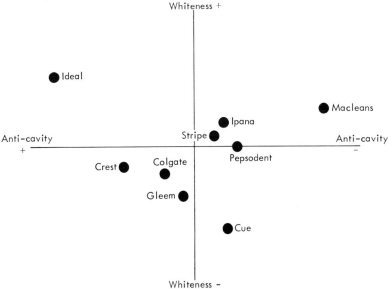

Source: Neidell and Teach (1969).

will gain in market share at the expense of Gleem, the brand closest to Cue in benefit space.

The mapping of ideal points into brand space makes an assumption that may be dangerous for new product development. It assumes that present brands, ideal brands, and possible new brands share the same attributes. Searching in brand space for a hole in the present offering of brands will never develop a product with a new attribute and may overlook marketing opportunities. Furthermore, brand positioning is a continuously dynamic concept. The introduction of a new brand will cause buyers to reevaluate old brands along old attributes as well as along new attributes. Therefore, marketers must track continuously the position of their brand in psychological space.

Developing promotional campaigns at General Motors

Promotional campaigns at General Motors are designed to induce changes in awareness, attitudes, and the probabilities of visiting a dealer and buying a car (Smith, 1965). Promotional goals are defined by comparing the attitude profiles of respondents who would consider buying a brand with those who would not consider buying the brand. One such comparison, shown here in Table 8–1, revealed that respondents held the erroneous

TABLE 8–1

Attitude profiles of prospects who would and who would not consider buying a brand of automobile (scale 1 to 100)

Attribute	Would not consider	Would consider	Difference
Smooth riding.	86	91	5
Styling	76	89	13
Overall comfort	81	87	6
Handling	83	86	3
Spacious interior	85	85	0
Luxurious interior	79	85	6
Quality of workmanship	80	83	3
Advanced engineering	77	83	6
Prestige.	73	82	9
Value for the money	76	79	3
Trade-in value	59	77	18
Cost of upkeep and maintenance.	63	67	4
Gas economy	58	58	0

Source: Adapted from Smith (1965).

attitude that the trade-in value of the brand in question was low. The goal of the promotion, therefore, was to improve the attitude toward trade-in value from 59 to 77 within the next year, thereby moving prospects into the classification of "will consider the brand." The incentive for moving the prospect into this classification may be seen in Table 8–2. A prospect whose attitudes toward the brand will lead him to consider it has a 0.62 probability of visiting the dealer and a 0.22 probability of buying the brand, while a person who initially states that he would not consider the brand has probabilities of 0.40 and 0.09 respectively.

TABLE 8–2

Relating attitude states to behavioral states

Attitude states	Percent of sample	Behavioral states* probability of–	
		Visiting dealer	Buying
Brand is first choice	5	0.840	0.560
Will consider brand	7	0.620	0.220
Will not consider brand.	8	0.400	0.090
Aware of brand	14	0.240	0.050
Not aware of brand.	66	0.015	0.004
	100		

* Proportion of prospects who reported that they had visited the dealer or bought the brand since the earlier interview.
Source: Adapted from Smith (1965).

The most efficient medium may be selected by computing the cost per 1,000 changes in awareness, attitudes, or probability. Table 8–3 illustrates the effectiveness of two media in making prospects aware of a brand of automobile. Medium B is clearly more efficient. Using the data in Table 8–2 it is possible to compute the expected value of the campaign in medium B as $3,187,280, assuming that G.M. nets $100 on each car.[5]

TABLE 8–3
Comparing the efficiency of two promotional media

	Medium A	Medium B
Reach (net unduplicated per target audience of 19 million men).	9%	33%
Target audience reached	1.72 million	6.3 million
Cost of medium.	$11,000	$39,000
Level of awareness:		
Before advertisement.	24%	25%
After advertisement	27	36
Accomplishment	3%	11%
Number of prospects made aware.	51,600	693,000
Cost per 1,000 prospects made aware	$213	$56

Source: Adapted from Smith (1965).

The greatest strength of the G.M. approach is the linking of attitude states to behavior states by reinterviewing a panel of respondents over time. The method suffers from not measuring attribute salience, yet the goal of promotional effort may be a restructuring of attribute saliences in the minds of prospects. For instance, an automobile salesman may have to admit that his brand gets poor gasoline mileage, but he may point out to the prospect that his car has better styling. Because of styling the brand enjoys a better trade-in value which more than offsets the higher gasoline costs. The salesman has attempted to reduce the salience of gasoline mileage and increase the salience of trade-in value, all to the advantage of his brand.

IDENTIFYING THE DEMAND FOR POSTAL SERVICES

A study of the demand for postal services had never been conducted until 1968 when the President's Commission on Postal Organization contracted with Arthur D. Little, Inc. to conduct a study to determine the

---

[5] The expected value before the campaign would be $277,200 [(693,000)(0.004)($100)] and $3,465,000 after the campaign [(693,000)(0.05)($100)], an increase of $3,187,280.

market for postal services (Arthur D. Little, Inc., 1968).[6] Some of the important findings, previously unknown, were that 74 percent of all mail originates with businesses, personal correspondence accounts for only 14 percent of all mail, and the largest category of mail, 40 percent, is for transactions—bills, checks, statements, etc. Beliefs and attitudes about the present service revealed some surprises. Only 28 percent of the respondents knew that the Post Office operates at a loss. Seven percent of the respondents thought the service had improved recently, while 8 percent thought that it was poorer than a year ago. Respondents were generally unaware of the services provided. Money orders were mentioned most frequently, but by only 58 percent of the respondents. As the result of this Commission, the United States Postal Service was established. The new organization contains a Deputy Assistant Postmaster General for Marketing who supervises functions that are familiar to marketers—planning, market research, customer service, advertising, and customer complaint.

To summarize, attitudes are the end product of an individual's processing information in accordance with his value system. This processing includes the steps common to all learning processes—the acquisition, rationalization, and forgetting of information. The information may be supplied by his culture, reference groups, opinion leaders, education, promotion, and casual acquaintances. After processing information about a product or service, the consumer forms attitudes and is motivated to acquire or not to acquire the product or service. Thus, the search for information is central to an understanding of buying behavior.

BUYER SEARCH FOR INFORMATION

There are basically three ways for supplying a buyer with information: moving the goods to the buyer (samples), moving the buyer to the goods (shopping), or moving information about the goods (promotion). Marketing systems become more efficient as they reduce the search required by buyers and sellers. The rise of shopping centers, for example, may be explained by a reduction in the buyers' time required to search for a desired assortment of goods (Alderson, 1957). The movement of information, the lowest cost technique for supplying information to a buyer, has several important prerequisites. Product descriptions must be standardized and clearly understood by buyers and sellers. Secondly, there must be a high level of integrity in the system to buy and sell without seeing the product. A decay in integrity will reduce an efficient marketing system to an ineffi-

---

[6] The author is indebted to Benson Jay Simon, of the Postal Rate Commission, for this example of marketing research.

cient system of barter. Much of the consumer movement has been concerned with establishing standards, providing a supply of information independent of the seller, and maintaining integrity.

Information and perceived risk

Personality variables have not been successful in predicting buyer behavior (Cohen, 1968; Jacoby, 1971; Kassarjian, 1970; Robertson, 1968; and Wells, 1970), but one personality variable, risk-taking propensity, is related to information processing leading to buyer behavior. Much of the research that explains a buyer's behavior in terms of perceived risk may be traced to Bauer (1960) and his students (Cox, 1967). These studies led to the proposition "that the amount and nature of perceived risk will define consumer information needs, and consumers will seek out sources, types, and amounts of information needs" (ibid., p. 604). The risk attributed to the product may be for its ability to function, its social acceptability, or its ability to meet psychological needs. Buyers' perceptions of risk will vary according to their experience with the product, their self-confidence in buying, and their self-involvement in the buying process (Robertson, 1970, p. 24). Other personality variables which have helped to explain buyer behavior and which seem to be closely related to perceived risk include self-confidence (Bell, 1967), dogmatism (Jacoby, 1971), and the need for certainty (Wilson and Mathews, 1971).[7]

Methods for reducing risk include using past experience, seeking new information, rationalizing stored information, and depending on guarantees. New information may be sought actively as in shopping, or through selectively perceiving information from unsolicited messages, such as TV advertising. Sources of information may be dominated by the marketer (promotion), the consumer (word-of-mouth), independent sources (rating services), and the consumer's memory (Cox, 1967). Experiments in consumer information handling revealed that persons who perceive high risk in a product's performance are brand loyal (i.e., used past experience) and are sensitive to word-of-mouth information (ibid.).

[7] Much of the confusion surrounding research into perceived risk could be eliminated by defining *information, uncertainty,* and *transmission* in terms of their respective descriptive statistical formulae. ". . . *information* describes a single probability, *uncertainty* describes a set of probabilities, and *transmission* describes the constraint between two (or more) sets of probabilities" (Coombs, Dawes, and Tversky, 1970, p. 311). The probabilities used in these formulae (ibid., pp. 307–50) would be *perceived* probabilities. Models of these probabilities and individual differences that determine perceived probabilities have been explored (Hughes, 1971a). Basic research in information processing would seem to have direct applications to marketing. For instance, the length of deliberation prior to purchase seems to be identical to the concept of latency associated with stimulus uncertainty (ibid., pp. 337–40).

The search process

The amount of information sought by buyers of cars and major appliances and the time required for them to make a decision are not determined by demographic variables but by their prior experience with purchasing the generic product and the brand, by the condition of their old products, and by their need to trust the opinions of others rather than evaluate the product themselves (Newman and Staelin, 1971). The length of time required for a decision has important implications for marketing strategies. Newman and Staelin (1971) found that one half of the buyers of cars and major appliances had a decision period of less than two weeks. Furthermore, two thirds of this group bought the generic product for the first time or switched brands. These findings suggest that manufacturers must advertise frequently so as to catch the buyer during his short decision period.

The concept of considering a buyer as an information processor is new and lacks the neatness of anything approaching a general theory or model, but it is a practical approach for delivering attitudinal information to management. Basically there are two approaches toward studying information processing. One considers the gathering of information and the other examines the mental processing of the information. The latter approach is the topic of Chapter 9.

Studies of the search for information require detailed protocols which are summarized as learning models (Haines, 1969) or flowcharts. The process by which women shopped for clothing is charted in Figure 8–4. The women recycled through the lower part of the search until they purchased the garment or abandoned the search. In the latter case, the revision of their data base would include a downgrading of the stores they shopped and, perhaps, the lowering of their criteria for buying the garment.

IDENTIFYING SALIENT ATTRIBUTES AND BENEFITS

The positioning of a brand in space begins with the identification of salient product attributes and buyer benefits. The procedures available for this identification range from personal approaches such as experience, introspection, and creativity to unstructured and structured techniques. One commonly used unstructured approach is the depth interview. Multivariate statistical methods represent frequently used structured techniques.

To discover needs that are not adequately met by products presently available, Yoell (1965) asks the consumer to recreate her behavior when performing household tasks and when shopping. These depth interviews

FIGURE 8–4

An overview of women shopping for clothing

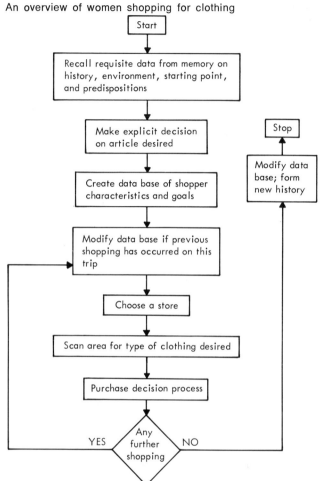

Source: Alexis, Haines, and Simon (1968).

last from three to five hours. The need for liquid soap emerged in 1943 when he discovered that women were in the habit of scooping up dissolved soap from the soap dish to wash dishes. In another case the need for a free pouring product was revealed by interviewees describing how they tapped the package on the counter while pouring.

The Automatic Interaction Detection (AID) algorithm is a useful multivariate method for identifying salient attributes and benefits. It will be recalled from an earlier discussion (Chapter 4) that this algorithm identifies the characteristics of those market segments with the highest probability of buying a brand. The technique is particularly useful with psychological variables because the measuring instruments frequently produce data that form only nominal scales[8] and are discontinuous, intercorrelated, and nonlinear.

Although the technique is new there have been many commercial and academic marketing applications of AID (Assael, 1970; Ostlund, 1970;

FIGURE 8–5
Attitude segmentation for a commonly used beverage using the AID technique

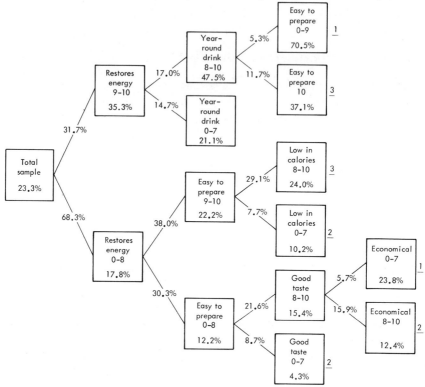

Stopping rules invoked:
 1 = *Sample size too small.*
 2̄ = *Split eligibility criterion not met.*
 3̄ = *Split reducibility criterion not met.*
  Source: Assael (1970).

and Snowbarger and Suits, 1967). An example of AID for attitude segmentation appears in Figure 8–5. The data in this figure are interpreted in the following manner. The percentages in the boxes are the proportion of that group which uses the beverage in question and are interpreted as the probability of using the product. For example, the probability of any-

---

[8] See Chapter 10 and Hughes (1971) for a discussion of scales of measurement and appropriate statistical methods.

one in the sample using the beverage is 0.233. Reading across the top branch it may be seen that the probability increases to 0.705 when the respondent thinks that the beverage restores energy, is a year-round drink, and is not easy to prepare (a guilt complex with regard to convenience foods). The percentages along the lines are the percent of the sample in that group. For instance, the high probability segment is only 5.3 percent of the sample. This application of the AID model will help the marketing planner to position his brand along attitudes toward attributes so as to maximize the probability of his brand's being purchased.[9]

DEVELOPING MULTIDISCIPLINARY STRATEGIES

To simplify the presentation of applications, models, and measures, each discipline has been presented separately. It will be recalled from an earlier example (Chapter 1) that the marketing strategist must consider simultaneously variables that are demographic, economic, social, and psychological. The two final examples represent multidisciplinary market segmentation for toothpaste brands and the Chicago beer market.

Segmenting the toothpaste market

The multidisciplinary characteristics of four market segments for toothpaste brands are summarized in Table 8–4. The sensory, sociable, worri-

TABLE 8–4
Multidisciplinary segmentation of the toothpaste market

	Segments			
Discipline	*Sensory*	*Sociable*	*Worrisome*	*Independent*
Demographic	Children	Teens, young people	Large families	Men, higher educated
Personality	High self-involvement	High sociability	High hypochondriasis	High autonomy
Activity (life style)	Hedonistic	Active	Conservative	Value oriented
Most important attributes	Flavor, product appearance	Brightener	Decay preventor	Price
Probability of buying brand (hypothetical)	Colgate. . 0.50 Stripe. . . 0.30 Others . . 0.20	Ultra Brite . . 0.65 MacLeans . . 0.25 Others 0.10	Crest . . . 0.70 Colgate . . 0.20 Others . . 0.10	Sale brand. . 0.85 Other. . . 0.15

Source: Adapted from Haley (1968).

[9] Additional methods for attribute identification are discussed in Chapter 9.

some, and independent segments may be distinguished according to their demographic variables, their personalities, their activities (life style), the product attributes they consider important, and their probabilities of buying brands. A table such as this one identifies appropriate strategies for brands not capturing an adequate share of a market segment. If a brand does not possess the attribute valued by a segment, one appropriate strategy is to add the attribute and promote the improvement. For example, Colgate added a decay preventor and Crest improved its flavor. An alternative strategy for Crest would be promotions to change the weights given to attributes, so as to downgrade the flavor attribute in the mind of the sensory segment and upgrade decay prevention.

Segmenting the Chicago beer market

A study of the Chicago beer market (Johnson, 1969 and 1971) revealed that 35 attributes could be reduced to two-dimensional space.[10] These dimensions, popular price/premium price and light/heavy, are shown in Figure 8–6 along with the position of brands and ideal points in two-dimensional space. (Four brands are disguised.) The size of the

FIGURE 8–6
Ideal points and brand space for the Chicago beer market

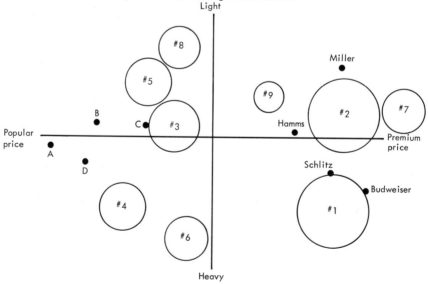

Source: Johnson (1971).

---

[10] Using multiple discriminant analysis, two dimensions accounted for 90 percent of the discrimination among brands. For a discussion of multiple discriminant analysis, see Massy (1965); and Sheth (1970).

circles in this figure reflects the number of people in that cluster who hold that position in space as their ideal product. (This density is sometimes shown as a contour map.) A marketing plan for a brand of beer would include changes in the product or promotion that would reposition the brand in this space so that it would be closer to the ideal points of a sizable market segment, farther from competitors, and along dimensions considered important by consumers (Johnson, 1971, p. 18).

TABLE 8–5
Multidisciplinary segmentation of the Chicago beer market

	Segments		
Discipline	*Sociable*	*Striving*	*Compulsive*
Demographic	Blue collar, less than 35	Much college	Less college
Activity (life style)	Sociable, enjoy doing favors for others	Independent, success important	Order-authority seeking, enjoy doing favors for others, inferiority feelings
Attitudes toward ideal brand	Quality, prestigious, popular, full-bodied, comfortable, national brew	Robust, not bland, high alcohol, man's beer	Quality, bland, not filling, not bitter, low alcohol, national brew
Brands drunk most often	Budweiser, Schlitz	Budweiser, Meister Brau	Hamm's, Schlitz
Market statistics: Cluster size (% of market).	16%	6%	6%
Bottles per week	12	10	5

Source: Adapted from Johnson (1969).

To aid in this repositioning a multidisciplinary segmentation of the market was prepared (Johnson, 1969), which is shown in Table 8–5. The demographic characteristics suggest appropriate media. The activities suggest the message. Attitudes toward the ideal brand may indicate the need for product redesign. Potential competition is revealed by the brands drunk most often. The market statistics indicate whether the demand of the segment is worth a special product or promotion.

SUMMARY

The most important application of psychological concepts to demand analysis is the positioning of a brand in psychological and competitive space. The brand may be new or an old brand that is being repositioned through product development and promotion. Positioning requires first the identification of product attributes and consumer benefits that are important during the decision process and secondly the positioning of buyers' perceptions of competitive brands along these dimensions. In psychological terms, these brand positions are buyers' attitudes toward the brands.

An attitude is a learned mental state that reflects a person's attraction toward or repulsion from an object, a person, or a concept. In marketing research the current trend is to regard an attitude as containing two elements—beliefs and values.

Applications of attitude measurement are illustrated by examples from the private sector of the economy (margarine, toothpaste brands, and automobiles) and the public sector (presidential candidates and postal services). Attitudes are formed as the result of the processing of information, which includes the acquisition, rationalization, and forgetting of information. Perceived risk influences the search for and the processing of information.

The salient attributes are identified by unstructured techniques, such as depth interviews, and multivariate statistical techniques, such as the Automatic Interaction Detection (AID) algorithm.

The discussion of the appropriateness of demographic, economic, social, and psychological concepts to demand analysis is simplified by considering each discipline separately, but in practice the marketing strategist must consider all of these disciplines simultaneously. Two examples, for toothpaste and beer, illustrated how markets may be segmented by taking a multidisciplinary approach.

READING QUESTIONS

1. Define an attitude. How does it differ from a belief?
2. What kind of marketing decisions require a knowledge of psychological variables?
3. Do you think that it would be easier to change beliefs or attitudes toward a brand?
4. What is the meaning of *positioning a brand?*
5. How do you translate a change in attitude into an expected value?
6. How do you identify the attributes of a product that are important to the buyer?

CLASS DISCUSSION QUESTIONS

1. Develop a model for predicting the probability of Irish housewives' buying the new brand of margarine with butter.

2. Develop a marketing strategy for brand B beer in Figure 8–4.

3. Examine recent advertising for Schlitz beer. Is the strategy consistent with Figure 8–6 and Table 8–5?

4. Develop a map of voters like Figure 8–5 for a local election. (Refer to Chapter 9 for low-cost means for identifying salient attributes of candidates and instruments for measuring voters' attitudes toward candidates.) Develop a strategy that will move your candidate closer to the image of the ideal candidate.

5. Create tables like Tables 8–1, 8–2, and 8–3 for the marketer of a desktop electronic calculator. Indicate how you would collect the data for such tables.

6. After gaining the permission of the supermarket manager, ask shoppers to let you follow them through the store while they verbalize their decision processes. Keep notes on the types of information that are used for each decision.

SUGGESTED CASES

Aqua-Craft Corporation (A): Determining purchasing influences. Blackwell, Engel, and Kollat (1969), pp. 163–166.

The major uses for boats were cruising, fishing, and skiing; but little was known about the criteria used when buying and the buying influences.

1. What are the motivations for buying boats?

2. How would you identify the decision makers and the attributes they consider important?

3. Does the present media mix reach the decision maker that you identified?

Armour Company: Attitude change. Blackwell, Engel, and Kollat (1969), pp. 75–81.

Changes in awareness and attitudes were used to measure the effectiveness of 12 advertisements in *Better Homes and Gardens*.

1. Compute the significance levels of the changes in awareness, Table 5–1.

2. What are the advantages and disadvantages of using a telephone survey to measure attitudes? To measure awareness?

3. Which of the attributes in Table 5–3 would you use as the basis for future campaigns? Why?

Brewer Company. Boyd and Davis (1971), pp. 3–27.

The Brewer Company sells malt beverages in Arizona, New Mexico, and Texas. Studies of the profiles of typical beer consumers provide direction for a marketing plan. Extensive psychological research measured recall of advertising themes, attitudes toward the attributes of Brewer and competitive brands of beer, sources of information about beers, and motivations for drinking beer.

1. Develop a marketing strategy for Brewer Company.
2. Do you think the company should expand into new markets?
3. Create a complete marketing plan. Indicate the copy themes, media, and goals as they change over time.

Hatfield versus Duncan. Boyd and Davis (1971), pp. 526–59.

In 1966, Republican Mark O. Hatfield and Democrat Robert B. Duncan were competing for one of Oregon's seats in the U.S. Senate. The former was a dove and the latter was a hawk on the controversial issue of the war in Viet Nam. A survey revealed the following preferences: Duncan, 46 percent; Hatfield, 40 percent; and uncommitted, 14 percent.

1. Based on the data in the case, develop a campaign strategy for Hatfield for key target segments. What copy themes and media would you use?
2. How would you measure the effectiveness of your strategy?

Playskool Manufacturing Company. Boyd and Davis (1971), pp. 523–25.

Playskool produces wooden educational toys for children from age 2 to age 10, with an emphasis on preschool children. The annual advertising budget is $200,000.

1. How should Playskool measure the effectiveness of its advertising?
2. Do you recommend any changes in its advertising plan?

W. T. Grant Company (A): Attitudes toward a retail chain. Blackwell, Engel, and Kollat (1969), pp. 82–88.

A store awareness and image study was conducted among Grant shoppers and nonshoppers. Attitudes were classified according to demographic characteristics.

1. How would you use the findings to develop strategies for locating sites for new stores?
2. What applications do these findings have for planning promotional campaigns?

SUGGESTED READINGS

"Ad Recall? P&G Couldn't Care Less," *Marketing/Communications,* August 1971, pp. 22–26.

BERDY, DAVID. "Order Effects in Taste Tests," *Journal of the Market Research Society,* Vol. 11, No. 4 (October 1969), pp. 361–71.

BETTMAN, JAMES R. "Information Processing Models of Consumer Behavior," *Journal of Marketing Research,* Vol. 7 (August 1970), pp. 370–76.

———. "The Structure of Consumer Choice Processes," *Journal of Marketing Research,* Vol. 8 (November 1971), pp. 465–71.

BRITT, STEUART HENDERSON (ed.). *Psychological Experiments in Consumer Behavior.* New York: John Wiley & Sons, Inc., 1970.

COLLINS, LESLIE, and MONTGOMERY, CAROLINE. "Whatever Happened to Motivation Research? End of the Messianic Hope," *Journal of the Market Research Society,* Vol. 12, No. 1 (January 1970), pp. 1–11.

DOLICH, IRA J. "Congruence Relationships between Self Images and Product Brands," *Journal of Marketing Research,* Vol. 6 (February 1969), pp. 80–84.

ENGEL, JAMES F.; BLACKWELL, ROGER D.; and KEGERREIS, ROBERT J. "How Information Is Used to Adopt an Innovation," *Journal of Advertising Research,* Vol. 9 (December 1969), pp. 3–8.

FARLEY, JOHN U. "Brand Loyalty and the Economics of Information," *Journal of Business,* Vol. 37 (October 1964), pp. 370–79.

GROSSACK, MARTIN M. (ed.). *Understanding Consumer Behavior.* Boston: The Christopher Publishing House, 1964.

———. *Consumer Psychology: Theory and Practice.* Boston: Branden Press, Inc., 1971.

JOHNSON, R. M. "Techniques of Market Segmentation: Cluster Analysis vs. Quantitative Analysis." Paper delivered at the 1969 International Marketing Congress, American Marketing Association (June 1969), mimeo.

KAMEN, J. M. "Quick Clustering," *Journal of Marketing Research,* Vol. 7 (May 1970), pp. 199–204.

KERNAN, J. B., and HAINES, G. H. "Environmental Search, an Information-Theoretic Approach," *Decision Sciences,* Vol. 2 (April 1971), pp. 161–71.

KOLLAT, D. T.; ENGEL, J. F.; and BLACKWELL, R. D. "Current Problems in Consumer Behavior Research," *Journal of Marketing Research,* Vol. 7 (August 1970), pp. 327–32.

McNEAL, J. U. (ed.) *Dimensions of Consumer Behavior.* 2d ed. New York: Appleton-Century-Crofts, 1969.

OXENFELDT, A. R. "A Marketing Manager Looks at Attitude Research," in King and Tigert (1971), pp. 13–25.

PERRY, M. "Discriminant Analysis of Relations between Consumers' Attitudes, Behavior, and Intentions," *Journal of Advertising Research,* Vol. 9 (April 1969), pp. 34–39.

REYNOLDS, F. D., and DARDEN, W. R. "Mutually Adaptive Effects of Interpersonal Communication," *Journal of Marketing Research,* Vol. 8 (November 1971), pp. 449–54.

SAMPSON, P. "Can Consumers Create New Products?" *Journal of the Market Research Society,* Vol. 12 (January 1970), pp. 40–52.

STIDSEN, B. "Some Thoughts on the Advertising Process," *Journal of Marketing,* Vol. 34 (January 1970), pp. 47–53.

THORELLI, H. B. "Concentration of Information Power among Consumers," *Journal of Marketing Research,* Vol. 8 (November 1971), pp. 427–32.

WHITE, W. JAMES. "An Index for Determining the Relative Importance of Information Sources," *Public Opinion Quarterly,* Vol. 33 (Winter 1969–70), pp. 607–10.

9

Psychological theories, models, and measures relevant to demand

Psychological theories, models, and measures provide the foundation for most explanations of buyer behavior. Theories relevant to demand analysis include those of motivation, need hierarchy, cognitive balance, and communication. Models of attitude change are important when a marketer is attempting to track the repositioning of his brand in psychological space (Chapter 8). Models to explain marketing behavior can be traced to a long history of psychological models. To implement these models and test these theories it is necessary to develop instruments for measuring attitudes.

BEHAVIORAL THEORIES

Motivation

Studies of human behavior may be traced to Aristotle, Descartes, Hobbes, Adam Smith, and Jeremy Bentham.[1] Common to the explanations of these authors is the concept of *hedonism*—man's desire for comfort and pleasure and his avoidance of discomfort and pain. The father of American psychology, William James, identified two sources of motivation—unconscious *instincts* and *habits,* which are learned. The instinct theory of motivation stimulated important research in human behavior.

---

[1] This discussion follows the excellent summary by Graffam (1963).

167

Perhaps the most famous instincts are two identified by Freud, sex and self-preservation.

Several forces in the early 1920s led to the decline of instinct theory. Instead of generating a general theory of behavior, the theory degenerated to lists of instincts, totaling nearly 6,000 separate ones. Secondly, the rise of experimental psychology emphasized the importance of learning. Finally, anthropologists demonstrated that behavior is greatly influenced by environment, especially culture. *Instinct* was replaced by *drive,* a term borrowed from mechanics, to denote a supply and direction of energy. But *drive* fell into a state of confusion because of a proliferation of meanings, which classified *incentive* and *habit* as drive. *Motive* has been introduced to include social and psychological drives as well as physiological ones. Maslow (1954) identified five motives: physiological, safety, belongingness (and love), esteem, and self-actualization. *Motives* and *needs* are synonyms when social and psychological needs are acknowledged. In this book *drive* has a specific meaning—an awareness of a need (Engel et al., 1968).

Incentives, systems of rewards and punishments designed to influence behavior, are a legacy of hedonism. Incentives perform central roles in learning theories and inducements to production. Closely related to reward, and perhaps part of it, is the concept of *reinforcement.* Being correct is a reward. When informed of his achievement an individual will raise his standards. Reinforcement, therefore, is an important part of learning. Reinforcement makes motivation a dynamic concept. It is important to note that reinforcement consists of two elements—achievement and valid reports of having achieved (e.g., Cummings, Schwab, and Rosen, in press).

While the theories of motivation are complex and frequently conflicting, the concept of motivation can be defined quite simply. It is the awareness of a need *and* the awareness of an acceptable means for meeting the need.

In reviewing theories of motivation Graffam (1963) makes an important generalization. Each new theory of motivation involves a higher level of consciousness or awareness. Instinct requires no conscious attention by the organism for its operation, drive involves at least a dim awareness, and incentive "requires perceptual contact with outer reality, learning, reinforcement, and in humans, at least, conscious attention" (p. 9). *Habits* may be placed midway along this continuum of awareness/unawareness because they "apparently provide their own motivation even when the original motives which caused them to be formed no longer exist." Attention and later refinements of selective exposure and selective perception are important to communication theories, as will become apparent later in this chapter.

Need hierarchy

Early definitions of needs focused on physical deprivation. These needs were concerned with maintaining the proper balances required for life, such as body temperature. acidity of blood, and water content. "It is, however, possible also to conceive of real or imagined deprivations in a purely *psychological* context where no question of organic survival is raised" (Viteles, 1953, p. 70). Even information deprivation has been shown to function as a drive variable in the same manner as the homeostatic drives of hunger, pain, and thirst (Jones, Wilkinson, and Braden, 1961).

It has been customary to classify needs as primary (biological) and secondary (social), but the usefulness of this classification is doubtful because it does not predict or explain behavioral differences among individuals or groups (Taylor, 1960). A better classification scheme would be a hierarchy of needs within groups. Such a classification would reflect differences in values, which are an important determinant of perceived needs and means for meeting them.

If sustenance were the only need, marketing systems could be reduced to linear programming models (Smith, 1959) and systems of logistics. But economic activity is complicated by consumers' preference for variety. The capriciousness of their preference precludes a simple model of economic equilibrium (Chipman, 1965).

The concept of a hierarchy of needs may be traced to Plato (*The Republic,* Book II).

"Come then," I said, "let us proceed with our imaginary sketch of the origin of the state. It springs, as we have seen, from our needs."

"And our first and greatest need is clearly the provision of food to keep us alive."

"Our second need is shelter, and our third clothing of various kinds."

"And we must no longer confine ourselves to the bare necessities of our earlier description, houses, clothing, and shoes, but must add the fine arts of painting and embroidery, introduce materials like gold and ivory."

Knight (1935, p. 22) expressed a need hierarchy in terms of a latent desire for better wants:

The chief thing which the common-sense individual actually wants is not satisfaction for the wants which he has, but more and better wants. There is always really present and operative, though in the background of consciousness, the idea of, and desire for a new want to be striven for when the present objective is out of the way.

In developing a hierarchy of needs Maslow (1954) builds a strong case for considering nonphysical needs when attempting to explain human behavior. He notes that most needs are cultural, not physical. Furthermore, ". . . from a full knowledge of the need for love we can learn more about general human motivation (including the hunger drive) than we could from a thorough study of the hunger drive" (p. 65). His strongest point,

FIGURE 9–1

Patterns of human needs according to Maslow (1954)

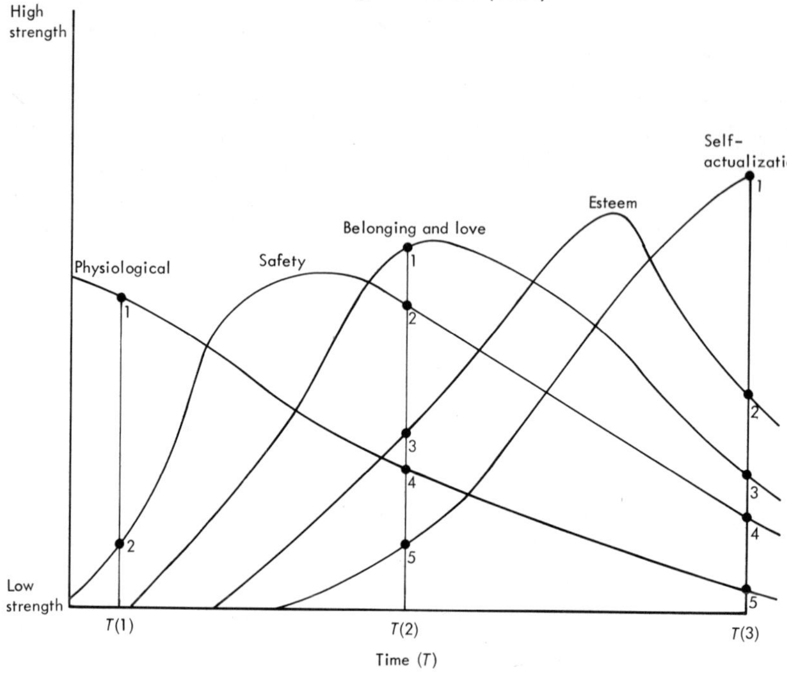

Source: Adapted from Krech, Crutchfield, and Ballachey (1962), p. 77.

however, is the concept of hierarchy. "Man is a wanting animal and rarely reaches a state of complete satisfaction except for a short time. As one desire is satisfied, another pops up to take its place. It is characteristic of the human being throughout his whole life that he is practically always desiring something" (p. 69).

The complexity of this hierarchy and its relevance to marketing planning may be illustrated with the aid of Figure 9–1 which graphs the changes in the relative strength of needs through time. To illustrate changes in the ranks of needs, three points in time are considered. At time $T(1)$ the needs are basic physical ones and the ranking is simple: (1) physiological and (2) safety. By the time $T(2)$ is reached the basic needs have been met and the relative strengths of needs have changed to the following ranking: (1) belonging, (2) safety, (3) esteem, (4) physiological, and (5) self-actualization. A completely different pattern of need strength emerges at $T(3)$: (1) self-actualization, (2) esteem, (3) belonging, (4) safety, and (5) physiological. These patterns may represent the needs of one market segment as they change over time or they may represent the needs of three market segments at a point in time. To the marketing planner each pattern requires a different strategy for product development and promotion.

Cognitive balance

The concept of physiological homeostasis appears in motivation theories as balance, tension, equilibrium, and closure. An individual is thought to have a social and psychological balance. Motivation is regarded as the process of restoring balance when it is disturbed. This concept is central to many motivation theories, such as the Gestalt theory, Lewin's person model, congruity models, and Festinger's (1957) theory of cognitive dissonance.[2] Thus, motivation is an imbalance between perceived needs and perceived goals.

The concept of balance has been challenged by recent authors (e.g., Argyris, 1964; and Berkowitz, 1969). The basis for this challenge has been the failure of balance models to explain curiosity and innovative and creative behavior. The latter seems to represent the seeking of change and the avoidance of balance. This challenge of the balance concept seems to disappear when needs such as self-actualization are considered. Thus, instead of two classifications of models, need-reduction and balance models, there are only need-reduction models tending toward balance. Innovative behavior is explained by acknowledging that some individuals have a higher order of needs than other individuals.

COMMUNICATION THEORIES

Communication includes the acquisition of new information. The process has been studied extensively beginning with the Yale Communication and Attitude Change group in the 1950s (Hovland, Janis, and Kelley, 1953). Topics of this research included attention, comprehension, the acceptance of messages, source-message interaction, the effectiveness of the order of messages, and persuasible personalities.[3]

---

[2] For a discussion of Gestalt, Lewin's, and balance theories, see Heider (1960). Congruity models and the theory of cognitive dissonance are discussed in Insko (1967).

[3] For discussions and citations, see Crane (1965); Dance (1967); Insko (1967); and Klapper (1961).

Cognitive organization of information involves the coding of new information into classifications that have been formed by presently stored information. Values determine what is classified as good and bad. Beliefs and attitudes are formed at this stage.[4]

Decision making is the evaluation of alternatives and final choice. The process has been studied extensively in the context of economic and management decisions (Bross, 1961; Raiffa, 1968; and Becker and Mc-Clintock, 1967).

Communication theories help us understand how advertising works. The effectiveness of advertising is influenced by two communication concepts—selective exposure and selective perception. Studies reveal that the individual is not a robot who responds to stimuli in a mechanical fashion. He retains some control over the information to which he is exposed and considerable control over the information that enters his short-term and long-term memories.

Selective exposure

Information may be passively received (e.g., a TV commercial) or actively sought (e.g., reading the supermarket specials before shopping). The latter is selective exposure. Selective exposure increases as an individual's awareness of his need increases. A man will read more automobile advertisements as his present automobile becomes less reliable. Selective exposure is not limited to physical needs. The social-psychological need for change and innovation drives some persons to expose themselves to more information than the less innovative person (Summers and King, 1969).

Selective exposure to supportive information is suggested by one type of cognitive dissonance, the approach-approach conflict (Festinger, 1957). This conflict occurs in marketing when a buyer must choose between two brands. If he selects A he restores consonance between his behavior and his attitudes by revaluating his attitudes so that A is clearly superior. Research supports the hypothesis that this revaluation occurs (Insko, 1967, p. 201). The theory also suggests that the dissonant buyer will seek supportive information to resolve the dissonance. Laboratory evidence does not support this selective exposure hypothesis (Freedman and Sears, 1965), and the evidence in marketing experiments is conflicting.[5]

The concept of attention is important during the acquisition of information. *Attention* is the focusing of the mind on one set of stimuli while being

---

[4] For a discussion and citations, see Norman (1969); and Niesser (1967).

[5] For recent discussions and citations of cognitive dissonance theory as it applies to marketing, see Oshikawa (1969); and Venkatesan (in press).

exposed to many stimuli. While the concept seems obvious, an understanding and a modeling of the process of attention is most difficult. Psychologists have yet to agree on models of the process (Norman, 1969, pp. 7–36).

Attention has been central to many models of marketing behavior. For instance, the new salesman is reminded that attention, interest, desire, and action (AIDA) represent the buying process and that his presentation should move the prospect along this sequence. This process has been expressed more formally by McQuire (1969) as follows:

$$\text{Probability of buying} = P(p) \times P(a) \times P(c) \times P(y) \times P(r) \times P(b) \tag{9–1}$$

where P is a probability and p, a, c, y, r, and b mean presentation, attention, comprehension, yielding, retention, and behavior. If attention $P(a)$ is 0.00, the probability of buying will be 0.00. Thus, Equation 9–1 is a series of probabilities that are conditional upon all prior states.

Selective perception

Present states of knowledge act as filters when an individual is exposed to new information. This process is known as *selective perception*.[6] This selectivity takes many forms in marketing. Brand loyal persons misperceived information as more favorable to their brands than it actually was (Hughes et al., 1969). Changes in the probabilities of buying a brand are greatly influenced by the initial probability of buying the brand (Hughes and Guerrero, 1971c). Reinforcing information induces greater attitude changes than nonreinforcing information. For example, when the initial attitude is positive, favorable information will induce a larger positive change than negative unfavorable information will induce a negative change. Conversely, when the initial attitude is negative, negative information will induce a greater negative change than positive information will induce a positive change. In marketing, reinforcement theory explains why it is more difficult for an advertiser to change the attitudes of persons using a competitive brand than those of persons using his brand. Reinforcement may be explained also by threshold theory. Persons lower their perceptual thresholds for favorable information and raise them for threatening information. The latter is known as *perceptual defense*.

Communication research stimulated largely by Hovland et al. (1953) has generated considerable investigation of the effect on attitudes of the credibility of the source, fear-arousing communications, and message pri-

---

[6] For a discussion and citations, see Engel et al. (1968, chap. 6).

macy versus recency. After a review of the literature Insko (1967) reached the following conclusions. The literature is highly consistent with regard to source credibility—highly credible sources are more influential than sources of low credibility (p. 48). The evidence is conflicting with regard to fear-arousing communication (p. 41). A low fear-arousing communication may stimulate an awareness of a need and make subsequent messages more effective, but a high fear-arousing communication may lack effectiveness because of perceptual defense. The findings with regard to primacy and recency (the effect of the initial message versus the final message) are inconsistent (p. 60). They permit no generalization that the last or the first message is the more effective.

MODELS OF ATTITUDE CHANGE

The least understood part of information processing is the manner in which an individual combines new information with his present beliefs, values, and attitudes to form new beliefs, values, and attitudes. The process is one of judgment, where new stimuli are coded according to learned classifications (Norman, 1969, p. 80). The few available models of this process have tended to be balance and congruity models that compare mental states at two points in time. (Two period models in economics are known as models of comparative statics.) The Heider (1958) balance model and the Osgood-Tannenbaum (1955) congruity model assume that the goal of the individual is a psychological homeostasis. Two additional central processing models, the St. James model and the Coombs unfolding model, assume that the goal of the individual is an ideal product.

Balance and congruity models

The Heider (1946) balance model explains changes in attitudes in terms of a restoration of balance in attitudes toward the concept, attitudes toward the medium communicating the message, and the content of the message. The model may be explained easily with the aid of Figure 9–2. The PC link indicates that the person (P) has an unfavorable attitude $(-)$ toward the concept (C). The PM link is positive $(+)$, which means he holds a favorable attitude toward the medium. This favored medium, however, communicates a favorable message about the concept $(+MC)$. This puts the person in an unbalanced state. To restore balance he must change his attitudes toward the medium or the concept. Since there are two states $(+ \text{ or } -)$ and three links, there are eight possible states (2^3), four balanced and four unbalanced. The balanced and unbalanced states

FIGURE 9–2
The Heider (a) and Osgood-Tannenbaum (b)
models of balance and congruity

Note: *P* is the person, *M* is the medium, and *C* is the concept.

may be identified easily by multiplying the signs of the three links. A state is balanced if the product of the signs is positive and unbalanced if it is negative.

The Osgood-Tannenbaum (1955) congruity model is a refinement of the Heider model. It is generally expressed algebraically, but it can be explained more easily with a graph (the right-hand portion of Figure 9–2).[7] The *PM* and *PC* links are refined by scaling the person's attitude along a semantic differential attitude scale. This scale, to be discussed below, yields three levels of positive and three levels of negative attitudes. The message link, *MC*, remains either + or −. In contrast to the Heider model, the congruity model predicts the amount of change in the attitudes toward the medium and the concept. While this model suggests useful hypotheses for marketing communication models, it is rarely used because of the *ad hoc* corrections required to improve predictions and because multiple regression models make better predictions (Hughes and Guerrero, 1971c). The latter models are also open to variables that reflect individual differences in information processing (Hughes, 1971a).

The Heider model and the Osgood-Tannenbaum model were compared with a multiple regression model of the following form:

$$\Delta Pr_1 = b_1 PM + b_2 S_i MC_i + b_3 R + b_4 N \qquad (9\text{–}2)$$

where ΔPr_1 is the change in probability, b_1 through b_4 are the regression coefficients to be estimated, *PM* is the attitude toward the medium, S_i is the salience of attribute i, MC_i is the favorability of the message toward attribute i, and *R* and *N* reflect reinforcement and nonreinforcement states (Hughes and Guerrero, 1971c). Equation 9–2 was found to be the best of the three models. Later models introduced variables for prior probabilities and measures of need.

---

[7] For a discussion of the algebra, see Hughes and Guerrero (1971c). For a discussion with examples, see Hughes (1971b).

Congruity in the models discussed above was between an individual's attitudes and the information supplied by the message and the medium. Another type of congruity which has received considerable attention in marketing is self-congruity. Models of self-congruity attempt to explain brand behavior as a search for a brand image that matches self-image. Self-congruity models are controversial. Some researchers have found congruence between self and brand images (Birdwell, 1968; Dolich, 1969; and Grubb and Hupp, 1968). Others suggest that social congruity would be more appropriate than self-congruity when the product is consumed socially (Hughes and Guerrero, 1971b).

St. James model

Several models of consumer preferences relate the probability of buying a brand to the cognitive distance between this brand and the ideal brand. The St. James model (Marchant, 1971) expresses the relationship as follows:

$$\frac{1}{Pr_j} = [S_1 f(|B_{1j} - I_1|) + \cdots + S_i f(|B_{ij} - I_i|) + \cdots$$
$$+ S_n f(|B_{nj} - I_i|) + 1] \tag{9-3}$$

where Pr_j is the probability of buying brand j, S_i is the salience of attribute i, B_{ij} is the perception of brand j along attribute i, I_i is the perception of the ideal brand along attribute i, and there are n attributes. This model states that the probability of purchase is inversely proportional to the distance between brand j and the ideal brand. Thus, the closer brand j is to the ideal, the higher the probability of buying brand j. This model is the sum of perceptions in unidimensional space. The next model considers perceptions in multidimensional space.

A multidimensional unfolding model

The Coombs (1964) unfolding model has been generalized (Carroll and Chang, 1967; Carroll, 1971) so that brands and the ideal product are projected in n-dimensional (Euclidean) space. For brand demand the model is as follows:[8]

$$\frac{1}{P_j} \approx b_0 + b_1 d_{Ij}^2 \tag{9-4}$$

$$d_{Ij} = \sqrt{\sum_{i=1}^{n} S_i (I_i - B_{ij})^2} \tag{9-5}$$

---

[8] The author is indebted to Professor Vithala R. Rao for this formulation.

where S_i, I_i, and B_{ij} have the same meaning as above; P_j is a preference rank given by a consumer to brand j; d_{lj} is the Euclidean distance between brand j and the ideal brand, modified by the salience of attribute i; and b_0 and b_1 are parameters to be estimated by regression.[9] Market share (M_{jt}) will be a function of $1/P_j$, thus, $M_{jt} = f(1/P_{jt})$. P_j may also be interpreted as the probability of buying brand j.

The St. James and unfolding models are static models in that they do not account for learning over time. Learning can occur over an infinite number of periods. Each new mental state is determined by the new information and the mental state prior to receiving the new information. A subjective probability learning model appears as follows:

$$Pr_j = L_i M_i + (1 - L_i)Pr_{j,t-1} \qquad (9\text{--}6)$$

where Pr_j is the subjective probability of buying brand j, L_i is the learning rate for message M_i, $(1 - L_i)$ is the foregetting rate, and $Pr_{j,\,t-1}$ is the probability of buying brand j prior to receiving the message. This is a linear operator model like those used in learning theory (Anderson, 1968, p. 733). It is central to many models of choice behavior (Coombs, Dawes, and Tversky, 1970).

BEHAVIORAL MODELS

A discussion of behavioral models will reveal the variables and some of the functional relationships that should be included in models of buyer behavior.[10] This review also illustrates how new behavioral models emerge as weaknesses in previous models are discovered.

Early psychological models—Hull, Spence, and Hilgard

Many models of buyer behavior can be traced to Hull (1943), who provided the following behavioral model:

$$_sE_R = f(D_S \cdot H_R) \qquad (9\text{--}7)$$

where E is expectancy, S is the stimulus, R is the response, D is the drive, and H is habit. The multiplicative function reflects the case when an indi-

---

[9] These parameters may be regarded as a linear utility function between preference ranks and squared distances.

[10] For a bibliography of the behavioral literature as it relates to marketing, see Britt (1966); Burk (1968); Engel, Kollat, and Blackwell (1968); Howard (1965); Howard and Sheth (1969); Kassarjian and Robertson (1968); Myers and Reynolds (1967); Nicosia (1966); and Sheth (1967).

vidual has a habitual form of behavior but lacks a need. For instance, his past behavior may indicate that there is 0.90 probability that he will buy Dole brand canned pineapple, but his need for pineapple may be 0.00; therefore the multiplicative function yields a 0.00 expectancy of buying Dole canned pineapple at this instant. This model should remind marketers that buyer behavior is determined by both generic and brand demand.

Equation 9–7 fails to consider the incentive (or means for meeting the need). To correct this deficiency Spence (1956) added K, a variable to represent incentive. His model for expected behavior may be stated as follows:

$$E = (D + K)H \qquad (9\text{–}8)$$

The Hull and the Spence models treat the stimulus as a variable that is external to the system. Hilgard (1956) makes the stimulus part of the model by adding V, a variable for stimulus intensity.

$$E = D \times K \times H \times V \qquad (9\text{–}9)$$

A change in the functional relationship should be noted. K has been changed to a multiplicative function. The introduction of a stimulus variable makes the behavior model more dynamic and opens the model to known communication effects. The model is quite simplistic, however, because it fails to explain how the stimulus affects D and K. Models of attitude change, to be discussed below, deal directly with this problem.

Recent psychological models—Atkinson and Fishbein

Earlier models fail to reflect the uncertainty that is associated with the decision process that leads to behavior. To correct this limitation, Atkinson (1964) proposed the following model:

$$T_{r,g} = {}_sH_r \times E_{r,g} \times I_g \times M_G \qquad (9\text{–}10)$$

where $T_{r,g}$ is the tendency to respond to a particular goal (g), ${}_sH_r$ is habit, $E_{r,g}$ is the expectancy (i.e., subjective probability) that response r toward incentive I_g will fulfill motive (i.e., need) M_G. The product of the middle elements $(E \times I)$ is very similar to Edwards' (1961) formulation of subjective expected utility (SEU), which is as follows:

$$\text{SEU} = \sum_{i=1}^{n} p_i{}^*u_i \qquad (9\text{–}11)$$

where $p_i{}^*$ is the subjective probability of outcome i and u_i is the utility or subjective value of this outcome.[11] Equation 9–11 is identical to the Fishbein model of an attitude, discussed in Chapter 8

$$A_0 = \sum_{i=1}^{n} B_i a_i \qquad (9\text{–}12)$$

when the belief component is expressed as a subjective probability and when values are expressed as utils. Thus, an attitude toward an object or an act is the subjective expected utility associated with the object or act.

Equation 9–11 is limited in its ability to explain behavior because it does not identify habit or needs. Atkinson and Feather (1966) present a more complete model of decision under uncertainty in which the needs are the motive to succeed (M_S) and the motive to avoid failure (M_{AF}). The model is

$$T = T_s + T_{-f} = (M_S \times P_s \times I_s) + (M_{AF} \times P_f \times I_f) \qquad (9\text{–}13)$$

where T is the tendency to behave in an achievement-oriented activity, T_s is the tendency to approach success, T_{-f} is the tendency to avoid failure, P is the subjective probability that success or failure will follow from the activity, and I is the incentive gain or loss from the activity. A positive T indicates that the individual is attracted to the activity while a negative T predicts that he will avoid it. By separating the motives for success and avoidance of failure, Equation 9–13 distinguishes between risk takers and risk averters. This distinction can be important when studying innovative behavior.

The Fishbein (1967) model of behavior that was presented during discussions of values (Chapter 7, Equation 7–2) should be presented in this section for completeness. Furthermore, using models presented in Chapter 8 and in this chapter, this single equation model may be disected into a set of equations that more completely explains behavior. The model, it will be recalled, was as follows:

$$BI = b_1 A_{\text{act}} + b_2(NB \times Mc) \qquad (9\text{–}14)$$

where BI represents behavior intention, A_{act} is the attitude toward the activity, NB is the normative belief, and Mc is the motive to conform. In disecting Equation 9–14, known functional relationships will be used where they are supported by theory or experiments.

The first element, A_{act}, may be defined further as

$$A_{\text{act}} = T \times H \qquad (9\text{–}15)$$

---

[11] Feather (1962) compares models by Lewin, Tolman, Rotter, Edwards, and Atkinson as they relate to subjective probability and decision under uncertainty.

where T is the tendency to act as the result of mentally processing information about motives, subjective probabilities, and incentives, as defined in Equation 9–13, and H is habit. In accordance with Maslow (1954), motives must include the social and psychological needs as well as physical ones. Similarly, the incentives must include the physical, social, and psychological gains and losses. In economic behavior the cost of the object and the cost of making the decision (e.g., shopping) must be deducted from I_s or added to I_f to determine if the net tendency (T) is one of attraction to or avoidance of the act.

Habit (H) may be computed using a lagged variable model borrowed from econometrics (Koyck, 1954), as follows:

$$BI(t) = H[BI(t - 1)] \qquad (9\text{--}16)$$

where $BI(t - 1)$ is the behavioral intention in the previous time period and H is an estimate of habit, the cumulative effective of behavioral intentions prior to t. $BI(t - 1)$, known also as prior probabilities, has been shown to influence $BI(t)$ strongly (Alker and Hermann, 1971; Hughes, 1971a).

M_S and M_{AF} are perceived needs and could be measured with one of the scaling instruments discussed later in this chapter. P_s and P_f, the subjective probabilities that the act will lead to success or failure, could also be measured with scaling devices. For practical reasons these probabilities would probably be estimated in the aggregate despite the fact they contain variables such as the probability of attainment, perceived opportunities to act, and information about previous successes and failures.

The expected value associated with the act ($P \times I$) could be estimated in the aggregate using an attitudinal scale or the components could be estimated using a probability scale for P and a value scale (Chapter 7) for I. Aggregate measures are adequate for prediction, but disaggregate measures give better explanations of behavior.

The last two elements in Equation 9–14 could be measured directly. NB, normative beliefs, represent the perceived range of acceptable behavior for a given situation in a culture. Mc, the motivation to conform, is a personality measure and could be measured using the activity instruments discussed in Chapter 7.

This summary of behavioral models reveals several important points. First, there is more agreement among behavioral scientists than is readily apparent from a cursory reading of the literature. Second, because motivation is determined by changes in the perception of needs and the means for meeting them, attitude models become an important part of behavioral models. Motivation may be aroused by external stimuli, such as new information, or the cognitive processing of stored information. Third, and perhaps the most startling finding of this summary, is the realization that marketers have not adequately considered motivation. They emphasize attitudes and the means for meeting needs, but until recently they have considered needs only by implication (Eysenck, 1960). Finally, values are central to behavior, yet their appearance in models of buyer behavior as activity variables (Chapter 7) has been very recent.

Marketing models

The links between models of attitudes and models of choice behavior are tenuous. Theoretical models of information processing tend to stop with attitude formation. Commercial marketing models of the process emphasize choice behavior and frequently ignore central processing entirely by linking an awareness of an advertisement to final brand choice.[12] Models developed by marketers tend to be of three types—hierarchy, dynamic, and comprehensive. The comprehensive models attempt to bridge the gap between theory and practice.

Hierarchy models. Consumer behavior has been viewed by many researchers as a series of mental states that lead step-by-step to behavior. A sequence quoted frequently in marketing suggested by Lavidge and Steiner (1961) is as follows: awareness, knowledge, liking, preference, conviction, and purchase. Colley (1961), writing on the subject of measuring advertising effectiveness, suggested a shorter sequence—awareness, comprehension, conviction, and action. Both can be reduced to the states which have been discussed in this book—beliefs, attitudes, and choice behavior.

The Fishbein model (Equation 9–14) links attitudes and expected behavior. Empirical evidence linking attitudes and purchase behavior has been reported in many commercial studies (e.g., Achenbaum, 1966; and Day, 1970).[13]

Dynamic learning models. Models of brand choice behavior are incomplete models of information processing. The basic Markov brand switching model emphasizes habit because its predictions are based on previous switching behavior, with no provision for new stimuli. Applications of the Bush-Mosteller learning model to consumer behavior (Kuehn, 1962) relate the probability of purchase or nonpurchase of a brand in time t to the probability of purchase in time $t + 1$. It is the basic stimulus-response model that is used to model the behavior of rats in a T maze (Coombs,

---

[12] For a discussion of theoretical and practical models, see Hughes (1971b).

[13] For a criticism of Palda's (1966) discussion of the "hierarchy of effects," see Hughes (1971b).

Dowes, and Tversky, 1970, pp. 259–79), where the stimulus is the previous experience with the product. The model makes no provision for interaction with new information or the central processing of such information into attitudes. Models based on immediate previous behavior tend to be good predictors but poor explainers of behavior because they omit the intervening states or assume that they are constant during the time period examined.[14]

Dynamic models can be applied to states of central information processing as well as states of buying behavior. The Markov model may be used to model changes in the states of beliefs, attitudes, and probabilities (Lazarsfeld, 1957, p. 29; and Day, 1969). Simulation has been used to model the complex patterns of information processing in consumer products (Amstutz, 1965) and the prescription-drug field (Claycamp and Amstutz, 1968). Generally speaking, however, models of buyer central processing have been comparative-static and models of buyer behavior have been dynamic.

Comprehensive models.   Models of buyer behavior incorporate to various degrees the models of behavior and information processing that have been outlined here. The Howard-Sheth (1969) theory of buyer behavior is the most comprehensive one available in terms of the present discussion. It builds on Hull's theory of behavior and uses stimulus-response concepts with intervening variables of information processing. The Nicosia (1966) model is expressed neatly by four equations that relate brand buying behavior, motivation, previous behavior, attitudes, and the level of communication (i.e., stimuli). The Andreasen (1965) model focuses on the early and central stages of information processing. Central information processing dominates the model by Engel, Kollat, and Blackwell (1968). It is encouraging to see some convergence of thought among these authors. One common fault, however, is that these models are too comprehensive to apply readily to problems of marketing management, such as demand analysis. Some authors (Hughes, 1971b; and Tintera, 1971) are urging the validation of subsystems of buyer behavior so that marketing managers may build models for their specific markets. Cohen and Barban (1970) note two characteristics of present comprehensive models that limit their ability to explain consumer decision making. First, they do not clearly state consumer motivation in operational terms, such as an objective function of expected value. Secondly, these comprehensive models emphasize the

---

[14] For an excellent discussion of the Markov and learning models, later variations, and their limitations, see Kotler (1968); and Montgomery and Urban (1969), pp. 53–84. For an extensive technical discussion of stochastic models of buying behavior, see Massy, Montgomery, and Morrison (1970). For a discussion of simulation models of market response, see Montgomery and Urban (1969), pp. 29–53.

mental processes (perceiving, thinking, learning, forgetting, and choice) rather than content (*what* was perceived, thought, learned, forgotten, and chosen). A similar criticism has been leveled by Schroder, Driver, and Streufert (1967, p. 5) against all information processing models when they noted that too little emphasis has been placed on "*how* a person thinks or uses an attitude as a structure for processing new information, as opposed to an emphasis upon content, upon *what* a person thinks, what his attitudes are, and so forth."

MEASURING ATTITUDES

The measurement of attitudes consists of two steps—the identification of the dimension along which the attitude will be measured and the development of an instrument to measure the attitude. The present discussion will be limited to those techniques which are used most frequently in marketing planning. Detailed discussions, with examples, may be found in Hughes (1971b, chaps. 5 and 6).

Identifying attributes

Methods for attribute identification are classified according to their degree of structure—structured, partially structured, and unstructured. The structured methods include statistical procedures such as factor analysis, cluster analysis, nonmetric multidimensional scaling, and the Automatic Interaction Detection algorithm discussed previously (Chapters 4 and 8).[15]

A partially structured technique that is receiving increased attention in marketing is the Kelly repertory grid (Frost and Braine, 1967; Sampson, 1971). To identify brand attributes the technique would consist of the following steps: (1) the respondent culls from a pack of cards all unfamiliar brands; (2) three cards are selected randomly from the remaining cards; (3) the respondent is asked to describe how two of the brands are similar to each other and different from the third; (4) using the dimension established in step (3) the respondent is asked to rate the remaining brands along this dimension; (5) three more brands are selected and the procedure is repeated until the respondent exhausts his attributes. Generally, only 40 interviews are required to identify the salient attributes (p. 166). The responses are summarized as a grid (i.e., matrix) in which the columns are brands (or concepts, packages, advertisements, etc.), the rows are attributes, and the cell entries are attitude measurements. These measurements may be the result of paired comparisons or other scaling tech-

---

[15] For a discussion of multivariate statistical methods, see Gatty (1966); and Sheth (1971).

niques. An analysis of this matrix reveals competitive brands (columns) and duplication of attributes (rows). The grid technique is superior to structured and unstructured techniques in that the respondent, not the researcher, identifies and names the attributes. This removes experimenter bias and names the attribute in terms familiar to the respondent.

Unstructured techniques, borrowed from clinical psychology, include depth interviews and projective techniques. During the 1950s they were known among marketing researchers as *motivation research* techniques (Ferber and Wales, 1958; and Smith, 1954). The term was unfortunate because they measure motivation only by vague inference. Their primary function is to elicit attributes that are not available by more direct methods. For instance, it may not be socially acceptable to admit directly to an interviewer that a cake mix was used because it requires less work, but "ease of preparation" may emerge as an attribute when a cartoon or sentence completion stimulus is given. Unstructured techniques may be defined as vague or incomplete stimuli. The most vague are the Rorschach ink blot tests and the thematic apperception test (TAT). The respondent reveals attributes that are salient to him by responding to the vague stimulus.

A cartoon projective technique for a cake mix appears in Figure 9–3. In completing the conversation the housewife who does not use the brand

FIGURE 9–3
A cartoon projective technique for cake mixes

may reveal that she thinks using a cake mix reflects laziness or neglecting her family (generic demand) or that the brand in question is too dry, lacks flavor, or is high priced (brand demand). The following sentence completion tests represent a slightly more structured approach to understanding the demand for cake mixes:

Cake mixes are for	[family use only; any occasion]
	[busy people; working mothers]
	[lazy women; mothers who neglect their family]
Astro brand cake mix	[is modern; is used by young sophisticates]
	[is dry; crumbles]
	[bakes a perfect cake every time; never fails]

Another unstructured technique that is useful when developing new products and promotional campaigns is the *focused interview*. In the cake mix example, small groups of housewives would be encouraged to discuss their experiences with desserts, entertaining, baking, and finally with cake mixes.

Measuring attribute beliefs

Market opportunities are frequently identified by measuring buyers' beliefs about existing brands. In this context a belief is the perceived probability that a brand possesses an attribute. If no existing brand is perceived as possessing a salient attribute, and if a sufficient proportion of the respondents regard this attribute as salient, then there is an opportunity for a new brand or modification of an existing brand. Beliefs may be measured as a simple dichotomy of aware/unaware or as a perceived probability of existing. Awareness would be measured as follows:

Check the attributes possessed by Astro brand cake mix.

_____	Moist	_____	Full flavored
_____	Modern	_____	Like homemade

Perceived probability would be measured with the same list but with the following instructions: "Using a scale from 0 to 100, indicate the percent chance that Astro brand cake mix possesses the following attributes." Whenever possible the probability scale should be used because it gives more information about the respondent.

Instruments for measuring attitudes

Instruments for measuring attitudes yield either relative or absolute measures. Paired comparison and ranking procedures produce relative measures while the Likert and semantic differential scales attempt to give absolute measures. It is doubtful that the latter scales give an absolute measure because they lack anchors that are common to all respondents.

A temperature scale is clearly anchored in the freezing and boiling of water, but an attitude scale of cold/hot will be interpreted differently by each individual. Relative instruments are frequently anchored by introducing the concept of an ideal brand.

Attitude measurement is part of a field of study known as psychometrics, which is part of psychophysics. Because psychometrics is over 50 years old and psychophysics has been in existence for more than a century (Guilford, 1954), the present discussion of instruments must be regarded as a representation of only those devices used frequently in marketing research.

Paired comparisons. The paired comparison technique consists of giving all pairs of objects to the respondent who reports which one he prefers according to some attribute such as product flavor, package design, or possible effectiveness of an advertisement.[16] When paired comparisons are used to generate data for nonmetric multidimensional scaling methods, the respondent is not required to make judgments along specified attributes. The attributes are identified by the scaling algorithm and named by the researcher.

The paired comparison is used to generate similarities data for nonmetric mapping of perceptions in n-dimensional space. In this case the subject is asked to identify the more similar pair of brands, given pairs such as *AB* and *CD*.[17] The computer algorithm then projects the brands into perceptual space.

The constant-sum scaling method is an extension of a paired comparison. The respondent is required to indicate the degree of his preference by allocating points, usually 10 or 100. For instance,

> Divide 100 points between each of the following brands according to your preference for each pair of brands.
>
> Brand A [45]   Brand B [55]
> Brand B [30]   Brand C [70]
> Brand A [12]   Brand C [88]

This scale indicates the degree to which one brand is preferred over another.[18]

---

[16] Scoring may be simple percentages or the psychological distance between stimuli may be computed using Thurstone's law of comparative judgment. A brief nontechnical discussion may be found in Hughes (1971b), pp. 103–4. Detailed discussions and examples may be found in Guilford (1954); and Green and Tull (1966).

[17] For a more complete discussion of methods for collecting similarities data, see Coombs (1964); Hughes (1971b); and Taylor (1969).

[18] Scoring techniques are discussed in Guilford (1954), pp. 214–20; Hughes (1971b), pp. 105–7; and Torgerson (1958), pp. 104–12.

The advantages of the paired comparison technique are the simplicity of the task assigned the respondent and the ability to generate interval scales, thereby permitting the use of more powerful statistical methods. The disadvantage is respondent fatigue because all possible pairs must be compared. If 10 brands are involved the respondent must make 45 comparisons $[n(n-1)/2]$.

Rank-order methods. Rank-order methods require the respondent to rank brands according to overall preference or along specific attributes. When the ranking task is used to generate similarities data for nonmetric mapping of perceptions in space, respondents are instructed to rank all pairs of brands in terms of increasing or decreasing similarity.

Ranking methods are relative, that is, they are unique to each individual because they have no common anchor. Anchor-point methods of ranking have been used to overcome this limitation. One brand may be designated as the anchor, and other brands will be ranked above or below this brand.

There are several advantages to ranking procedures. They are less fatiguing for respondents. For instance, it is easier to rank 10 brands than compare 45 pairs. Ranking methods avoid intransitivities. An intransitivity occurs in paired comparisons when a respondent selects brand A over brand B and brand B over brand C, but then selects brand C over brand A. The limitation of rank-order methods is the measurement scale that they generate. The data are ordinal, which precludes using familiar statistics such as the arithmetic mean and variance and significance tests such as the *t* and *F* tests. Rather than develop methods for transforming the data into interval scales, recent effort has been directed toward developing nonmetric statistical techniques (e.g., Siegel, 1956; and Green and Rao, 1970).

The Likert scale. The Likert scale contains many statements which are relevant to the brand, package, or advertisement. The respondent is asked to indicate his degree of agreement or disagreement. An example of the Likert scale appears in Table 9–1. In marketing the customary scoring procedure of the Likert scale is to compute the percent of respondents in each state of agreement or to identify the median state.[19]

The semantic differential. The semantic differential scale (Osgood, Suci, and Tannenbaum, 1957) is probably the most widely used scale in marketing research. It consists essentially of pairs of antonyms with cues spaced in between. In their original form the cues were graphic, but later scales have had verbal and numerical cues. Examples of each of these cues appear in Table 9–2. There is some controversy about the reversing of

---

[19] For a discussion of the summated scoring procedure and other methods, see Edwards (1957).

TABLE 9–1
A Likert scale for cake mixes

The following statements describe cake mixes. If you agree strongly with the statement underscore "Strongly agree," if you are uncertain, underscore "Uncertain," and so on.

1. Astro brand mix makes a perfect cake every time.
   Strongly agree   Agree   Uncertain   Disagree   Strongly disagree

2. Ready mix cakes can be as good as cakes made from scratch.
   Strongly agree   Agree   Uncertain   Disagree   Strongly disagree

3. A cake mix should not be used for special occasions.
   Strongly agree   Agree   Uncertain   Disagree   Strongly disagree

---

alternate cues to eliminate response errors. Some researchers recommend reversing cues while others (e.g., Guilford, 1954) report that the reversing of cues confused respondents and introduced errors of an unknown magnitude.

A balanced verbal scale has an equal number of cues on either side of the midpoint. Frequently respondents use only a few cues at the extreme end of a scale, causing a response pattern known as end piling. To eliminate end piling and generate more useful measures of attitudes the extreme end of a scale is stretched by adding more cues. For example, the unbalanced scale in Table 9–2 has been stretched on the unfavorable end of the scale.

There is general agreement that six to eight cues are appropriate. Reliability increases as the number of cues increases, but it levels off at seven cues (Nunnaly, 1967, p. 521). Green and Rao (1970) concluded that little additional information is gained beyond six points on a scale. Even-numbered scales are used to force the respondent off the midpoint of the scale.

The first three scales in Table 9–2 are known as forced-choice scales because they require the respondent to express an attitude. It has been shown (Hughes, 1969) that these scales confound indifferent attitudes and unawareness when some respondents have no knowledge of the concept being scaled. In such cases provision should be made for respondents to report the fact that they have no opinion, as in the last scale in the table.

Measuring buying tendencies. The final stages of information processing leading to choice behavior in marketing are measured as buying tendencies. Two types of instruments have been used to measure these tendencies. Buying *expectations* are used by the Survey Research Center, University of Michigan (Katona et al., 1969), and prior to 1966, by the U.S. Bureau of the Census in its quarterly survey of consumer buying plans

TABLE 9–2
Examples of the semantic differential scale
_____

Graphic cues

Please evaluate the window service at your local post office by placing an X on the line that represents your attitude.

Efficient ____: ____ : ____ : ____ : ____ : ____ : ____ Inefficient
Friendly ____: ____ : ____ : ____ : ____ : ____ : ____ Unfriendly

Balanced verbal cues

Please check the adjective that represents your overall attitude toward your local post office.

_____ Very progressive
_____ Progressive
_____ Moderately progressive
_____ Neither progressive nor conservative
_____ Moderately conservative
_____ Conservative
_____ Very conservative

Unbalanced verbal cues

Please check the adjective that represents your overall attitude toward your local post office.

_____ Moderately progressive
_____ Neither progressive nor conservative
_____ Moderately conservative
_____ Conservative
_____ Very conservative
_____ Old-fashioned

Numerical cues

Please circle the number that reflects your attitude toward the window service at your local post office. Circle 0 if you have no opinion.

							No opinion
Inefficient 1	2	3	4	5	6	Efficient	0
Unfriendly 1	2	3	4	5	6	Friendly	0

(see Chapter 5). Subjective *probabilities* are presently used by the Bureau of Census and many commercial researchers.

Buying expectations scales are essentially a semantic differential scale. The respondent is asked to report his expectations of buying specific products by checking one of the following verbal cues (Katona et al., 1969): No; Don't know; Maybe; Yes, probably; or Yes, definitely. The vagueness of these cues has reduced their ability to predict. Stapel (1968) has found less vague cues to yield valid indications of actual purchasing.[20]

Probability scales ask the respondents to report their "percent chance" of buying a specific product. Respondents seem to have no trouble thinking in terms of percentages. Perhaps they have been conditioned by weather

_____
[20] For a discussion of expectations measures and citations, see Ferber (1966).

reports such as "there is a 40 percent chance of rain today." The following verbal and numerical cues are used by the U.S. Bureau of the Census (1967):

100	Absolutely certain
90	
80	Strong possibility
70	
60	
50	
40	
30	
20	Slight possibility
10	
0	Absolutely no chance

In one study the U.S. Bureau of the Census (1969) found that the mean probability of buying an automobile was less than 65 percent of the actual purchase rate during the subsequent six-month period. (One explanation may be breakdowns that force unplanned automobile purchases.) However, probabilities are useful for short-term forecasting of consumer durable goods because these biases tend to be constant during the period of the forecast. For instance, 76 percent of the variance in subsequent automobile purchases was associated with the variance in purchase probabilities and a dummy variable to reflect supply shortages caused by strikes (ibid.).

Nonverbal instruments to measure attitudes

Physiologists have developed measures and laboratory instruments that monitor physical reactions to mental activities, such as the processing of information. For decades measures of advertising effectiveness have been sought by using galvanic skin response to various advertisements (e.g., Eckstrand and Gilliland, 1948). Recently Hess (1965) has argued that attitude is related to dilation of the pupil of a respondent's eye as he views an advertisement. While pupillary dilations have been used by some advertisers to pretest advertisements, the technique has been the subject of much criticism and confusion (Blackwell, Hensel, and Sternthal, 1970).

All of the techniques discussed so far have been reactive measures—the subject knew he was being measured. This awareness may affect the measurement. This measurement problem is like the problem in physics of measuring the velocity of a particle without altering its velocity. In the behavioral sciences there is a class of procedures known as nonreactive or unobtrusive measures (Webb, Campbell, Schwartz, and Sechrest, 1966). These include hidden cameras and microphones to monitor the salesman-buyer interaction in an appliance store, one-way mirrors, and checking the wear on the floor tiles in front of museum exhibits. In observational techniques such as these the measurement is free from subject bias.

THE BUYER AS AN INFORMATION PROCESSOR

The final decision to buy a product or a brand is the result of the buyer's processing of information about his needs and the attribute benefits of a product. Even an objective stimulus such as price is perceived subjectively. To study the dynamics of the buying decision, researchers are now viewing the buyer as a processor of information. Measures of values, beliefs, and perceived benefits are emerging as better predictors of buying behavior than demographic and economic variables (Halley, 1972; and Yankelovich, 1971).

The concept of information is extremely broad. Its physical properties of channel capacity and noise were the focus of the pioneering work of Shannon and Weaver (1949). Psycholinguists consider the influence of beliefs and values on language and the communication of messages (e.g., Krauss, 1968). Psychologists have used information theory to reformulate basic concepts such as motivation (Taylor, 1960) and intelligence (Guilford, 1967; and Schroder, Driver, and Streufert, 1967).

The role of information in marketing systems has received considerable attention among marketing scholars. Consumer goods have been classified as convenience goods, shopping goods, and specialty goods according to the amount of effort the consumer is willing to put into the search for the product and information about it (Copeland, 1923; Holton, 1958; and Bucklin, 1963 and 1966). Channels of distribution have as one of their functions the supplying of information in the form of promotion and market analysis (Aspinwall, 1962; Breyer, 1949; and Vaile, Grether, and Cox, 1952). Recent experiments have related prechoice information seeking to brand loyalty (Swan, 1969). Consumer rating services tend to establish a market for information which is separate from the product. Thus, viewing the buyer as an information processor is a logical extension of other marketing theories.

SUMMARY

Psychological theories of motivation, need hierarchy, cognitive balance, communication, and attitude change are central to an understanding of the dynamics of demand in the marketplace. Models and measures for applying these theories to marketing are also derived from psychological research.

Behavioral theories have their origins in hedonism. *Pleasure* and *pain avoidance* were replaced by *instincts* and *habits*, which yielded to *drives*, which, in turn, were replaced by *motivation*. Motivation consists of two elements, a perception of needs and the evaluation of the means for meeting these needs. Needs may be arrayed as a hierarchy ranging from the physiological to the psychological. Behavioral models must reflect motivation and the environment in which the behavior will take place.

Behavioral models are in a constant state of refinement. Spence added *incentive* to Hull's concepts of drive and habit. Hilgard introduced a variable for *stimulus intensity,* which had been outside previous models. Atkinson's model provided for *uncertainty.* Motives are defined with greater precision in the model by Atkinson and Feather. McGuire has included variables that reflect the communication process, but he omits variables that reflect motivation and the environment. The marketing planner must accept the fact that there is no general model of behavior and must develop his own models by using generally accepted variables and functions, when they are known. There is some convergence, however, between behavioral models, attitude models, and decision theory.

The principal limitation of measures of attitudes toward objects is their inability to predict behavior toward objects. Rather than search for links between these attitudes and behavior, Fishbein has taken the approach of identifying the components of behavior. The independent variables in his behavioral model are attitudes (toward the behavior), values (normative beliefs), and social pressures (motivation to comply).

Most of the information to which a person is potentially exposed is filtered during the first stage of processing through selective exposure and selective perception. An awareness of a need reduces the filtering out of information. Models of attitude change seem to have been inspired by the physiological concept of homeostasis. They view the buyer as seeking a balance with previously held attitudes, a self-image, or an image of an ideal brand. This concept of balance has been challenged because it does not explain innovative behavior, which is a movement away from balance. Models of choice behavior tend to emphasize previous behavior, and thus are habit models rather than models of information processing.

Attributes must be identified before attitudes can be measured. Statistical methods for attribute identification include the AID algorithm, nonmetric multidimensional scaling, factor analysis, and cluster analysis. The Kelly repertory grid method, a partially structured technique, has the advantage over other methods of requiring the respondent to identify the attributes and name them in his own terms. Unstructured techniques for identifying deep or socially sensitive attributes include depth and focused interviews, and the projective techniques of cartoon tests and sentence completion tests.

The techniques used most frequently in marketing research to measure attitudes include variations on the paired-comparison method, ranking techniques, Likert scales, and the semantic differential. Nonmetric multi-dimensional scaling is gaining popularity as its advantages become known to marketing planners. It requires only ordinal data, and in one operation it identifies the attributes and places brands in perceptual space. Probability scales of buying tendencies provide useful data for short-term forecasting.

READING QUESTIONS

1. What is motivation in the context of marketing?
2. What is a need hierarchy? How is it related to values?
3. How do the theories of selective exposure and selective perception relate to advertising?
4. Which of the attitude change models would you use for brand promotion?
5. How does the Fishbein model relate to the Atkinson model and subjective expected utility?
6. What are the standard methods for identifying psychological product attributes? Which do you recommend?
7. What instruments are used frequently in marketing to measure beliefs and attitudes?

CLASS DISCUSSION QUESTIONS

1. Trace the refinements in the theories of motivation. What do you think will be the next refinement, or do you think that the concept of motivation is a fully developed theory?
2. Identify products and services that will be demanded at various points in time in the Maslow hierarchy of needs (Figure 9–1).
3. Develop a behavioral model for buying a house.
4. With the cooperation of a local appliance retailer, depth interview couples who recently purchased refrigerators, washers, dryers, dishwashing machines, or TV sets. Identify the source and the content of the information that was used by the husband and the wife during each stage of the decision process.
5. Develop a communication model for a promotional campaign opposing drug abuse.
6. Which areas in buyer/consumer information processing do you think should receive priority among researchers?

7. Identify product attributes for hot drinks using the Kelly repertory grid and a projective technique. What are the advantages and disadvantages of each technique?

8. Which attitude scaling instrument would you recommend to measure attitudes toward a political candidate?

9. An analysis of perceptions of a representative sample of consuming units (i.e., potential and present customers) of six major brands of color television sets revealed the following configuration in two-dimensional space. The dimensions were interpreted as technical complexity and convenience in use.

Brand	Configuration dimension	
	1	*2*
A	1.0	2.0
B	2.0	-1.0
C	1.0	-2.0
D	-2.0	1.0
E	-1.0	-1.0
F	-1.0	1.0

For the purposes of this exercise, assume that the six brands comprise the whole market and that the two dimensions exhaust the possible ways of describing the brand space.

In the same analysis, five distinct market segments were identified. Their characteristics and the locations of their ideal points are shown below:

Segment	Description	Market share	Location of ideal point	
			1	*2*
I	All institutions such as hotels, motels	30%	1.0	1.0
II	Households with income less than $15,000 and nonSMSA residents	20	1.0	-1.5
III	Households with income less than $15,000 and SMSA residents	15	1.5	1.5
IV	Households with income over $15,000 and nonSMSA residents	10	2.0	1.5
V	Households with income over $15,000 and SMSA residents	25	2.0	2.0

It is further estimated that P_{ij}, the probability of purchase of a brand j by the segment i, is inversely proportional to:

$$1.0 + 2.0d_{ij}^2$$

where

d_{ij}^2 = squared Euclidean distance between the ideal point for the segment and the j-th brand in the brand space.

That is,

$$\frac{1}{P_{ij}} = k(1 + 2d_{ij}^2),$$

k being a constant of proportionality so chosen to make the probabilities of purchase add to 1.0.

a) Estimate the probabilities of purchase of the institutional segment for brand B.

b) Estimate the expected market share for brand B.

c) Plot the ideal points of several segments in the brand space. What product modification ideas follow from this?

d) Suppose a new brand, G, with coordinate values (2.0, 1.0) is introduced in the market. What market share can this brand be expected to capture? Which segment would be most attracted to this brand? Which brand would be most affected by brand G?

(Answers for (a) and (b) may be found in Appendix B.) *

SUGGESTED CASES

Algonquin Advertising Agency. Bursk and Greyser (1968), pp. 1–18.

The agency must evaluate existing motivational studies to determine if it should seek the account of the Sunsweet (prune) Growers Association.

1. Evaluate the motivational studies. Was the problem the identification of attributes or the measurement of attitudes?

2. Evaluate the methods used to determine motivations for buying and consuming prunes. What new techniques would you recommend?

Eastern Air Lines: Attitude change. Blackwell, Engel, and Kollat (1969), pp. 94–102.

To correct an unfavorable image of Eastern Airlines, an extensive promotional campaign was planned and executed. Attitude research was used during the planning stages.

1. Do you agree with the strategy of concentrating on the business flier?

2. How were the salient attributes identified? How would you identify them for an airline?

---
* The problem and the solution were contributed by Professor Vithala R. Rao. The author gratefully acknowledges this contribution.

3. Are the strategic goals "In Support of Customer Satisfaction" (Table 5–11) operational?

4. How were the needs of the traveling public identified?

5. Develop a questionnaire to measure the effect of the promotional effort.

Lectromatic Corporation: Analyzing problem recognition—purchasing relationships. Blackwell, Engel, and Kollat (1969), pp. 169–81.

A large manufacturer of electrical appliances used longitudinal (re-interview) data to examine buyer purchasing processes.

1. Evaluate the data that were collected. Do they adequately describe buyer information processing? What changes would you make, if any?

2. What changes would you make to improve the predictive ability of buying intentions?

Miss Ritz Cosmetics (B): Comprehensive review of consumer influence on marketing strategy. Blackwell, Engel, and Kollat (1969), pp. 363–427.

Nondirective interviews were conducted with 52 coeds to determine collegiate preferences for cosmetics.

1. Using the verbatim raw data (Appendix B in the case), identify coeds' motivations for using cosmetics. What are the salient attributes?

2. What other techniques would you consider for identifying salient attributes?

National Liberty Life Insurance Company: Personality and Direct Mail Buying. Blackwell, Engel, and Kollat (1969), pp. 61–74.

Perceived risk was measured to determine if it was a barrier to the purchase of mail-order insurance.

1. What kinds of risk do the instruments measure?

2. What changes would you make in the instruments to make them more precise? (Hint: Note the confounding effect in the present instruments.)

3. Would more precise instruments change the findings and therefore change the action to be taken by the marketing management?

W. T. Grant Company (B). Blackwell, Engel, and Kollat (1969), pp. 88–94.

Grey Advertising, Inc. designed a campaign to change customers' image toward Grants to one that corresponded with the vastly changed merchandising policy of the chain. Copy research was used to pretest advertisements.

1. Relate the measures of impact and attitudes used by Grey Advertising, Inc. to the concept of buyer information processing.

2. What is the advantage of *Difference Score Analysis* over *Usage Weight Score Analysis,* as used by Grey?

3. How does Grey identify salient attributes? What other methods would you recommend?

SUGGESTED READINGS

ALPERT, M. I. "Identification of Determinant Attributes: A Comparison of Methods," *Journal of Marketing Research,* Vol. 8 (May 1971), pp. 184–91.

ATKINSON, J. W., and FEATHER, N. (eds.). *The Theory of Achievement Motivation.* New York: John Wiley & Sons, Inc., 1966.

BECKER, BORIS W., and MYERS, JOHN C. "Yeasaying Response Style," *Journal of Advertising Research,* Vol. 10, No. 6 (December 1970), pp. 31–37.

BETTMAN, J. R. "Methods for Analyzing Consumer Information Processing Models," in Gardner (1971), pp. 197–207.

CARMAN, J. M., and NICOSIA, F. M. "Analog Experiments with a Model of Consumer Attitude Change," *Proceedings: American Marketing Association,* December 1964, pp. 246–57.

COHEN, J. B., and ABTOLA, O. T. "An Expectancy X Value Analysis of the Relationship between Consumer Attitudes and Behavior," in Gardner (1971), pp. 344–64.

CRAVENS, D. W. "An Exploratory Analysis of Individual Information Processing," *Management Science,* Vol. 16 (June 1970), pp. B656–70.

DAY, G. S. "Changes in Attitudes and Intentions as Predictors of New Product Acceptance," in King and Tigert (1971), pp. 92–110.

EHRENBERG, A. S. C. "Towards an Integrated Theory of Consumer Behaviour," *Journal of the Market Research Society,* Vol. 11 (October 1969), pp. 305–37.

FENDRICH, J. M. "A Study of the Association among Verbal Attitudes, Commitment, and Overt Behavior in Different Experimental Situations," *Journal of Social Forces,* Vol. 45 (1967), pp. 347–55.

GOLDBERG, M. E. "A Cognitive Model of Innovative Behavior: The Interaction of Product and Self-Attitudes," in Gardner (1971), pp. 313–30.

GREEN, P. E., and CARMONE, F. J. "Multidimensional Scaling: An Introduction and Comparison of Nonmetric Unfolding Techniques," *Journal of Marketing Research,* Vol. 6 (August 1969), pp. 330–41.

————, and RAO, V. R. "A Note on Proximity Measures and Cluster Analysis," *Journal of Marketing Research,* Vol. 6 (August 1969), pp. 359–64.

HANSEN, F., and BOLLAND, T. "The Relationship between Cognitive Models of Choice and Non-Metric Multidimensional Scaling," in Gardner (1971), pp. 376–88.

HARRIS, R. J. "Dissonance or Sour Grapes? Post-'Decision Charges' in Ratings and Choice Frequencies," *Journal of Personality and Social Psychology,* Vol. 11 (April 1969), pp. 334–44.

HEISE, DAVID R. "Some Methodological Issues in Semantic Differential Research," *Psychological Bulletin,* Vol. 72 (December 1969), pp. 406–22.

―――. "The Semantic Differential and Attitude Research," in *Attitude Measurement* (ed. G. Summers). Skokie, Ill.: Rand McNally & Co., 1970.

HUGHES, G. D. *Attitude Measurement for Marketing Strategies.* Glenview, Ill.: Scott, Foresman and Co., 1971.

JONES, J. M. "A Comparison of Three Models of Brand Choice," *Journal of Marketing Research,* Vol. 7 (November 1970), pp. 466–73.

KERNAN, J. B. "The CAD Instrument in Behavioral Diagnosis," in Gardner (1971), pp. 307–12.

KIESLER, C. A.; COLLINS, B. E.; and MILLER, N. *Attitude Change.* New York: John Wiley & Sons, Inc., 1969.

―――. *The Psychology of Commitment.* New York: Academic Press, 1971.

KING, C. W., and TIGERT, D. J. (eds.). *Attitude Research Reaches New Heights.* Marketing Research Techniques, Bibliography Series No. 14. Chicago: American Marketing Association, 1971.

KLAHR, D. "Decision Making in a Complex Environment: The Use of Similarity Judgments to Predict Preferences," *Management Science,* Vol. 15 (July 1969), pp. 595–618.

LEHMANN, D. R.; FARLEY, J. U.; and HOWARD, J. A. "Testing of Buyer Behavior Models," in Gardner (1971), pp. 232–42.

McGUIRE, W. J. "An Information-Processing Model of Advertising Effectiveness." Paper read at the Symposium on Behavior and Management Science in Marketing. Chicago: Center for Continuing Education, the University of Chicago, June 11, 1969.

―――. "The Guiding Theories Behind Attitude Change Research," in King and Tigert (1971), pp. 26–48.

MATHEWS, H. L.; SLOCUM, J. W., JR.; and WOODSIDE, A. G. "Perceived Risk, Individual Differences, and Shopping Orientations," in Gardner (1971), pp. 299–306.

MISCHEL, W. *Personality and Assessment.* New York: John Wiley & Sons, Inc., 1968.

―――. "Continuity and Change in Personality," *American Psychologist,* Vol. 24 (1969), pp. 1012–18.

MOINPOUR, R., and MACLACHLAN, D. L. "The Relations among Attribute and Importance Components of Rosenberg-Fishbein Type Attitude Model: An Empirical Investigation," in Gardner (1971), pp. 365–75.

MURRAY, J. A. "Utilizing Consumer Expectational Data to Allocate Promotional Efforts," *Journal of Marketing,* Vol. 33 (April 1969), pp. 26–33.

NAKANISHI, MASSAO. "Consumer Learning in Awareness and Trial of New Products," in Gardner (1971), pp. 186–96.

NEIDELL, L. A. "The Use of Nonmetric Multidimensional Scaling in Marketing Analysis," *Journal of Marketing,* Vol. 33 (October 1969), pp. 37–43.

O'BRIEN, T. "Stages of Consumer Decision Making," *Journal of Marketing Research,* Vol. 8 (August 1971), pp. 283–89.

PERLOFF, R. "Consumer Analysis," in *Annual Review of Psychology* (eds. Paul R. Farnsworth, Mark R. Rosenzweig, and Judith T. Polefka), pp. 437–66. Palo Alto, Calif.: Annual Reviews, Inc., 1968.

RAMSAY, J. O., and CASE, B. "Attitude Measurement and the Linear Model," *Psychological Bulletin,* Vol. 74 (September 1970), pp. 185–92.

RAPOPORT, A., and WALLSTEN, T. "Individual Decision Making," in *Annual Review of Psychology,* Vol. 23. Palo Alto, Calif.: Annual Reviews, Inc., 1972.

ROKEACH, M. *Beliefs, Attitudes, and Values: A Theory of Organization and Change.* San Francisco: Jossey-Bass, Inc., Publishers, 1968.

RUSS, F. A. "Evaluation Process Models and the Prediction of Preference," in Gardner (1971), pp. 256–61.

SIMON, H. A. *Models of Man, Social and Rational.* New York: John Wiley & Sons, Inc., 1957.

STEFFLRE, V. J. "Some Implications of Multidimensional Scaling to Social Science Problems," in King and Tigert (1971), pp. 300–311.

SWANSON, C. E. "The Frontiers of Consumer Psychology, 1964–70," in *The Frontiers of Management Psychology* (ed. George Fisk), pp. 188–208. New York: Harper & Row, Publishers, 1964.

TANNENBAUM, P. H., and GREENBERG, B. S. "Mass Communication," in *Annual Review of Psychology* (eds. Paul R. Farnsworth, Mark R. Rosenzweig, and Judith T. Polefka), pp. 351–86. Palo Alto, Calif.: Annual Reviews, Inc., 1968.

WICKER, A. W. "Attitudes versus Action: The Relationship of Verbal and Overt Behavioral Responses to Attitude Objects," *Journal of Social Issues* Vol. 25 (1969), pp. 41–78.

10

Measuring and modeling
for planning

PLANNING SCIENTIFICALLY

The discussion in the previous chapters leads to three conclusions. First, all marketing plans are built on an understanding of demand. Secondly, an understanding of demand requires a multidisciplinary approach, which includes demography, economics, sociology, and psychology. Thirdly, there is no general, interdisciplinary model of demand that will apply to all products and services and in all market segments. The marketing planner, therefore, will find it necessary to build models of his own marketing system, using models and measures from these disciplines as building blocks. Thus, scientific planning requires an understanding of scientific processes of measuring and modeling.

THE ROLE OF MEASURES AND MODELS IN SCIENCE

To understand the behavior of a molecule, an animal, or a person, a scientist must be able to *describe* the object of his study without bias. Briefly, unbiased description is the function performed by measurement. A scientist must understand how the properties of the object interact with each other so that he can *predict* the behavior of the object. Models perform this task by summarizing the functional relationships of properties. To strengthen the inferences that follow from prediction, the scientist must *control* the variables in the object that led to its predicted change. Experimentation provides this control. Therefore, to explain the behavior of the systems he studies, the scientist must be able to describe them and predict their behavior under controlled conditions. Measures, models, and experiments provide the bases for description and prediction.

To illustrate the scientific process assume that the object to be studied is a familiar one—a book. It has many properties which can be measured by standard procedures. We might measure its weight; its length, width, or height; the reflective qualities of its paper; the wave length of the color of its cover; or we might use a nonnumerical system, the alphabet, and

FIGURE 10–1
The scientific process: Measuring volume

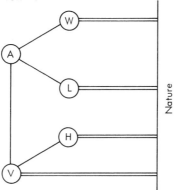

Note: Double lines are measures; single lines are the variables in the model. *W, L, H, A,* and *V* represent width, length, height, area, and volume respectively.
Source: Adapted from Margenau (1950), p. 85.

array it on a shelf with other books according to the first letter of the author's last name. We might combine several measures according to the appropriate geometric model and derive measures of area and volume; applying our knowledge of physics we could compute the average density of the book.

The number and kinds of properties we measure depend on the problem under investigation. If we are mailing the book, its weight is important; the color of the cover and the author's last name are unimportant. Conversely, if we are trying to locate it on our bookshelf, weight is unimportant but the color and author's name are vital properties. Thus, the problem determines which properties are important.

Continuing with the book example and with the aid of Figure 10–1 we may examine the relationships among measurement, models, deduction, prediction, validation, and experimentation. The double lines in the figure represent rules of correspondence, that is, measurement. The single lines represent formal logical relationships among properties which are shown in circles, that is, models.

Measuring the width of the book requires several decisions—specification of the desired measuring standard (a meter or a yard), specification of precision (centimeters, millimeters), manipulation of the measuring device, and recording of the observation. We repeat the process to measure the book's length and height. If we want to derive the area represented by the cover we must apply a model from plane geometry: length (L) times width (W) equals the area (A) of a rectangle. To derive the theoretical volume (V) of the book we multiply the area times the height. The result is a theoretically derived prediction of the volume of the book. There can be two sources of error in the prediction—the measurement process and the model. Measurement errors include those of observation and recording. While there is no reason to doubt the geometric models, we might have used the wrong model or made an error in calculation. To validate the entire system—measurement, model selection, and manipulation—we must compare our prediction of the book's volume with an observation of its volume in nature. This requires a direct measurement of volume, which is shown in Figure 10–1 by the double line between V and "nature."

To validate our prediction of the book's volume we could cut the book into cubic centimeters and count the pieces or we could apply Archimedes's Principle by immersing the book in water and observing the displacement. Errors of observation will prevent the findings of this experiment from agreeing with the prediction, so we will want to replicate the experiment many times and compare our average prediction with our average observed volume. If these agree, using appropriate statistical techniques, we have validated the scientific process.

To appreciate the advantage of a model, assume that we have the conditions shown in Figure 10–2. In this case we want to measure the volume of a book but we do not know geometry. Identification of the model becomes the problem. But prior to identification of the model we must identify the variables that are relevant to the model. One procedure would be as follows: take a sample of books and measure the properties shown in Figure 10–2, immerse the books in water and record the volume displaced, use the appropriate statistical technique (e.g., correlation, factor analysis, or cluster analysis) to reveal those properties that are most closely associated with volume. Color would be eliminated, but the thickness of paper might be correlated with the height of the book and emerge from

FIGURE 10–2
Properties of a book

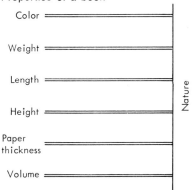

this analysis as a variable to be included in the model. Having identified three important and one minor variable, the scientist must then determine the functional relationship among the variables and volume. Because simple additive models

$$Y = a + b_1X_1 + b_2X_2 \cdots b_nX_n$$

are easy to compute, he will probably consider this model first.

Once the scientist has derived a model he must collect new data to validate it. The reader has recognized by this point that Figure 10–2 represents the present state of the behavior sciences and therefore the state of marketing. Marketers have derived a few laws or constants such as Reilly's (1931) law of retail gravitation, Agostini's (1962) constant of accumulative audience, and Ehrenberg's (1969) constants relating brand usage to intentions-of-buying; but general relationships of buyer behavior are unknown.

Which comes first, the measurement, the model, or the theory? The question cannot be answered because measurement, modeling, and theory building are inseparable parts of the scientific process. The researcher has a tentative theory in mind when he selects variables for measurement. This theory is based on earlier, less refined measures. Any models that he uses are logical summaries of previous measures. The new measures will yield more refined models and theories, which will suggest the need for new measurement, and thus the process of scientific refinement continues. Each level of knowledge is built upon less refined measures, models, and theories (Hughes, 1968).

MEASUREMENT

Measurement defined

The measurement process generally assigns numbers to the properties of an object according to certain rules so that the numbers reflect the magnitudes of the properties. The casual observer might conclude that measurement requires the use of a numerical system. While this is the general practice, measurement can be accomplished by using other logical systems. For instance, the verbal scale of hot, warm, and cold provides a crude measure of temperature. In addition, measurement can be performed using graph or set theory. Numerical measures are the most common, however, because they are more precise than verbal measures and easier to manipulate than graphic and set theoretical ones.

An object can have discrete and continuous properties. A discrete property would be an attribute such as male or female. A continuous property would be a variable such as height or weight. Measurement is not limited to physical objects; in earlier chapters we saw that instruments have been developed for measuring the mental processes of beliefs, attitudes, and action tendencies.

Measurement can be described in set theoretical terms as the process by which the properties of the observed object are mapped into the properties of a system of logic according to some rules of correspondence (i.e., functions). Ideally, this mapping yields a one-to-one correspondence between the two systems, but isomorphism is rarely achieved.

Measurement is crucial to abstract analysis. It is the process by which observations in nature are transformed into logical models. The manipulation of these models reveals new relationships among variables, which are known as predictions. These predictions are validated by relating the logical system back to the object, a process requiring measurement. This sequence was illustrated in Figure 10–1. Vannevar Bush (1965) observed that:

Logic can proceed only when the entities with which it is concerned are strictly defined. Science can proceed only when it can observe with precision, and when it can measure. Mathematics becomes useful only when the quantities it manipulates have precise meaning.

The functions of measurement

Measuring instruments perform two important functions during the process of observing the behavior of a system. In the first place, an instrument is frequently necessary to bring a variable within the range of human perception. A microscope and an audio amplifier perform this function. Instruments perform a second function, that of standardizing observations so that information can be communicated and stored. A metric rule provides a means by which physical scientists around the world can communicate their observations of physical systems.

Without some form of measurement it would be necessary for everyone in the marketing system to gather his own information. For buyers and sellers this would mean transporting individuals or at least samples of the goods so that appropriate observations could be made. Instead, measurement enables information about the goods to be communicated by printed or electronic media. Thus, measurement reduces the cost of marketing by substituting the movement of information for the movement of people and goods. Without measurement, scholarly research in marketing would be limited to the observations of each scholar.

Measuring instruments and their related standards are frequently very colorful. If a woman was thought to be a witch, she was thrown in a river; if she sank, she was a witch. Before chronometers were invented, small units of time were measured in terms of heartbeats. The speed of a ship is presently measured in "knots" because the only method available to early sailors for measuring speed was to drag a funnel tied to a line, letting the line slide through the fingers. By counting equally spaced knots in the line they could estimate the speed of the ship. The Beaufort scale for the naming of wind forces provides graphic descriptions for those lacking equipment. Beaufort number 0 designates a calm, a wind force of less than one mile per hour, which can be recognized by smoke rising vertically. A number 9 represents a strong gale, a wind force from 47 to 54 miles per hour, which can remove chimney pots and slates. In the future, our present measures of mental processes and human behavior may appear as crude as the ones noted above.

Scientists frequently are preoccupied with a measuring instrument or a model. Kaplan (1964, p. 28) describes this as the law of the instrument. "Give a small boy a hammer, and he will find that everything he encounters needs pounding." Kaplan notes further that scientists tend to formulate problems in terms of the techniques they know and that the price of training is the incapacity to learn to attack a problem differently. "Electronic computers, game-theoretic models, and statistical formulas are but instruments after all; it is not *they* that produce scientific results but the investigator who uses them scientifically." Maslow (1954, p. 13) observes that the stress on elegance and technique plays down the significance of the problem and scientific creativity to the point that a polished methodological study would never be criticized for considering a trivial problem.

MODELS

Models defined

A model can be defined most easily by contrasting its function with the one performed by measurement. Measurement establishes an isomorphism with the magnitude of some property of an object and a system of logic, generally a numerical system. The number serves the function of describing the magnitude of the property. A model goes beyond magnitudes of properties to describe the structural relationships among the magnitudes of two or more properties. Thus, a model establishes an isomorphism between the structure of the object and the structure of some system of logic. As with measurement, this system need not be numerical; it can be verbal, symbolic, or graphic. Massy and Savvas (1964) provide an excellent example of a verbal, a mathematical, and a graphic model of a single concept—a competitor's reaction to a price cut. These three models are reproduced in Figure 10–3.

A model is a generalization of relationships, that is, structure is generalized. In abstracting the relationships of an object, a good model considers only those relationships that are necessary for the problem at hand. Bross notes, ". . . an apple has many properties, size, shape, color, etc. but only a few are considered before making the decision to eat it or not" (Bross, 1961, p. 170). A parsimonious model is easier to manipulate and cheaper to implement when making the necessary measurements, but naive critics like to emphasize where such a model fails to represent the object. Unfortunately they miss the point. "Science always simplifies; its aim is not to reproduce the reality in all its complexity, but only to formulate what is essential for understanding, prediction, or control" with respect to a specific problem (Kaplan, 1964, p. 280).

Identifying the structure of the model

The procedures for identifying the structural relationships that form models are the least defined steps in the scientific process. Here is where the history of science reports discoveries that were accidental or that were flashes of insight after long periods of dreary work. This is the creative step in the scientific process.

FIGURE 10–3

Three models of a competitor's reaction to a price cut

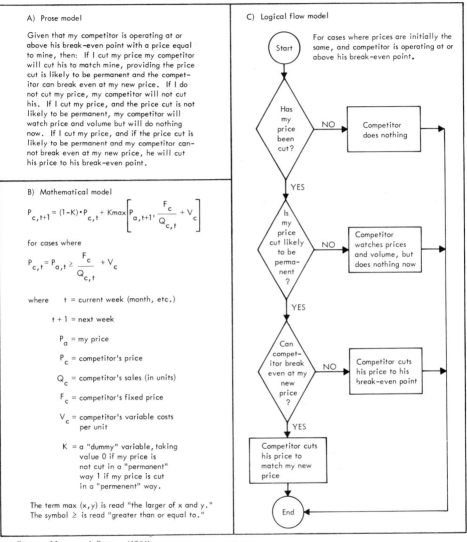

Source: Massy and Savvas (1964).

The structural relationships among variables in a model of the marketing system can be established by one or more of the following procedures: (1) definition, (2) law or rule, (3) physical relationships between input and output in a system, and (4) description of decision processes. The models that result by following these procedures are known respectively as definitional, institutional, technical, and behavioral models (Koopmans,

1945). Examples of each of these procedures will clarify the process of building models.

Definitional models are identities that establish exact relationships between variables. The equations used in accounting are definitional models—profit (π) equals sales (S) minus total cost (TC). Sales may be defined further as price (P) times quantity (Q) sold. Total costs include fixed costs (FC) and variable costs (VC). Variable costs are the costs that vary with the quantity (Q). With these definitions, profit can be defined as follows:

$$\pi = PQ - (FC + VC \times Q) \tag{10-1}$$

which reduces to

$$\pi = Q(P - VC) - FC \tag{10-2}$$

Additional relationships may be derived from Equation 10–2 using algebra. To determine the quantity of goods that must be sold to break even (i.e., zero profits), set Equation 10–2 equal to zero and solve for Q. Thus,

$$0 = Q(P - VC) - FC \tag{10-3}$$

$$Q = \frac{FC}{P - VC} \tag{10-4}$$

Equation 10–4 is used frequently when making pricing decisions. Assume that a product has a fixed cost of $25,000, variable costs per unit of $3, and a selling price of $8 is being considered. How many units must be sold to break even? Using Equation 10–4,

$$Q = \frac{25,000}{8 - 3} = 5,000 \text{ units}.$$

If competition were to force the price to $7, break-even would increase to 6,250 units.

The structure of institutional models is determined by laws, rules, and policies. These models constrain the decision maker. A company may limit market penetration to a fixed percentage of the market, say 50 percent, to avoid an antitrust injunction. The upper limit of company sales (S_c) would be equal to or less than 0.50 times industry sales (S_i), that is

$$S_c \lessgtr 0.50 \, S_i$$

Department store buyers are frequently instructed to maintain a margin of profit for their department and to sell within a limited range of price (known as a price line). If policy establishes the margin as one third of selling price (P) and the buyer is expected to sell men's slacks for about $15 each, he knows that he should buy them (VC) for about $10 each, calculated as follows:

$$\frac{1}{3} P = P - VC \tag{10-5}$$

$$P - \frac{1}{3} P = VC$$

$$\frac{2}{3} (15) = VC$$

$$VC = \$10$$

Budget constraints are institutional models. For example, a marketing manager might be given a budget limit of $250,000 which he must allocate to product development (PD), marketing research (MR), advertising (A), and personal selling (PS). The budget model may be expressed as

$$PD + MR + A + PS \leq \$250,000 \tag{10-6}$$

Previous experience, competition, and marketing policy will set upper and lower limits on expenditures for each element of the marketing mix, which could be expressed as follows:

$$\$20,000 \leq PD \leq \$60,000 \tag{10-7}$$
$$\$15,000 \leq MR \leq \$70,000 \tag{10-8}$$
$$\$60,000 \leq A \leq \$100,000 \tag{10-9}$$
$$\$85,000 \leq PS \leq \$110,000 \tag{10-10}$$

Equation 10–7 states, for example, that at least $20,000, but not more than $60,000, is to be spent on product development. To the extent that Equations 10–7 through 10–10 are based on competition and experience with previous consumer reaction, these models are behavioral ones.

Technical models express physical relationships between the input and output of a system and therefore reflect the state of technology in the system. A production function is a technical model because it expresses the relationship between units of labor (L) and capital (C) inputs to output (O). The Cobb-Douglas (1928) production function for the entire United States as computed in 1928 was:

$$O = 1.10 \ L^{0.75} \ C^{0.25}$$

Input-output models are being applied with increasing frequency to the marketing problems of demand analysis and forecasting. They are particularly useful when analyzing the derived demand for intermediate goods that follow an increase in consumer demand. Thus, some of the most enthusiastic supporters of these techniques have been firms that produce intermediate products—paper, chemicals, public utilities, etc. The structure of input-output models is determined by technology. The technical coefficients are summarized in the technology matrix. An example for the Dutch economy is shown in Table 10–1 (Theil, Boot, and Klock, 1965, p. 61).

TABLE 10–1
Input-output example from the Dutch economy

From sector	To sector		
	Agriculture	*Industry*	*Services*
Agriculture	0.2	0.09	0.01
Industry	0.4	0.24	0.05
Services	0.04	0.12	0.09

Source: Theil, Boot, and Klock (1965).

The nine technical coefficients may be interpreted in the following manner: 20 percent of agricultural output consists of inputs from agriculture, 40 percent from industry, and 4 percent from the service industry; 9 percent of the industrial output consists of inputs from agriculture, 24 percent from industry, and 12 percent from the services; and 1 percent of the output of services comes from agriculture, 5 percent from industry, and 9 percent from the services. Each of these coefficients reflects the state of technology in the Dutch economy in the 1950s.[1]

Behavioral models summarize the structural relationships among decision makers' cognitive processes and information which leads to changes in behavior. Models of learning and forgetting, brand switching, adoption of new products, and information searching represent attempts to describe, predict, and control the consumer's decision process, and therefore his behavior. These consumer models are an important part of the manager's decision model as he searches for an optimal allocation of promotional effort. In addition to the consumer models, the manager needs models that describe the productivity of promotional effort, the strategic and tactical goals of the firm, competitive reactions, and constraints, such as budgets and policy. The regulator has crude models of the consumer and the manager in mind as he attempts to determine if the competitive system is being

[1] For an application of input-output analysis to the auto industry, see *Measuring Markets,* pp. 77–83.

maintained. In short, behavioral models are central to marketing decisions and therefore to the marketing system, yet they are the least developed of the four types of models. Their structures lack the precision of the models that are determined by definition, fiat, or technology. In addition, considerable variance is introduced by the crudeness of measures associated with these models. Marketers must improve their behavioral models and measures before they can develop general theories of market behavior.

SYSTEMS

Systems defined

A system is more than a set of models. It may be defined as a super model which describes the structural relationships among models, and therefore among their properties. Because of the interrelationships among models within a system it ". . . has properties, functions or purposes distinct from its constituent objects, relationships and attributes" (Hall and Fagen, 1956, p. 18). Thus a system is more than the sum of its parts, a phenomenon known as *synergism*.

Methods for representing systems

A system, like a model, may be represented by many different methods. It may be a physically scaled-down version of the system in question, such as the physical system developed by Dutch hydraulic engineers to study the relationships among the waters of the North Sea, the Rivers Rhine and Maas, and the effects of wind, tide, sea bed, and seven new dams (Villiers, 1968). The relationships among variables in the system may be transformed so that angles on a graph or ratios of current in an analog computer are isomorphic, thereby creating a system that can be manipulated to reveal new relationships. A system may be portrayed verbally or symbolically.

The method used for portraying a system becomes more precise as the scientist gains knowledge of how the system operates. An example is provided by the economic system for eggs (Gerra, 1959). The first approximation of the system is graphic (Figure 10–4). Physical quantities appear in boxes, and economic variables appear in circles. The degree and direction of influence is shown by arrows.

The market system for eggs can be described by 11 verbal models. For illustrative purposes the discussion here will be limited to the model for

FIGURE 10–4

The economic system for eggs

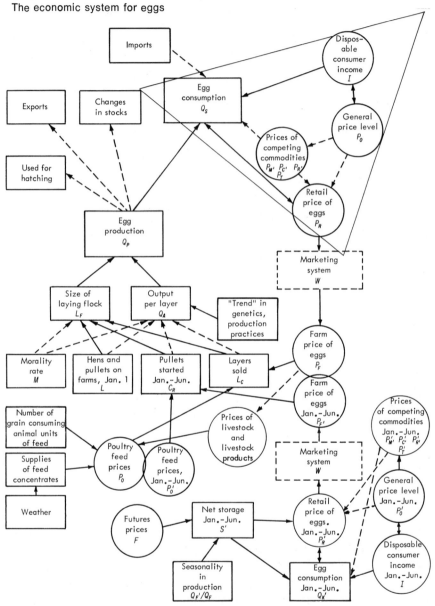

Physical quantities are shown in boxes. Prices and income are shown in circles. Solid lines indicate important paths of influence. Broken lines portray minor influences.

Source: Gerra (1959).

egg consumption, which includes the upper, right-hand part of the system shown in Figure 10–4 (within the triangle). The verbal model is as follows:

The civilian consumption of eggs per capita (QE/H) is influenced by: the price of eggs (P_R); disposable income (I) and population (H) expressed as disposable income per capita (I/H); prices of substitute and complementary goods such as meats, poultry, and fish (P_M), cheese (P_C), bacon (P_B), and ready-to-eat cereals (P_T); and the consumer price index (P_o).

The model may be expressed with greater precision by using available data and multiple regression techniques. Thus,

$$\frac{\Delta Q_E}{H} = -3.05 - 0.84\Delta P_R - \frac{0.03\Delta I}{H} + 0.07\Delta P_M$$
$$+ 0.52\Delta P_C - 0.61\Delta P_B - 1.77\Delta P_T + 5.11\Delta P_o \quad (10\text{–}11)$$

where the symbols are the same as in the verbal model, and Δ indicates changes in the variables. The first variable, P_R, indicates that a decline in price will increase the civilian consumption of eggs. The complete system was represented by a total of seven models like Equation 10–11.

The marketing system for eggs demonstrates that a graph can be an important first step in building a mathematical system of behavior in the marketplace. The Howard-Sheth (1969) model of buyer behavior was a graphic and a verbal system until Farley and Ring (1970) translated it into a system of simultaneous estimation equations and tested it with available data. The Nicosia (1966) model is expressed graphically and mathematically. (Procedures for theory construction—from verbal, through graph, to mathematical formulations—are presented in Blalock, 1969.)

Laws, theories, and systems

The establishment of general laws is the function of science; thus, we must note briefly the relationship between laws, theories, and systems. A law asserts a relationship between properties of a system. Laws make it possible to predict the behavior of a system with a minimum amount of information. A theory is more than a stable relationship because it explains as well as predicts the behavior of the system. "A scientific theory is a deductive system in which observable consequences logically follow from the conjunction of observed facts with the set of fundamental hypotheses of the system" (Braithwaite, 1953, p. 10). It is important to note that a scientific theory requires a deductive system, observed facts, and observable consequences. Thus, we have not developed a theory if only the deductive system exists.

ADVANTAGES AND DISADVANTAGES OF A MEASURES, MODELS, AND SYSTEMS APPROACH

Many of the advantages and disadvantages of a measures, models, and systems approach to marketing have been implicit, but it seems advisable to summarize them. Stevens (1959) has succinctly outlined the advantage of measurement by noting, "Measurement permits accurate, or objective, and communicable descriptions that can be readily manipulated in thinking." Objectivity occurs when the rules of measurement reduce the personal biases of observers. Because these rules provide a common language, descriptions are more efficiently communicated. By transforming the properties of an observable system into those of a logical system, measurement permits logical manipulation. This manipulation leads to new understanding and explanations of the structure of the real system.

Advantages of the systems approach follow from those of measurement. Masses of data are reduced to a general theory which is more capable of manipulation than the real system as found in nature. Through the manipulation of the reduced system, complex relationships become understandable. Nagel (1961) observed that Newtonian mechanics enable young students to analyze problems in the motion of bodies that previously had been too complex for the best minds of experienced scholars.

The disadvantages of these approaches accrue largely from the manner in which the researcher uses them. There is the danger that scientific marketers will become preoccupied with their methods and lose sight of their subject matter—people in the process of exchanging value. Another limitation is scientific myopia. The requirements of a model tend to introduce rigidities in scientific thinking at a point when the system should remain open for new hypotheses. Then there is the problem of the naive model. While a model is intended to simplify reality, there is the danger of oversimplification. The scientist must compromise between reality and data gathering problems on one hand, and workable, simplified models on the other.

Perhaps the most serious danger occurs when a scientist has a substantial investment of time and effort in a model and is unwilling to relinquish it for a fresh approach. Instead, he continues to modify an old model. Bross notes that this condition existed in astronomy when the earth was thought to be the center of the solar system and other bodies were thought to move in circles. When this model failed to predict the movement of other bodies, Ptolemaic astronomers changed the model from circles to epicycles, and then to epicycles on epicycles. Only after many years of poor predictions and struggling with the difficult calculations associated

with this model did they try the model which put the sun in the center.
Bross (1961) describes "epicyclitis" as a symptom of scientific senility.
The symptom may be observed in scientists of all ages and in all fields.

THE DEVELOPMENT OF A SCIENCE OF MARKETING

Whether a discipline is more or less scientific than another discipline
depends on the procedures used to explain the structural relationships
among properties, that is, its models. The more scientific discipline
searches beyond observables and explains the behavior of its systems with
deductive relationships (e.g., Figure 10–1). The less scientific discipline,
in contrast, depends on methods such as the correlation of observables
to explain its systems (e.g., Figure 10–2). Margenau (1950) places the
behavioral sciences among those which lack structure beyond the
observable.

Nagel's (1961) classifications of scientific explanations suggest that
marketing is not as crude a science as the Margenau observation would
suggest. The Nagel classifications, ranked from the most to the least scientific explanation, are as follows (pp. 20–26):

1. Deductive explanations using the formal structure of deductive argument in which the explicandum is a logical consequence of the
   premises.
2. Probabilistic explanations in which the ". . . premises do not
   formally imply their explicanda," but they make it probable.
3. Functional explanations (common in the biological and social sciences) which describe the role of subsystems in maintaining or achieving the goal of a system.
4. Genetic explanations which describe how a sequence of earlier events
   were transformed into later ones.

In general, marketing is moving from the functional to the probabilistic
level of scientific development. This movement is encouraging because
many observers consider probabilistic explanations as halfway stations to
deductive explanations.

In their search for a more scientific understanding of marketing systems,
marketing scholars should be encouraged by the fact that the highly refined
sciences of today have their origins in the practical problems of daily living.
Nagel points out that the problems of measuring and surveying fields resulted in geometry, the needs of architectural and military arts produced
the science of mechanics, problems in health and animal husbandry yielded

biology, the needs of the metallurgical and dyeing industries contributed to the development of chemistry, and household and political management brought about economics. Thus, marketers should not be disturbed by the practical and humble origins of their problems—the marketplace.

Using Boulding's (1956) nine levels of a general systems theory we see that the task facing the social scientists, and therefore marketers, is much greater than the one faced by the physical scientists. Marketing would be included among the behavior described in his level number eight, social organizations. (The distinction between the plant and animal kingdoms occurs at level six and the distinction between living and nonliving entities occurs at level four, where the concept of the open system is introduced.)

Marketers should not be discouraged by the magnitude of the task because considerable understanding is available through the lower level systems. Boulding places descriptive models for geography, chemistry, geology, anatomy, and the social sciences in level one. Physics is placed at level two, which includes dynamic systems that afford precise predictions. Economics approaches level three as it attempts to use cybernetic systems. Psychometric techniques, despite all of their crudeness, are attempts to measure a sixth level concept, that of image. Thus, if marketing could make contributions at level eight, as well as the lower levels, we would achieve a new interdisciplinary approach in marketing—that of marketing's *contributing* to other disciplines (Hughes, 1968).

THREE VIEWS OF THE MARKETING SYSTEM

Three quite different groups have a need for measures and models of the marketing system.[2] These include: market participants (buyers and sellers), regulators of the socioeconomic system (e.g., the Justice Department and the FTC), and marketing scholars. Each has a different perspective of the marketing system and therefore demands a different set of data. Their viewpoints may be distinguished by four characteristics: (1) their time horizons, (2) their levels of aggregation, (3) their goals, and (4) their rankings of three steps in the scientific process—description, prediction, and control.

The time horizon of the marketing manager is shorter than that of the regulator. The marketing scholar, in contrast, is interested in both long- and short-run behavior in the marketplace because he is concerned with the entire marketing system. With regard to aggregation, the perspective of the regulator is broader than that of the administrator in the firm.

---

[2] This discussion follows Hughes (1968).

The greatest differences among these three groups may be found in their goals. The manager is concerned with the optimization of his firm's system, the regulator is charged with maintaining the socioeconomic system in accordance with the values of society, and the scholar tries to explain the behavior of the entire system. The distinctions become more obvious when we examine their reasons for using measures. A marketing manager is concerned first with controlling his system, secondly with predicting how it will behave, and in a distant third, describing this behavior. Therefore, the manager is concerned with measures such as the productivity of the marketing mix. The scholar ranks these steps in the opposite order. He begins by describing marketing behavior. Prediction is a means for validating his explanations. Experimentation enables him to control variables to test the predictive ability of his model. The regulator or public administrator shares with the manager the sequence of reasons for needing measures of the marketing system—control, prediction, and description. But his measurement needs differ from the manager's because of differences in time horizon, aggregation, and goals. In addition, control has a different meaning at the public policy level. The regulator, in theory, is less concerned with controlling the socioeconomic system than assuring that it reflects the desires of society, not the power system of a few individuals. Therefore, measuring competition becomes central to many of the problems of the regulator.

SUMMARY

Scientific planning in marketing requires an appreciation of the roles of measures and models in the scientific process. To understand and explain behavior in the marketplace it is necessary to follow this process, which requires an unbiased description of the marketing system and predictions of its behavior under controlled conditions. Measures, models, and experimentation are the scientific procedures for achieving these ends.

Measurement is the process by which the magnitudes of the properties of an object are mapped into a system of logic, generally a numerical system. The goal of this process is to establish a one-to-one correspondence (i.e., isomorphism) between the magnitudes of the object and those of the numerical system so that the numbers represent the magnitude of the properties possessed by the object.

A model goes beyond a representation of the magnitude of properties by describing the structural relationship among properties. To model is to establish an isomorphism between the structure of the object and the structure of some system of logic. As with measurement, this system may be numerical, verbal, symbolic, physical, or graphic. The structure may be established by definition, rule, input-output relationships, or decision processes.

A system is a super model because it describes the structural relationships among many models. Graphs are frequently used as first approximations of a system. These graphs are replaced by a system of mathematical models as an understanding of the system improves.

The advantages of the scientific process are several. It permits accurate, objective, and communicable descriptions. It facilitates logical manipulation which leads to new insights into the behavior of the real system. The disadvantages accrue from the manner in which the scientist uses the process. Preoccupation with the process may emphasize structure to the exclusion of content. A scientist who has a substantial personal investment in a model may continue to modify it long past the point where he should have abandoned it and started afresh.

Marketing, like the behavioral sciences on which it builds, has a long way to go to achieve the scientific status of the physical sciences. Marketers' use of probabilistic explanations suggests that they are well on the way to deductive explanations, but Boulding's nine levels of a general system reveal that their task is more difficult than that of the physical scientists.

It is difficult to build a single marketing system that will meet the needs of buyers and sellers, regulators, and scholars. The view of each of these groups differs according to its time horizon, level of aggregation, goals, and its ranking of the importance of the three steps in the scientific process—description, prediction, and control.

READING QUESTIONS

1. What roles do measures and models perform?
2. How are the structures of models determined?
3. What is a system? Name several methods for representing systems.
4. What are some advantages and disadvantages of a measures, models, and systems approach to the study of marketing behavior?
5. Why is there a lack of communication between market participants, regulators of the socioeconomic system, and marketing scholars?

CLASS DISCUSSION QUESTIONS

1. Select some object and illustrate how the decision to be made determines the properties that will be measured.

2. You have been put in charge of a research project to improve marketing measuring instruments. Rank five instruments that you would select for research in decreasing order of the amount of money that you would allocate to each. Explain your choices and rankings.

3. What are some limitations of input-output analysis in demand analysis? Compare your discussion with that of Theil, Boot, and Klock (1965).

4. Why are behavioral models less developed than other marketing models?

5. Rank the behavioral sciences from the most to the least scientific and explain your ranking. What changes must take place in the lowest rank discipline to move it higher in your ranking?

SUGGESTED CASES

Continental Appliance Company. Bursk (1965), pp. 27–34.

A mobile demonstration unit and questionnaires were used to estimate the potential for three new types of dishwashers.

1. Analyze the strengths and weaknesses of the procedures used to select the best product. Did these procedures estimate market potential?

2. What changes, if any, would you make in the questionnaire?

Evaluating alternative modes of travel. Blackwell, Engel, and Kollat (1969), pp. 182–95.

Consumer research was sponsored by airlines to learn more about the air travel market.

1. Develop a model describing the probabilities of flying for each of the market segments in the case.

2. Develop a model for airline brand demand.

3. In each of the models indicate your estimate of standardized beta coefficients.

Falstaff Brewing Corporation (B). Newman (1967), pp. 123–42.

A consumer taste test of beers was conducted in Oakland, California, in an attempt to understand the poor sales of Falstaff in California.

1. Evaluate the sampling procedures.

2. Evaluate the measuring instruments. What additional ones would you recommend?

3. Was the statistical analysis appropriate for the instrument? Was the analysis complete?

General Foods Corporation—Maxim. Boyd and Davis (1971), pp. 267–306.

The Maxwell House Division of General Foods is formulating a marketing plan for its new instant coffee, Maxim, which uses the freeze-dry process.

1. Assume that you have been assigned the task of developing a computer simulation to help develop the plan. What variables would you consider? Distinguish between the independent and dependent variables.
2. From your knowledge of the behavioral sciences indicate the functional relationships between independent and dependent variables.

Pure Test Farms Dairy. Bursk (1965), pp. 19–23.

A market test and survey of preferences was used to test the attributes of a new cranberry-orange drink.

1. Evaluate the questionnaire and analysis.
2. Should the dairy make a decision or gather more information?
3. Did the dairy proceed in a scientific manner?

SUGGESTED READINGS

BLACKETT, G. H. "Measuring Raw Materials Needs to the Year 2000," *The Conference Board RECORD*, January 1971, pp. 23–28.

BLALOCK, H. M. JR., "The Measurement Problem: A Gap between the Languages of Theory and Research," in *Methodology in Social Research* (eds. H. M. Blalock and Ann B. Blalock), Chap. 1. New York: McGraw-Hill Book Co., 1968.

———. *Theory Construction: From Verbal to Mathematical Formulations.* Englewood Cliffs, N.J.: Prentice-Hall, Inc., 1969.

DUNCAN, O. D. "Path Analysis: Sociological Examples," *American Journal of Sociology,* Vol. 72 (1966), pp. 1–16.

———. "Contingencies in Constructing Causal Models," in *Sociological Methodology* (ed. E. F. Borgatta), San Francisco: Jossey-Bass, Inc., 1969.

EHRENBERG, A. S. C. "The Discovery and Use of Laws of Marketing," *Journal of Advertising Research,* Vol. 9, No. 2 (June 1969), pp. 11–17.

———. "Models of Fact: Examples from Marketing," *Management Science,* Vol. 16, No. 7. (March 1970), Theory Series, pp. 435–45.

ELLIOTT-JONES, M. F. "An Introduction to Input-Output Analysis," *The Conference Board RECORD*, January 1971, pp. 16–19.

EMSHOFF, JAMES R., and MERCER, ALAN. "Aggregate Models of Consumer Purchases," *Journal of the Royal Statistical Society, Series A. General,* Vol. 133, Part 1 (1970), pp. 14–32.

GREEN, P. E., and RAO, V. R. *Applied Multidimensional Scaling: A Comparison of Approaches and Algorithms.* New York: Holt, Rinehart & Winston, Inc., 1972.

LAVINGTON, MICHAEL R. "A Practical Microsimulation Model for Consumer Marketing," *Operational Research Quarterly,* Vol. 21, No. 1 (March 1970), pp. 25–45.

LIPSTEIN, BENJAMIN. "Modeling and New Product Birth," *Journal of Advertising Research,* Vol. 10, No. 5 (October 1970), pp. 3–11.

ZALTMAN, GERALD; ANGELMAR, REINHARD; and PINSON, CHRISTIAN. "Metatheory in Consumer Behavior Research," in Gardner (1971), pp. 476–97.

11

New trends in demand analyses

There are dramatic trends in the demographic, economic, sociological, and psychological forces that determine rates of consumption and production. These trends include reductions in the rate of population growth, a preference for leisure over consumption, introduction of the quality of life (e.g., ecology and health care) into economic and political decisions, and changing values toward materialism, productivity, interpersonal relations, and current institutions. The trends relevant to the demand for goods and services will be considered in this chapter.

The environment for demand analysis is influenced also by changes in styles of management. There is a shift from the tactics of problem solving to long-range planning, which includes the seeking of problems that lead to marketing opportunities. Thus, there is a greater need for improving the techniques of demand analysis. Two important trends in technique development will be noted.

NEW TRENDS IN THE DETERMINANTS OF DEMAND

Demographic trends

The most predictable characteristic of the population is its future age distribution because of the predictability with which crests and troughs move across age classifications. During the 1970s there will be a decline of one million persons in the 10–19 age classification, an increase of 9 million persons in the 20–29 age classification, and an increase of 9 million persons in the 30–39 age classification. In the 1960s there was an increase of 9 million persons in the 10- to 19-year-old classification, the 20–29 classification remained almost constant, and the 30–39 classification declined by approximately 2 million persons (Mayer, 1971; and U.S. Department of Commerce, Bureau of the Census, 1971).

The unanswered question for planners is one of values. Will the values of teen-agers become conservative as they move through the life cycle, or are some life styles permanent? The answer to this question will influence the strategy of those firms which focused on a youth market. Some authors predict the 1970s will be conservative (e.g., Wells, 1970; and Drucker, 1971).

Less certain is the rate of population growth. The rate will probably continue to decline because of basic changes in attitudes toward family formation and size. Marriages and the birth of the first child are being postponed, and there is a trend toward smaller families. "Automatic approval of large families has quietly gone out of style" (Mayer, 1971, p. 81).

There seems to be a desire to enjoy the good life before settling down. Mayer (1971) contrasts the typical life cycle with the emerging one. The present typical middle-class life cycle is an early marriage, three to four children, a house in the suburbs, two cars, commuting, the wife working part time when the children are in the teens, and trying to squeeze from a limited budget some travel, savings, and a college education for the children. The emerging cycle is a later marriage, the wife working longer before the first child and returning to work after the second child reaches six years of age, living nearer their work since both are working, and having more discretionary income. Planners whose products are related to the life cycle (Chapter 6) must reflect these changes in their long-range plans.

Present trends in education will continue, but there seems to be less of a commitment to college. Possible explanations include changing values and the fact that educational requirements for hiring exceed educational levels necessary for job performance, leading to frustrations and a misallocation of educational resources.

Changing determinants of GNP

The forces that determine the size of the Gross National Product (GNP) are changing on the demand and the supply sides of the equation. The important variables are no longer solely economic. New projections must reflect changes in attitudes and values. Silberman (1971) noted that accurate forecasts for the 1960s of first-time automobile owners made by *Fortune* magazine were based on consumer income, trends in scrappage rates, rates of growth in multiple car ownership, and judgments about styles and tastes. But such projections in the 1970s are questionable "in a decade in which nonmarket forces may be critical for both supply and demand" (ibid., p. 77).

Demand determinants. Two major influences on new patterns of demand are the role of government and changes in individual values. The public decision process is beginning to dominate areas that were largely private decisions (e.g., health care) and areas that were outside formal decision processes (e.g., ecology and the environment). To understand the demand patterns in these and related industries it will be necessary to include variables that reflect the political power structures and decision processes. Concurrent with this public influence are signs of privatization—industry's taking over services that were exclusively in the public sector, such as mail delivery, weather forecasting, remedial education in public schools, and private community security patrols.

Personal values seem to be influencing the direction of causality between income and spending. Consumption patterns are determining income. A family decides its life style and consumption patterns (Nicosia and Glock, 1968). The husband moonlights and the wife works to support this desired level of consumption (Silberman, 1971). Thus, the typical economic sequence of income's determining expenditures has been reversed. Evidence supporting this new direction of causality is found in the fact that more than half of the married men in the 25–44 age group have working wives, 40 percent work overtime, and about 10 percent moonlight (Silberman, 1971b).

Supply determinants. GNP projections based on the size of the labor force are influenced by the decisions of women to stay in the labor force by postponing marriage and families and by returning to work before their youngest child is a teen-ager. Productivity rates which influence GNP are subject to individual values toward work. There is no clear measure of the trends in these values. Some of the conflicting hypotheses have been summarized by Silberman (1971) and Mayer (1971). On one hand, the Protestant ethic may be giving way to an era of antimaterialism and a demand for more leisure and time with the family. On the other hand, there is a segment of Americans who have not become disillusioned with materialism because they have had so little of it. Professor Zbigniew Brezzinski of Columbia University views this segment as the preindustrial Americans, composed of sharecroppers, migrant farmers, and black immigrants to the city (quoted in Silberman, 1971, p. 76). Given the opportunity, this segment would be motivated toward high rates of productivity if they led to improved patterns of consumption. Somewhat counter to the latter hypothesis is the notion that the poorer youth may lack some drive because an affluent and humane society has relieved them of some of the responsibilities of family care (Mayer, 1971). Lacking evidence, we can conclude only that there is a need for measures and models of the influence of changing values on the productivity rates of workers. The work force of the 1970s will be young, so there is some urgency in understanding these values.

Changing values

The origins of changing values may be traced to the affluence generated by the Industrial Revolution. We seem to be experiencing an event previously unknown to man—the transition to a post-industrial society. Values such as the Protestant ethic, economic efficiency, and a preference for rational behavior are reinforced by the industrial society, but they seem to be inconsistent with the values of the post-industrial society. The transition of cultural values, organizational philosophies, ecological strategies associated with the move from an industrial society to a post-industrial society have been discussed by Schmidt (1970) and are summarized in Table 11–1. A careful examination of this table will suggest sectors of society

TABLE 11–1
The transition to post-industrialism

Type of change	From	Toward
Cultural values	Achievement Self-control Independence Endurance of distress	Self-actualization Self-expression Interdependence Capacity for joy
Organizational philosophies	Mechanistic forms Competitive relations Separate objectives Own resources regarded as owned absolutely	Organic forms Collaborative relations Linked objectives Own resources regarded also as society's
Ecological strategies	Responsive to crisis Specific measures Requiring consent Short planning horizon Damping conflict Detailed central control Small local government units Standardized administration Separate services	Anticipative of crisis Comprehensive measures Requiring participation Long planning horizon Confronting conflict Generalized central control Enlarged local government units Innovative administration Coordinated services

Source: Schmidt (1970), p. 32.

that subscribe to the older values and other sectors that have adopted the new values. The interaction of such sectors can be described simply as an inability to communicate. In the extreme, the conflict of values takes on the irreconcilable state of a religious war.

The emerging intellectual, moral, and cultural era has been characterized as a weakening of the Protestant ethic; a revolution in sex mores; an emphasis on the immediate; a questioning of authority, tradition, and customs; and a search for a meaning and purpose in life outside work (Silberman, 1971). The implication of these changing values to marketing planning is only beginning to be appreciated. For instance, there is less emotional attachment toward automobiles among the higher income, better educated young adults; therefore they will be insensitive to promotion based on the status of a brand. Market segments may be based on buyers' societal orientation—the degree to which they are willing to forego personal satisfaction for the well-being of society (Kelley, 1971). The fragmentation of the formerly homogeneous middle class complicates the merchandising policies of department stores. What is the optimal assortment of men's clothing and furnishings? Should the latest styles be in the same department with conservative styles or should there be separate style boutiques? In conclusion, the changing of values requires a revaluation of present marketing strategies.

"The marketer has no satisfactory source of information to draw upon for relevant changes in the social environment—changes in the consumers' needs, values, and life styles. And yet, increasingly in recent years, here is where the action is" (Yankelovich, 1971, p. 37).

Two broad approaches for measuring trends in values have been identified by Yankelovich—the futurist and social indicators (pp. 42–43). The futurist approach deduces changes in values from projected changes in technology, population, and institutions. This approach draws on experts with diverse backgrounds, frequently using the Delphi method to sift through the ideas (e.g., North and Pyke, 1969). The social indicators approach searches for leading indicators of social change, similar to leading indicators of business cycles (Bauer, 1966). There has been little formal effort in marketing to measure values, with the exception of Yankelovich, and Pessemier, whose work will be summarized shortly. Psychographic and activity measures (Chapter 7) are situation-specific personality measures which permit only an inference of values, not a direct measurement.

Yankelovich stresses the need to measure directly trends in consumer needs, values, attitudes, beliefs, and behavior. Unstructured approaches are necessary to identify new trends, while structured methods are required to measure changes in the composition and rate of growth of a trend. Thus, many of the methods discussed in Chapter 9 may be adapted to measuring values.

Thirty-one social trends that tend to alter consumption have been reported by Yankelovich (1971) and summarized in Table 11–2. A trend

TABLE 11–2
Social trends that alter consumption

Psychology of affluence
  Physical self-enhancement
  Personalization through new life styles
  Physical health and well-being ·
  Antimaterialism
  Personal and cultural self-expression
  Personal creativity
  Meaningful work
Quest for excitment and stimulation to counteract the practical and the mundane
  New romanticism, mystery, and adventure
  Search for novelty and change
  Stress on beauty
  Sensuousness, moving away from linear, logical, and visual
  Search for spiritual experience, mysticism
  Introspection and self-understanding
Reactions against the complexity of modern life
  Life simplification
  Return to nature
  Increased ethnicity
  Increased community involvement
  Distrust of tradition, confidence in science
  Departure from bigness is good
New values replacing puritanical values
  Pleasure for its own sake
  Blurring of the sexes
  Living for the present
  Liberal sexual attitudes
  Acceptance of stimulants and drugs for mood change, instead of strength of character alone
  Relaxation of standards for working and self-improvement
  Substitution of personal experience for institutionalized religion
Values derived from the child-centered homes of the 1940s and 1950s
  Greater tolerance of chaos and disorder
  Challenging of authority
  Rejection of hyporcrisy
  Female careerism
  Renewed faith in the family as a social unit

Source: Yankelovich (1971).

may have marketing and nonmarketing implications. For example, a tolerance of chaos and disorder emerges in marketing as consumer acceptance of disorderly stores; unplanned meals; less compulsiveness about cleaning, polishing, and neat refrigerators; and unplanned travel. The nonmarketing effects of this tolerance emerge as campus disorders, social protests, and acceptance of taboo topics (ibid., 45). By studying Table 11–2, the long-range planner will gain new insight into the behavior of buyers in his market segments, especially those segments which are influenced by the youth culture.

Pessemier, DeBruicker, and Hustad (1971) have conducted an extensive survey of consumer behavior that will give insight into the relationships among demographic dimensions, attitudes, activities, values, and buying behavior. Values were measured using scales developed by Rokeach (1968–69) and found useful in public opinion research. These researchers converted the task given to the respondent from a ranking task to anchor-point scaling, so that the Rokeach scale could be used in a mail survey.[1]

The Rokeach scales measure instrumental and terminal values. Instrumental values are acceptable modes of behavior. Some of the values in the instrumental scale are as follows: ambitious, cheerful, forgiving, imaginative, obedient, and responsible. Terminal values, end states of existence, include the following: comfortable life, sense of accomplishment, equality, inner harmony, mature love, and social recognition.

NEW TRENDS IN MANAGEMENT STYLES

A shift from problem solving to problem anticipation

Until recently, marketing management techniques have emphasized the tactics of management, such as models for allocating resources to the marketing mix or selecting the optimal media mix. This type of management may be characterized as problem solving. As noted in Chapter 1, identification of opportunities and the development of a marketing strategy precedes the development of tactics. Long-range planning, therefore, may be defined as an application of the scientific method to problem anticipation. In the future, marketing planning will give greater emphasis to demand analysis than has been the general practice.

A concern for societal goals

Meaningful work and social ends have not replaced power and profit as the goals of administrators and corporations, but societal goals are acknowledged as constraints on profit maximization. For instance, it may be necessary to incorporate the ecology into a marketing strategy (Kassarjian, 1971). The recycling of solid wastes may require the develop-

---

[1] For a discussion of ranking and anchor-point techniques, see Hughes (1971b).

ment of costly reverse channels of distribution (Zikmund and Stanton, 1971).

Marketing techniques seem to have immediate application for organizations with societal goals. Kotler and Zaltman (1971) conclude that the techniques can be applied to planning for social change. The marketers of public services, such as health care, can benefit from a knowledge of marketing techniques (Zaltman and Vertinsky, 1971; White, 1970; Simon, 1968). The application of marketing techniques to family planning has been examined by many marketers (Farley and Leavitt, 1968 and 1971; O'Connor, 1970; Urban, 1970).

The concern for societal goals creates many needs that can lead to new products, such as soda drinks in biodegradable containers, or a freeze-dry soda drink to which water is added. But, as noted in Chapters 8 and 9, need is not motivation. Motivation is an awareness of a need *and* an acceptance of a means for meeting the need. Thus, promotional techniques must be used to make these new, socially desirable products more attractive to buyers than the products presently being used.

NEW TRENDS IN DEMAND ANALYSIS TECHNIQUES

The review of demand analysis techniques in previous chapters reveals two trends that should be emphasized. The first trend is the growing importance of multivariate and nonmetric techniques for identifying the dimensions and structure of demand. Market segmentation is accomplished using techniques such as factor analysis, cluster analysis, the AID algorithm, multiple regression, and multidimensional scaling. Examples of the AID algorithm were presented in earlier chapters because the characteristics of this technique are particularly appropriate for demand analysis (Chapter 4). Extensive examples of all multivariate methods are outside the pale of the present discussion, especially when excellent discussions of these methods are readily available.[2] Methods have been classified according to the number of variables, the dependency among variables, and whether they have been measured by metric or nonmetric techniques (Sheth, 1971; Kinnear and Taylor, 1971).

The second trend is in the development of instruments to measure activities. Activities, it will be recalled from Chapter 7, are situation-specific

---

[2] For a review of multivariate techniques as they apply to marketing, see Gatty (1966); Sheth (1971); and Aaker (1971). For a presentation of nonmetric multidimensional scaling see Green and Rao (1971). The need for nonmetric multivariate techniques is discussed by Green and Rao (1972). A nontechnical discussion of factor analysis as it applies to marketing may be found in Wells and Sheth (in press). Kotler (1971) provides a nontechnical presentation of multiple regression.

personality variables. The situation in the marketing case is the environment in which the product is bought and consumed. Pessemier and Bruno (1971) examined the reliability of activity scales that were common to eight surveys conducted between 1963 and 1970. They concluded that reliability was high and that it is now possible to develop standardized instruments to measure activities. The standardization of instruments represents an important step in any scientific effort.

SUMMARY

Demand analysis is the study of the decision processes that lead to the purchase and consumption of goods and services. There are three trends which will increase the need for demand analyses and alter the manner in which they will be conducted—shifts in the determinants of demand, changes in management styles, and new tools for conducting the analyses.

Plans for periods beyond 5 or 10 years should reflect a decline in the rate of population growth, which is the result of the tendency to postpone marriage and family formation and the preference for smaller families. This change in the typical middle-class life cycle will change the demand patterns for products related to family formation.

A new relationship between consumption and income seems to be emerging. Families select a life style that determines their consumption patterns and members of the family work at a level that will generate the income to support the consumption. Thus, the size of the labor force is determined partly by life styles. The productivity of the labor is determined by values toward materialism and leisure. While values are gaining importance as determinants of supply and demand, there has been little attempt to measure them directly and systematically over time.

Management styles are shifting from problem solving to problem anticipation. The former is tactical and must be preceded by the development of strategies. Strategies, in turn, require an assessment of opportunities. The function of demand analysis is the identification of marketing opportunities. Long-range planning may be defined as the application of the scientific process to anticipating problems and identifying opportunities. A concern with societal goals influences management styles by creating marketing opportunities for new products and services, by increasing the cost of producing and delivering a product, and through the introduction of public decision processes in areas that were formerly private.

Shifts in the determinants of demand and new management styles create a greater need for demand analyses. Future analyses will benefit from the development of multivariate statistical techniques and new measuring instruments, particularly those which measure marketing activities and individual values.

READING QUESTIONS

1. Which trend do you think will be the most influential in:
   —determining demand?
   —determining supply?
2. Of what importance to marketers are measures of values, personalities, and life styles?
3. How does the movement toward a post-industrial society affect marketing decisions?

CLASS DISCUSSION QUESTIONS

1. How will noneconomic forces determine the goals of marketing organizations?
2. How will noneconomic forces change the present methods of marketing management?
3. How should changing personal values be incorporated into a formal demand analysis? How will they change marketing strategies?
4. Identify the characteristics of the major market segments of the next decade.

SUGGESTED CASES

Donahue Sales Corporation (B). Newman (1967), pp. 159–89.

Depth interviews and projective techniques were used to determine the motivations for home sewing and to determine how the use of zippers might be promoted.

1. Redesign the study to lower the costs by eliminating the depth interviews.
2. What conclusions do the findings permit?
3. What additional variables would be required to update the study?

Foremost Dairies, Inc. (B). Newman (1967), pp. 143–49.

Flavor-concept testing was conducted to determine new flavors that should be offered in the following year, the name of the new flavors, and the promotional strategy.

1. Has the motivation for buying ice cream been identified adequately?
2. Is the interview guide adequate for the goals of the study?

3.   Do the findings permit the development of a promotional strategy? What additional information would you like and would it be worth the cost of generating it?

Sanka Coffee (B). Newman (1967), pp. 210–40.

To evaluate the product strategy for Sanka Coffee, a personal interview was conducted with 1,150 U.S. homemakers. An extensive questionnaire was used during the interviews.

1.   Assume you have been asked to conduct a new study for Sanka Coffee. Would you use any of the items in the old questionnaire? Give reasons for your answer.

2.   What new items would you add to the questionnaire as a result of new developments in attitude measurement?

3.   What type of analysis do you recommend?

SUGGESTED READINGS ──────────────────────────────────

AAKER, DAVID A. (ed.). *Multivariate Analysis in Marketing: Theory and Application.* Belmont, Calif.: Wadsworth Publishing Co., Inc., 1971.

BAUER, R. A., and GERGEN, K. J. *The Study of Policy Formation.* New York: Free Press, 1968.

BRZEZINSKI, A. K. "America in the Technotronic Age," *Encounter,* January 1968, pp. 16–26.

INGLIS, J., and JOHNSON, D. "Some Observations on, and Developments in, The Analysis of Multivariate Survey Data," *Journal of the Market Research Society,* Vol. 12, No. 2. (April 1970), pp. 75–98.

KATONA, GEORGE. *Aspiration and Affluence.* New York: McGraw-Hill Book Co., 1971.

PITTEL, S. M., and MENDELSOHN, G. A. "The Measurement of Moral Values," *Psychological Bulletin,* Vol. 66 (1966), pp. 22–35.

SHETH, J. N. "The Multivariate Revolution in Marketing Research," *Journal of Marketing,* Vol. 34 (January 1971), pp. 13–19.

SKINNER, B. F. *Beyond Freedom and Dignity.* New York: Alfred A. Knopf, Inc., 1971.

Appendix A

Selected sources of data for demand analyses

G. DAVID HUGHES AND
SUSANNE B. HENDSEY*

The following annotated sources have been compiled to provide a basic bibliography of data sources for the planner when he is conducting a demand analysis. The references are arranged by subject category and follow the outline of the text wherever possible. The sources were selected on the basis of their comprehensive coverage; however, some examples of specific data (e.g., media research) have been included for illustrative purposes.

I. GENERAL MARKETING SOURCES

A. Marketing bibliographies

American Newspaper Publishers Association. Bureau of Advertising. *Research Studies and Reports Published by Newspapers in the United States and Canada.* New York: American Newspaper Publishers Association, 1971. Irregular.

Listing and abstracts of studies done by newspapers arranged by:
1. Consumer analysis
2. Ten top brands
3. Continuing home audit
4. Special subjects

* Susanne B. Hendsey is the Senior Assistant Librarian, Business and Public Administration Library, Cornell University. The authors acknowledge with gratitude the assistance of Miss Betsy Ann Olive, Librarian, Business and Public Administration Library, Cornell University.

5. Audience and markets

6. Canada

"Available Market Data," *Advertising Age.* Chicago, Advertising Publications, Inc. Annual feature of an April or May issue.

Annotated bibliography of over 1,000 recent and/or to be published materials which are available by coupon order free of charge or for a nominal fee. Arranged by subjects including national markets, farm markets, regional and local markets, distribution markets, industrial markets, professional and institutional markets, Canadian market, and international markets.

Bibliography of Consumer Magazine Research. 3d ed. New York: Association of National Advertisers, 1969.

Subject index of material "done by and for magazines." Covers topics from apparel through beverages, office machines, sporting goods, and travel.

Carpenter, Robert N. *Guidelist for Marketing Research and Economic Forecasting.* New York: American Management Association, 1966.

Somewhat dated, but excellent annotated bibliography covering marketing and forecasting materials. Many government and private sources are cited. Arranged by bibliographies, forecasts, statistical summaries, maps and market guides, production, population, consumers, financial data, and associations. Subject index.

Coman, Edwin T. Jr. *Sources of Business Information.* Rev. ed. Berkeley: University of California Press, 1964.

Although an older work, it is still a useful bibliography covering general business sources. Arranged by broad chapter headings such as foreign trade, management, and statistical sources. Commentary on the usefulness of the various sources. Covers books, directories, periodicals, and services. The last chapter entitled "A Basic Bookshelf" gives a good checklist for personal use.

Disch, Wolfgang K. A. *Bibliothe Bibliographie zur Marktforschung. Bibliography on Marketing Research. Bibliographie sur l'Etude des Marchés.* 2. erweiterte Aufl. Hamburg: Welt-Wirtschafts-Archiv, 1964.

A little dated, but very thorough bibliography covering foreign language and English marketing materials. Covers fundamental works, methods, sales forecasting, sales planning, market research, etc. Arranged alphabetically under books and then periodicals. Bibliographies, glossaries, and periodicals are listed separately. Citations are mostly in English, French, or German. 2,477 items listed.

Encyclopedia of Business Information Sources. Edited by Paul Wasserman. Detroit: Gale Research Co., 1970. 2 vols.

Excellent sourcebook to be used as a guide for beginning marketing search. Subject arrangement is quite specific, including materials on adhesives through zoological gardens. Cites encyclopedias and dictionaries, periodicals, trade associations, handbooks, bibliographies, statistical sources, almanacs, yearbooks, general works, abstract services, indexes, and directories. Gives address, price, frequency.

Frank, Nathalie D. *Data Sources for Business and Market Analysis.* 2d ed. Metuchen, N.J.: Scarecrow Press, 1969.

Comprehensive annotated bibliography of current marketing and statistical sources. Included are market data guides, university programs, advertising media, periodicals, and abstracting services. The chapters on federal statistical publications are extremely informative, and Miss Frank's annotations and commentaries on use are very helpful to the uninitiated.

"Market Information Guide," *Industrial Marketing.* Chicago, Advertising Publications, Inc. Annual feature of a fall issue.

Annotated listing of marketing material on market size, trends, buyers, brand preferences, etc., published by business firms. Available free items are obtained by using Readers' Service Cards; others available directly from publisher. Arranged by broad industry headings.

Pennington, Allan, and Peterson, Robert A. *Reference Guide to Marketing Literature.* Braintree, Mass.: D. H. Mack Publishing Co., 1970.

Bibliography of current articles by author or title; numbered code gives subject. 3,000 articles from 12 journals including *Fortune, Journal of Marketing Research,* and *Business Horizons.*

Revzan, David A. *A Comprehensive Classified Marketing Bibliography.* Berkeley: University of California Press, 1951. 2 vols.

Excellent bibliography covering materials in books, journals, and government publications. Divided into material published prior to 1930 and that published 1930–50. Arranged by subjects such as marketing history, prices, sales analysis, government, trade marks, retailing, etc. Author index. Useful for retrospective searching.

Extended from 1950 through 1962 by:

Revzan, David A. *A Comprehensive Classified Marketing Bibliography,* Supplement 1, Parts 1 and 2. Berkeley: Institute of Business and Economic Research, University of California, 1963. 2 vols.

Revzan, David A. *A Geography of Marketing.* Berkeley: Institute of Business and Economic Research, University of California, 1968.

Retrospective bibliography covering 1880s to 1968. Arranged by broad subject classifications such as: locational determinants, trading area patterns, spatial competition, human populations, geographical variations, uses of geography, etc. Subdivided by books and articles. Each item is numbered for cross-referencing.

Special Libraries Association, Advertising and Marketing Division. *What's New in Advertising and Marketing.* New York, Special Libraries Association. Monthly.

Listing of recent books, marketing research projects, government, university, and trade publications in the marketing field. Many available free of charge from the publisher. Arranged by broad subject headings. Excellent means of keeping up with current marketing material.

Wasserman, Paul (ed.). *Statistics Sources.* 3d ed. Detroit: Gale Research Co., 1971.

Bibliography of statistical sources. Extensively indexed are *United Nations Statistical Yearbook* and *Statistical Abstract of the United States.* Includes many primary sources and some secondary statistical sources. Gives addresses. Arranged by subject with subdivisions, includes much geographical information. Very useful annotated bibliography of bibliographies, government publications, yearbooks, and international sources.

B. General government sources

1. GENERAL GUIDES

U.S. government agencies publish voluminous materials on a wide variety of subjects. To help understand the publishing program of the government, the following serve as excellent guides:

Boyd, Anne M. *United States Government Publications.* 3d ed. Revised by Rae Elizabeth Rips. New York: The H. W. Wilson Co., 1949.

Although a little dated, this reference work still serves as a basic handbook on public documents. Arranged by issuing agency with brief descriptions of that agency's typical publications.

Schmeckebier, Laurence, and Eastin, Ray B. *Government Publications and Their Use.* 2d ed. Washington, D.C.: Brookings Institute, 1969.

Definitive survey of U.S. government publications divided by type: congressional, federal laws, foreign affairs, etc. Tells how publications are issued and how to use them.

2. GUIDES TO FEDERAL STATISTICS

Androit, John L. *Guide to U.S. Government Serials & Periodicals.* McLean, Va.: Documents Index, 1971. 4 vols. in 3.

Useful annotated listing of government serial publications arranged by Superintendent of Documents number. Includes section on government agencies with brief historical description and a listing of publications of discontinued agencies.

Beginning in 1972 basic volumes are scheduled to be published annually in March and supplemented in September.

Directory of Non-Federal Statistics for States and Local Areas, a Guide to Sources. Washington, D.C.: U.S. Bureau of the Census, 1969.

Arranged by state and then by topic. Gives sources of primary statistics in serial publications or books with data no older than 1960. Covers social, political, and economic statistics.

U.S. Bureau of the Budget. Office of Statistical Standards. *Statistical Services of the United States Government.* Washington, D.C., U.S. Government Printing Office. Irregular.

Guide to the organization of U.S. government statistics. Explains which department is responsible for collecting data falling under broad subject headings of demography, social statistics, foreign trade, construction, etc.

Part III gives listing of federal agencies and an annotated listing of their principal publications. *Statistical Reporter* publishes current and future publications on statistical activities.

Bureau of the Budget now Office of Management and Budget.

U.S. Bureau of the Census. *Catalog of Publications.* Washington, D.C., U.S. Government Printing Office. Monthly. Cumulates annually from quarterly issues and monthly supplements.

Listing of Bureau publications arranged by census with special section of available data tabulations. Annotated citations.

————. *Census Bureau Programs and Publications Area and Subject Guide.* Washington, D.C.: U.S. Government Printing Office, 1968.

Catalog of Bureau of the Census publications under broad subject headings of agriculture, construction, distribution, foreign trade, etc. Gives program, title or report, area covered, and subjects included for each.

————. *Directory of Federal Statistics for Local Areas, a Guide to Sources.* Washington, D.C.: U.S. Government Printing Office, 1966.

Handbook to published federal statistical data on population, education, income, prices, banking, etc. for countries, cities, SMSA's.

————. *Directory of Federal Statistics for States.* Washington, D.C.: U.S. Government Printing Office, 1967.

A guide to federal sources of statistics on social, political, and economic subjects by states. Arranged by subject; gives sources and frequency.

U.S. Business and Defense Services Administration. *Measuring Markets: A Guide to the Use of Federal and State Statistical Data.* Washington, D.C.: U.S. Government Printing Office, 1966.

Handy publication giving data by topic such as population from federal and state sources. Also included are sample cases with citations as to source of statistics. Bibliography with addresses completes publication.

U.S. Superintendent of Documents. *Monthly Catalog: United States Public Documents.* Washington, D.C., U.S. Government Printing Office. Monthly. Index in each issue, with cumulative index in December issue.

Listing of recent government publications available from issuing office or U.S. Government Printing Office. Arranged by issuing department or bureau. Full bibliographic information given, including price.

C.   Directories

1.   TRADE DIRECTORIES

Guide to American Directories, a Guide to the Major Business Directories of the United States Covering All Industrial, Professional and Mercantile Categories. Edited by Bernard Klein. 7th ed. New York: B. Klein Co., 1968.

Annotated directory arranged alphabetically by topic. Comprehensive coverage on directories published by business and reference book publishers, magazines, government agencies, and trade associations. Annotations give price and address.

Handbook of Marketing Research in Europe. Amsterdam, European Society for Opinion and Marketing Research. Annual.

Directory of international organizations and individual country organizations. Gives addresses, personnel, services, and publications of marketing research organizations. Membership directory by country with individuals listed alphabetically with company affiliation.

National Directory of Newsletters and Reporting Services. Detroit: Gale Research Co., 1966.

A directory of newsletters, information services, financial services, bulletins, training and educational services in the following classifications: agriculture, conservation, natural resources, business, industry, economics, construction, real estate, education, hobbies, humanities, investment advisory services, law, insurance, taxation, public affairs, social services, religion, science, medicine, health, and training materials.

Trade Directories of the World. New York, Croner Publications, Inc. Monthly. Country arrangement and directories listed alphabetically under country. Price, annotation, address, frequency for each item. Indices by trade, profession, and country.

2. MARKETING RESEARCH AGENCIES DIRECTORIES

Advertising Research Foundation. *Directory of Research Organization Members.* New York: Advertising Research Foundation, 1968.

Alphabetical listing and brief description by member companies. Subject and geographic index.

American Marketing Association. *Directory of Marketing Services and Membership Roster.* Chicago, American Marketing Association. Annual.

Alphabetical and classified listings of marketing research organizations, includes address, personnel, and brief descriptions of services. The biographical section of AMA members is alphabetical with very brief biographical information.

Anderson, Ian Gibson. *Marketing and Management: A World Register of Organizations.* Edited by I. G. Anderson in cooperation with the Institute of Marketing. Beckenham: C.B.D. Research, 1969.

Directory of marketing organizations. Arranged by international organizations and then by country. Brief description includes founding date, address, publications. Abbreviations index, publications index, general index.

Bradford's Directory of Marketing Research Agencies and Management Consultants in the United States and the World. Fairfax, Va., Bradford's Directory of Marketing Research Agencies. Biennial.

Listing of over 500 marketing research agencies by state and city. Foreign firms are listed by country. Includes address, brief summary of services, and staff. Also has subject classification listing and index of personnel. Handy tabulation of population estimates and projections for the U.S. rounds out this fine directory.

Green Book: International Directory of Marketing Research Houses and Services. Chicago, American Marketing Association. Annual.

Alphabetical listing of marketing research agencies. Gives address, personnel, and brief summary of services. Geographic index is also included.

D. Indices

Applied Science & Technology Index. New York, H. W. Wilson, Co. Monthly, with quarterly and annual cumulations.

Subject index to periodicals in scientific and technological fields.

Business Periodicals Index. New York, H. W. Wilson Co. Monthly. Cumulative (except August).

Subject index to English language periodical articles in accounting, advertising and public relations, automation, banking, communications, economics, finance and investments, insurance, labor, management, marketing, taxation, and specific businesses, industries, and trades.

Funk and Scott Index. International. Cleveland, Ohio, Predicasts, Inc. Monthly with annual cumulation.

Worldwide abstracting service of over 800 foreign and U.S. business, trade, and bank publications. Over 75,000 abstracts for industries, countries, and firms for all countries except the United States are included.

Funk and Scott Index of Corporations and Industries. Cleveland, Ohio, Predicasts, Inc. Weekly, monthly, quarterly, semiannual, and annual cumulations.

Abstracting service of over 750 U.S. business and trade publications. Arranged by SIC number for industry and product with a separate company listing. Excellent source for information on American industry.

Market Research Abstracts. London, Market Research Society. Semiannual.

British abstracting service covering many American journals. Subject arrangement under broad headings such as techniques, attitude research, etc. Abstracts are quite extensive.

Complemented by:

Industrial Marketing Research Abstracts. Lechfield, Staffordshire, Industrial Marketing Research Association. Semiannual.

"Marketing Abstracts," *Journal of Marketing.* Quarterly.

Reviews of marketing articles found in business, trade, and government publications. All reviews are signed. Arrangement is alphabetical under 22 general subject headings. Published quarterly as part of the *Journal.*

Marketing Information Guide. Washington, D.C., U.S. Bureau of Domestic Commerce. Monthly.

Abstracting service of articles, books, and government publications related to marketing. Arranged by topic.

New York Times Index. New York, The New York Times Co. Semimonthly, annual cumulation.

Subject index of articles appearing in the Late City edition. Summaries of articles often give enough information that there is no necessity to consult paper. Many cross-references add to ease of use.

Predicasts. Cleveland, Ohio, Predicasts, Inc. Quarterly, annual cumulations.

One line abstracts on growth expectations of many detailed products from over 500 trade, financial, government sources. Arrangement is by Standard Industrial Classification number. Gives both short- and long-term forecasts. General projections on U.S. economic conditions giving population, employment, and GNP are very useful for quick reference.

Public Affairs Information Service Bulletin. New York, Public Affairs Information Service, Inc. Weekly, fortnightly in August. Cumulates five times a year.

A weekly subject list of the "latest books, pamphlets, government publications, reports of public and private agencies and periodical articles, relating to economic and social conditions, public administration, and international relations."

Wall Street Journal Index. Princeton, N.J., Dow Jones & Co., Inc. Monthly, yearly cumulations.

Subject index of news items appearing in final Eastern Edition. Brief summary of article helpful in identifying. Divided into two sections, one on the general news, and the other on corporation news. Handy inclusion is daily Dow Jones average.

World-Regional-Casts. Cleveland, Ohio, Predicasts, Inc. Quarterly.

Abstracting service covering foreign and U.S. government, trade, and bank publications. Arranged by region or country and by product. Each quarterly issue covers different world region.

Companion volume is *World-Product-Casts.* Quarterly.

Abstracting service covering "comparative country data for a single product." Each quarterly issue covers different products and industries.

E.   Criteria for evaluating research

Advertising Research Foundation. *Criteria for Marketing and Advertising Research.* New York: Advertising Research Foundation, 1963.

Useful checklist for evaluating research.

American Marketing Association. *Criteria to Assist Users of Marketing Research.* Chicago, 1962.

Simple, but handy guide to use in evaluating the worth and need for market research.

Gordon, William C. *Selecting Marketing Research Services.* Washington, D.C.: Small Business Administration, 1960.

Very general coverage of types of services and sources available in marketing. Tells how to choose one for your needs.

Mayer, Charles S. "Evaluating the Quality of Marketing Research Contractors," *Journal of Marketing Research,* Vol. 4 (May 1967), pp. 134–41.

Explanation of contractor rating system for evaluating marketing research.

National Industrial Conference Board. *Using Marketing Consultants and Research Agencies.* New York: National Industrial Conference Board, 1966.

Study of over 280 executives and their policies in selecting marketing research organizations. Gives information on selection, financial arrangements, and follow up.

II. DEMOGRAPHIC VARIABLES

A. Sources of data

United Nations. *Demographic Yearbook*. New York, United Nations. Annual.
Vital statistics data for countries of the world. Estimates given where data unavailable.

United Nations Educational, Scientific and Cultural Organization. *Statistical Yearbook*. Paris, UNESCO. Annual.
Social statistics for over 200 countries covering libraries, population, education, films, TV, etc.

U.S. Bureau of the Census. *Census of Population*. Washington, D.C.: U.S. Government Printing Office, 1970.
Basic source for demographic data. Consists of statistics on number of inhabitants, general population characteristics, general social and economic characteristics, and detailed characteristics.

————. *County and City Data Book*. Washington, D.C.: U.S. Government Printing Office, 1967.
Data on a variety of topics including vital statistics, employment, income, housing, manufacturers, and hospitals. Arranged by state, county, SMSA's, and cities.

————. *Current Population Reports*. Washington, D.C., U.S. Government Printing Office. Irregular population publications issued in separate series. Includes:
Population Characteristics (Series P-20)
Special Studies (Series P-23)
Population Estimates and Projections (Series P-25)
Federal State Cooperative Program for Population Estimates (Series P-26)
Farm Population (Series P-27)
Special Censuses (Series P-28)
Consumer Income (Series P-60)
Consumer Buying Indicators (Series P-65)

————. *Historical Statistics of the United States*. Washington, D.C.: U.S. Government Printing Office, 1960.
1960 supplement to *Statistical Abstract* giving historical data from 1610–1957. Covers vital and health statistics, migrations, labor, prices, consumer income,

etc. Most of the series are presented on an annual basis. Notes and sources given. Revised and updated by Bureau of the Census in its *Continuation to 1962 and Revisions.*

Both publications are available in one volume in *The Statistical History of the United States from Colonial Times to the Present.* Stamford, Conn.: Fairfield Publishers, 1965.

————. *Statistical Abstract of the United States.* Washington, D.C., U.S. Government Printing Office. Annual.

Since 1878 the *Statistical Abstract* has been the standard source for statistical data on the United States. Volume includes a variety of subjects including finance, transportation, vital statistics, welfare services, etc. in tabular form. Sources given for each table. Also included is a bibliography, "Guide to Sources of Statistics," which lists basic references for statistical data by subject.

U.S. Business and Defense Services Administration. *Facts for Marketers.* Washington, D.C.: U.S. Government Printing Office, 1966. 9 vols.

Nine regional volumes that include 100 Standard Metropolitan Statistical Area market studies. Brings together in a standard format data from selected government sources on population and housing characteristics, employment, income, industry sales by retail, wholesale, and selected service trades, and consumer expenditures.

B. Selected examples of applications

Additional statistical data can be found in many government publications. The U.S. Superintendent of Documents' *Monthly Catalog* and the Bureau of the Census' *Catalog of Publications* serve as indices to these publications. Examples of health, education, and housing statistics follow:

Health, Education and Welfare Indicators. Washington, D.C., U.S. Government Printing Office. Monthly; annual supplement.

Health, education, vital statistics, and social security statistical information and articles of current relevance. *Health, Education and Welfare Trends* supplements annually.

Monthly Vital Statistics Report. Washington, D.C., Public Health Service. Monthly.

Provisional data on mortality, marriage, birth, etc. by state and some cities.

U.S. Bureau of the Census. *Census of Housing.* Washington, D.C.: U.S. Government Printing Office, 1970.

Statistical data on tenure, vacancy, plumbing, rent and block statistics for 236 urbanized areas and 42 small cities in the United States.

————. *Current Housing Reports.* Washington, D.C., U.S. Government Printing Office.

Current statistics on housing vacancy rates and characteristics by geographic region are included in:

Housing Characteristics. Irregular.

Housing Vacancies. Quarterly.

U.S. National Center for Health Statistics. *Vital Statistics of the United States.* Washington, D.C., U.S. Government Printing Office. Annual.

Definitive publication of vital statistics containing extensive basic data.

U.S. Office of Education. *Digest of Educational Statistics.* Washington, D.C., U.S. Government Printing Office. Annual.

Compilation of statistical data on school enrollments, finances, federal programs, graduates, etc. Covers historical and current materials. Sources given.

————. *Projections of Educational Statistics.* Washington, D.C., U.S. Government Printing Office. Annual.

Annual publication which serves as a supplement to *Digest of Educational Statistics.* Statistics on finances, enrollments, graduates, etc. are projected for the next 10 years. Contains articles.

III.   ECONOMIC VARIABLES

A.   General economic conditions

The *Statistical Abstract of the United States* provides in one handy reference work extensive economic data. For more detailed statistics see the following citations:

Business Conditions Digest. Washington, D.C., U.S. Bureau of the Census. Monthly.

Economic time series for national income and product accounts, cyclical indicators, anticipations of consumers, and other indicators presented in graphic and tabular form. Also included are instructions on interpreting the data and methodology.

The Conference Board Statistical Bulletin. New York, The Conference Board. Monthly.

Statistics covering GNP, projections, diffusion indexes, and purchasing power trends.

Economic Indicators. Prepared for Joint Economic Committee by Council of Economic Advisors. Washington, D.C., U.S. Government Printing Office. Monthly.

Charts and graphs on personal income, corporate profits, new plant expenditures, wages, wholesale prices, etc. to provide an overview of the economy.

The Handbook of Basic Economic Statistics. Washington, D.C., Economics Statistics Bureau of Washington, D.C. Monthly. Cumulates each month. Handbook of 1,800 series based on government statistics with data on: employment and earnings, production, profits, prices, general business indicators, social security, national product, and income accounts.

National Industrial Conference Board. *Economic Almanac.* New York, The Macmillan Co. Irregular.

Source book of data covering population, industry, and government statistics. Includes a handy glossary of economic terms. Most of the statistical tables are based on U.S. government sources. Latest published, 1967–68.

U.S. Office of Business Economics. *Business Statistics.* Washington, D.C., U.S. Government Printing Office. Biennial.

Retrospective data with sources for statistical series in *Survey of Current Business.*

————. *Survey of Current Business.* Washington, D.C., U.S. Government Printing Office. Monthly.

Major source of current data with over 2,500 statistical series covering consumer price index, GNP, industry statistics, and articles on topics of current interest. Supplemented weekly by *Business Statistics.*

B. Industry demand

1. SOURCES

To facilitate the preparation of uniform statistics for various industries, the U.S. Bureau of the Budget has developed a classification scheme for all business establishments which has been published in:

U.S. Bureau of the Budget. *Standard Industrial Classification Manual.* Rev. ed. Washington, D.C.: U.S. Government Printing Office, 1967.

Industry classification scheme arranged by major group number with definitions of inclusions under that number. Subdivisions refined to four digits. Indices for nonmanufacturing and manufacturing industries arranged alphabetically aid in locating particular industry.

Many private and public concerns use this system when gathering industry information. Most of the citations noted in the next section make use of this scheme.

Predicasts, Inc. *Industry Studies.* Cleveland, Ohio, Predicasts, Inc. Irregular.

Studies which analyze market outlook, market structure, and historical development of industries such as recreational trailers, plastics, small computers, and institutional furniture. Fifty-three studies now available.

Standard & Poor's Corporation. New York.

The Outlook. Weekly. Forecasting service.

Standard & Poor's Industry Surveys; Basic Analysis. Weekly. Service covering major industries giving industry and company data.

Standard & Poor's Industry Surveys; Trends and Projections. Monthly. Forecasting service for economic expectations.

Standard & Poor's Trade & Securities Statistics. Annual. Updated by *Current Statistics.* Monthly. Gives basic statistics by industry, stock price, and historical data.

U.S. Bureau of the Census. *Annual Survey of Manufactures.* Washington, D.C., U.S. Bureau of the Census. Annual except for census years.

Updating statistics for *Census of Manufactures* providing data on employment, payroll, value of shipments and inventories, new plant expenditures, etc. Includes state, large county, SMSA's, and selected city data.

————. *Census of Agriculture.* Washington, D.C.: U.S. Government Printing Office, 1969.

Data on number of farms, land use, income, livestock, crops, employment, irrigation, etc. by county with state summary. Published every five years.

————. *Census of Business.* Washington, D.C.: U.S. Government Printing Office, 1967. 5 vols.

Detailed statistics of retail, wholesale, and selected services businesses. Published every five years. Includes volumes noted below:

Vol. 1   *Retail Trade—Subject Reports.* U.S. summary, sales, employment size and payroll statistics.

Vol. 2   *Retail Trade—Area Statistics.* Summary, sales, payroll, number of establishments by state, county, city, SMSA, and some towns.

Vol. 3   *Wholesale Trade—Subject Reports.* U.S. summary, sales employment, credit, customer, value, capital expenditures, and public warehousing.

Vol. 4   *Wholesale Trade—Area Statistics.* By state, county, city, SMSA, and some towns.

Vol. 5   *Selected Services—Area Statistics.* 3 parts.

————. *Census of Construction Industries.* Washington, D.C.: U.S. Government Printing Office, 1967. 2 vols.

1967 marks the first year since 1939 that census data on the construction industry has been collected. Data includes statistics on number of establishments, employment, new construction, location, and type of work by geographic area.

Vol. 1   *Industry Statistics and Special Reports.*

Vol. 2 *Area Statistics.*

————. *Census of Manufactures.* Washington, D.C.: U.S. Government Printing Office, 1967. 3 vols.

Basic government source for detailed statistics on U.S. manufacturing industries. Published every five years. Includes following three volumes:

Vol. 1 *Summary and Subject Statistics.* Size establishments, inventories, equipment, includes concentration ratios.

Vol. 2 *Industry Statistics.* Issued in three parts. Covers industry groups. Compares 1963 data. Gives data on capital expenditures, value of shipments, employment, payroll, etc.

Vol. 3 *Area Statistics.* Parts 1, 2. States, SMSA's, counties, and selected city data.

————. *County Business Patterns.* Washington, D.C., U.S. Government Printing Office. Annual.

Data on payrolls, employees, and establishments arranged by industry groups. Excludes data on government, railroad, and self-employed persons. Published in separate volumes for each state and U.S. summary volume.

————. *Current Construction Reports.* Washington, D.C.: U.S. Government Printing Office. Series of reports providing current construction data:

Authorized Construction—Washington, D.C. Area. Monthly.

Construction Expenditure of State and Local Tax Revenue. Quarterly.

Housing Authorized by Building Permits and Public Contracts. Monthly, annual summary.

Housing Completions. Monthly.

Housing Starts. Monthly.

Housing Units Authorized for Demolition in Permit—Issuing Places. Annual.

Residential Alterations and Repairs. Quarterly, annual summary.

Sales of New One-Family Homes. Monthly, quarterly supplements, annual summary.

Value of New Construction Put in Place. Monthly.

————. *Current Industrial Reports.* Washington, D.C., U.S. Government Printing Office. Monthly, quarterly, semiannual, annual.

Updating series for *Census of Manufactures* and *Annual Survey of Manufactures.* Statistics given for value of shipments and production figures. Extent of data varies according to industry covered.

————. *Enterprise Statistics.* Washington, D.C.: U.S. Government Printing Office, 1967.

Report derived from data of *Censuses of Business, Manufacturers, and Mineral Industries.* Covers industries as a whole and the changes which have occurred between censuses on the enterprise rather than establishment level.

———. *Retail Trade Report.* Washington, D.C., U.S. Government Printing Office. Weekly, monthly, annual.

Estimates of inventories, per capita sales, sales, cost of merchandise, and sales inventory ratios by type of retail business by geographic area.

———. *Selected Services Receipts.* Washington, D.C., U.S. Government Printing Office. Monthly.

Data on receipts of hotels, motels, motion pictures, automobile services, and repair services estimated monthly.

———. *U.S. Commodity Exports and Imports as Related to Output.* Washington, D.C., U.S. Government Printing Office. Annual.

Output, import, and export statistics for 2,100 commodities. Arranged by SIC number. Data from *Census of Manufactures, Current Industrial Reports,* and other government publications.

———. *Wholesale Trade Report; Sales and Inventories.* Washington, D.C., U.S. Government Printing Office. Monthly.

Sales, inventories, and stock sale ratio statistics for merchant wholesalers from sample of 5,000 reporting firms.

U.S. Bureau of Domestic Commerce. *Industry Profiles.* Washington, D.C., U.S. Government Printing Office. Annual.

Analysis of 527 manufacturing industries arranged by 4-digit SIC number. Includes data on year-end inventories, value added, wages, number of establishments, rankings, etc. for the years covered. 1958–69 latest published.

———. *U.S. Industrial Outlook.* Washington, D.C., U.S. Government Printing Office. Annual.

Useful publication giving an overall view of individual industries with predictions for developments in the coming year. Arranged by broad industry. Statistical tables for smaller industry subdivisions in appendices.

2.   INPUT-OUTPUT MATRICES

The use of input-output matrices to show the interrelationships of various industries has in recent years become a most useful marketing tool. Below are listed several publications which might be of use to the marketer:

Fortune. Fortune's Input/Output Portfolio. New York: Fortune, 1966. 2 vols.

Joint Study of C-E-I-R, Inc. and Fortune which updates the 1958 input-output matrix of the U.S. Office of Business Economics using 1966 data. Includes text and large input-output chart.

"Input-Output Structure of the U.S. Economy: 1963," *Survey of Current Business,* Vol. 51 (November 1969), pp. 16–17.

Summary of material appearing in three volumes.

Vol. 1   *Transactions Data for Detailed Industries.*

Vol. 2   *Direct Requirements for Detailed Industries.*

Vol. 3   *Total Requirements for Detailed Industries.*

The 1963 study has been expanded from the 84 industries covered in 1958 to include 367 industries.

"Personal Consumption Expenditures in the 1963 Input-Output Study," *Survey of Current Business,* Vol. 51 (January 1971), pp. 34–39.

Extension of 1963 input-output study to include the industrial composition of personal consumption expenditure data.

Young, Allan H., et al. "Interindustry Transactions in New Structures and Equipment, 1963," *Survey of Current Business,* Vol. 51 (August 1971), pp. 16+.

Update input-output table of 1963 giving capital flow of "new structure and equipment from producing industries to using industries."

C.   Competition

For additional information on corporate competition, see citations in section III, B. (industry demand) and section I, D. (indices):

Of special interest and use are *Funk and Scott Index* and *Wall Street Journal Index.*

Concentration Ratios in Manufacturing, 1967. Washington, D.C.: U.S. Government Printing Office, 1970–71. 3 pts.

Special Census report issued in three parts which gives information on the largest U.S. corporations and their concentration ratios in employment, payroll, capital expenditures, value added, value of shipments. Arranged by 4-digit SIC numbers. Although companies are not identified, the arrangement gives an overall view of the share of industry for largest U.S. corporations.

The Fortune Directory of the 500 Largest U.S. Industrial Corporations. New York, Fortune. Annual in May issue.

and

The Fortune Directory of the 501–1,000 Largest U.S. Industrial Corporations. New York, Fortune. Annual in June issue.

Ranking of American companies by sales, assets, net income, stockholder equity, employees, and earning per share. Also included are tables which condense data given in larger compilation such as those companies with biggest increase in sales for past year. assets per employee, and money losers.

Growth & Acquisition Digest. Cleveland, Ohio, Predicasts, Inc. Monthly. Annual cumulation.

Company information on mergers and acquisitions. Also includes industry and new product data.

Moody's Banks & Finance Manual. New York, Moody's Investors Service. Annual.

Moody's Industrial Manual. New York, Moody's Investors Service. Annual.

Moody's Municipal & Government Manual. New York, Moody's Investors Service. Annual.

Moody's OTC Industrial Manual. New York, Moody's Investors Service. Annual.

Moody's Public Utility Manual. New York, Moody's Investors Service. Annual.

Moody's Transportation Manual. New York, Moody's Investors Service. Annual.

Manuals give corporation histories, addresses, officers, type of business, subsidiaries, and financial statements. Included is a detailed summary section giving basic data on industries covered in a particular manual. Updated twice weekly by *News Reports.*

News Front. *25,000 Leading U.S. Corporations; a Computerized Analysis.* New York: Year, Inc., 1970.

Ranking of 25,000 firms by SIC number. Included are analyses of sales, employees, assets, earnings per share, and stockholder equity of both public and private firms and 1,100 leading foreign corporations. Based on 1967 data.

Standard & Poor's Corporation. New York.

Over-the-Counter and Regional Stock Reports. 5 vols.

Standard A.S.E. Stock Reports. 3 vols.

Standard Listed Stock Reports. 4 vols.

Looseleaf services covering American, New York, over-the-counter, and regional exchanges. Arranged alphabetically with continual revision. Brief history of firm, officers, products, and financial data given. Recent developments and prospects section of interest to prospective investor.

D.   Consumer demand

Additional sources cited in section II (demographic variables):

Editor & Publisher. *Market Guide.* New York, The Editor & Publisher Co., Inc. Annual.

Statistical compilation of city population, housing, automobile registrations, retail sales, etc. arranged by city and state.

A Guide to Consumer Markets. New York, The Conference Board. Annual.

Excellent source of data including over one thousand statistical series on consumer markets. Chapters on population, employment, income, expenditures, production and distribution, and prices in graphic and tabular form. Formerly *Graphic Guide to Consumer Markets.*

Rand McNally Commercial Atlas and Marketing Guide. New York, Rand McNally & Co. Annual.

General information and maps on transportation, retail trade, communications, and specific state maps with statistics on retail and wholesale trade and population. World section on airline distances, population, altitude, and gazetteer.

Sales Management. Conducts annual surveys covering a variety of market indicators. Below are noted examples:

"SM's Market Indicators; Metro Markets Drawing Power." March 1971.

"SM's Market Indicators; Metro Markets; High Income Households." May 1971.

"SM's Market Indicators; Metro Markets Untapped Potential." February 1971.

"SM's Market Indicators; Metropolitan Area Projections through 1975." November 1970.

"Survey of Newspaper Markets." September 1971.

"Survey of Television Markets." September 1971.

Sales Management. "Survey of Buying Power." New York, Sales Management, Inc. Annual.

Annual June or July issue of *Sales Management.* Comprehensive data on state, county, and city retail sales, population, income, and buying power indexes.

Standard Rate & Data Service, Inc. *Consumer Market Data.* Skokie, Ill., Standard Rate & Data Service, Inc. Monthly.

Monthly publication appearing in *Newspaper, Spot Television,* and *Spot Radio* publications. Includes population, income, and retail sales by state and city.

IV. SOCIAL PSYCHOLOGICAL VARIABLES

Consumer Attitudes and Buying Plans. New York, The Conference Board. Bimonthly.

Publication based on survey conducted by National Family Opinion, Inc. which gives consumer plans for coming months in relation to purchases of autos, homes, appliances, vacation plans, outlook on general business conditions.

Consumer Buying Prospects. Baltimore, Md., Commercial Credit Corporation. Quarterly.

Projections of consumer demand based on data from the U.S. Bureau of the Census' *Consumer Buying Indicators.* Survey of 15,000 random households every three months giving consumer expectations for autos, household durables, housing, etc.

Consumer Market Indicators. New York, The Conference Board. Monthly.

Total market statistics covering income, consumption, employment, and retail sales. Gives changes in percent over past year.

Sindlinger's Tuesday Report. Consumer Confidence. Swarthmore, Pa., Sindlinger & Co. Weekly.

Statistics based on sample of over 2,200 households covering current and expected income, employment, and business conditions.

Survey of Consumer Finances. Ann Arbor, Survey Research Center, University of Michigan. Annual.

Study based on interviews with 2,576 families covering topics such as housing, credit, durables, autos, mutual funds and stocks, outlook and demand.

U.S. Bureau of the Census. *Consumer Buying Indicators.* Washington, D.C., U.S. Government Printing Office. Quarterly. Current Population Reports P-65.

Statistics on purchases of cars, houses, and household durables by quarters, by income, age, race, and area. Tables on expected purchases also included.

V. SYNDICATED SOURCES OF SALES AND MARKET SHARE DATA

Below are listed examples of syndicated market surveys:

Audits & Surveys Co., Inc. New York

National Restaurant Market Index. Annual study of 6,000 restaurants covering brands used, potential volume, equipment, etc. Data divided by drugstore, hotel/motel/drive-ins, counter service, and table service, and then by geographic area.

National Retail Census of Product Distribution. Annual study of 40,000 retail outlets giving number of outlets carrying a particular product, percent stocking manufacturers' and competitors' brands. Gives data by city, geographic area, and outlet.

National Total-Market Audit. Bimonthly reports and home office presentations of consumer sales of a particular product, its market share, inventory, type of retail outlet by city and geographic division.

Brand Rating Research Corp. New York.

Brand Rating Index. Survey of approximately 15,000 users of various products. Demographic reports accompany each product.

Market Research Corporation of America. New York.

National Consumer Panel. Data on weekly family purchases of consumer products.

National Menu Census. Data on home food consumption.

Metro Trade Audits. Survey of 6,000 retail, drug, and discount retailers in various geographic areas.

A. C. Nielsen Company. Chicago.

Retail Index Services. Data on products sold through retail outlets.

Media Research Services. Data on television audiences.

Neodata Services, Inc. Circulation magazine data.

Nielsen Clearing House. Coupon processing service and promotion service.

Nielsen Special Research. Custom designed service for individual clients.

Selling Areas-Marketing, Inc. New York.

SAMI Reports. Reports warehouse withdrawals to food stores in selected market areas. 13 reports, 4 weeks after the end of the reporting period. Better than 85 percent of the total market volume is represented.

Simmons (WR) and Associates Research, Inc. *Selective Markets and Media Reaching Them.*

Annual series of reports covering television markets, sporting goods, proprietary drug, smoking products, food wraps, soft drinks, magazines, alcoholic beverages, etc. Excellent reports giving demographic data by sex, income, age, and brand preferences.

Daniel Starch and Staff. New York.

Annual Media Report of Audiences. Readership survey of 78 magazines giving education, occupation, age, sex, and race of readers.

Trendex, Inc. Westport, Conn.

Trendex Buyership Reports. Quarterly data gathered from 70,000 telephone interviews on consumer products.

Top of Mind Index Service. Data on brand awareness from 52,000 telephone interviews.

VI. DATA BANKS

The U.S. Bureau of the Census maintains a data file of materials used in its publications, and much that is not available in printed form. Many of these data files may be purchased on magnetic tape or on punch cards. The Bureau will also prepare special tabulations for individual needs.

Below are listed publications by the Bureau of the Census describing its services:

U.S. Bureau of the Census. *Census Tract Manual.* 5th ed. Washington, D.C.: U.S. Government Printing Office, 1966.

Publication which explains what census tracts are and how to use them. Included are several appendices listing census tracts and key personnel.

————. *Data Access Descriptions.* Washington, D.C., U.S. Government Printing Office. Irregular.

Series which describes U.S. Bureau of the Census tape data and tells how to use the tapes. Material covered is mostly the 1970 *Census of Population.*

————. "Data Files and Special Tabulations," in *Catalog of Publications.* Washington, D.C., U.S. Government Printing Office. Monthly.

Regular feature of the Bureau's *Catalog* which lists and describes data files and tabulations available for purchase.

————. *1970 Census Users' Guide.* Washington, D.C.: U.S. Government Printing Office, 1970.

Part I is a dictionary of terms. A comparison of materials found in tape and printed reports is also presented.

Part II contains information on technical conventions, character set, technical documentation of first to fourth count, and address coding guide.

Special tabulations of U.S. Censuses are available from nongovernment sources such as the following:

Consolidated Analysis Centers, Inc.
1815 N. Fort Myer Dr.
Arlington, Va. 22209

Data Use and Access Laboratories
Suite 916
1411 Jefferson Davis Highway
Arlington, Va.

National Planning Data Corp.
65 Broad Street
Rochester, N.Y. 14614

Westat Research, Inc.
11600 Nebel Street.
Rockville, Md. 20852

The following directories are useful sources of currently available data files:

Cohan, Leonard. *Directory of Computerized Information in Science and Technology.* New York: Science Associates International, Inc., 1968.

Entry by title of system. Index serves as guide to body of work. Descriptions very complete.

Kruzas, Anthony. *Encyclopedia of Information Systems and Services.* Ann Arbor: Edwards Brothers, 1971.

Catalog of information systems arranged by issuing agency. The descriptions are fairly complete and magnetic tape files are listed. Covers primarily scientific data.

Examples of commercially available data banks follow:

Dun & Bradstreet, Inc. New York.

Dun's Market Identifiers (DMI).

Covers approximately 3.5 million corporations including 398,000 manufacturing, 1,265,000 retailing and 295,000 business service establishments. Various selections can be made by size, location, line of business factors. Magnetic tape and punchcard formats available with very flexible tape blocking and card field arrangements.

Also available on tape and punchcards are selected data from Dun & Bradstreet's:

Metalworking Directory

Middle Market Directory

Million Dollar Directory

Chilton Company. Bala-Cynwyd, Pa.

Census of the Electronic Market in the U.S.A. Statistical data on electronic plants, employees, volume, and products by geographic area.

Census of U.S. Metalworking. Statistical data on metalworking plants, location, employment, size, etc. by geographical area.

Data available on magnetic tape and punchcards.

Year, Inc. New York.

News Front Corporate Data Bank.

Data from 1966–70 on manufacturing and nonmanufacturing corporations. Complete tape covers 25,000 corporations.

Information available on magnetic tapes, printouts, or punchcards.

Market Statistics, Inc. New York.

Sales Management's "Survey of Buying Power" data available on tape or IBM cards.

Predicasts, Inc. Cleveland, Ohio.

Magnetic tapes available covering *Predicasts'* complete files. Includes information by product, subject, country, and company. Analysis of data in many forms.

Standard & Poor's Corporation. New York.

Variety of financial information available on tape such as:

COMPUSTAT Tapes. Historical statistics on approximately 3,000 public companies. Updated daily.

CRSP Tapes. Month-end prices, dividends and volume for issues traded on N.Y. Stock Exchange since 1926. Continually revised.

CUSIP Tapes. Standard security identification directory codes and descriptions.

ISL Price Services. Prices for all N.Y., American, and Over-the-Counter Stock Exchanges. Updated daily.

Appendix B

Suggested answers to discussion questions and problems

Chapter 2
Suggested answers to the first three questions

1. A short-run analysis of the potential for videotape recorders should include the number of families with small children. A long-run analysis should include marriage and birth rates. The most important economic variable would probably be family income. The adequacy of distribution facilities in a territory could be measured by historical trends in the sales of TV sets.

2. Jay M. Gould (1963) identified the following segments for paints and the variables for measuring county potential:

Segment	Variable
1. Do-it-yourself market	Income in owner-occupied homes
2. Paint contracting	Income in renter-occupied homes
3. New construction	Number of new homes
4. Industrial	Number of employees in manufacturing, trade, and service industries

3. Gould (1963) suggests the following variables for measuring the potential for fire insurance:
   a) Residential—the number of homes, weighted by their value.
   b) Industrial—number of employees.
   c) Commercial—sales volume in dollars.

Chapter 3
Suggested solution to the case "locating bank branches"[1]

Predicting the performance of a branch is dependent upon the cost and revenue forecasts which are made; these forecasts in turn are largely a function of the volume of business a new branch is expected to generate. In developing a model to determine this volume, the first problem confronted is that of delineating the market area (around the branch) from which it is reasonable to expect the majority of accounts will come. Unfortunately, these market areas in the past have had vague and loosely constructed boundary lines, largely dependent on subjective factors. To facilitate the use of the model, the definition of trade areas must prevent variation due to personal whim. Thus, three methods of constructing these areas were considered and tested:

1. The trade area consisted of the census tract containing the branch office plus all the census tracts contiguous to the branch's tract.
2. A circular trade area with the branch as center was also examined. A previous market study questioned people about how far they traveled to their bank. Using population density figures it was possible to relate this distance information to our specific locations in determining an appropriate diameter for the circular area. In addition, each circle was modified to reflect natural barriers.
3. Using the hypothesis that a consumer bank is chosen solely for convenience of location, a trade area was formed by drawing the perpendicular bisectors of the lines joining the branch and all the surrounding banks.

All three trade areas were determined for 65 of the bank's present offices.

After developing these trade areas, variables had to be chosen which would relate the demographic factors of the area to the aggregate bank deposit potential of the area. In addition, several variables were chosen to reflect factors affecting the branch's share of the aggregate potential.

Income, population, competition, branch's age, a neighborhood evolution factor, the relative ages of our branches' competitors, and the number of new families moving into the area per month were selected. Two income numbers were used, one for the branch tract and another, a weighted average, for the contiguous tracts. Updated census information was the source of this data. Two population figures corresponding to the income figures were also obtained from updated census statistics. The competition variable consisted of the number of commercial competitors, savings bank competitors, and savings and loan institutions. The age of each of our branches was ascertained. This age represented the time when the office began collecting deposits, whether or not at that time it was one of the bank's offices. Each branch was assigned a -1, $+1$, or 0 neighborhood evolution factor depending on the socioeconomic

---

[1] This solution was written by Mr. Bertram H. Lowi, assistant vice-president and director of marketing research, Bankers Trust Co., New York.

change of the market area since the branch was established. The opening date of each bank designated as a competitor was compared to the age of the bank's branch and given a grade—on a five-point scale—by the branch's employees. Tabulations by zip code were obtained on the number of new families moving into an area each month. These data were obtained for each of the three trade areas drawn around the branches selected for the study.

Once this information was collected for the 65 branch offices for each of the three trade area definitions, the figures were used as the independent variables in a step-wise regression analysis. Four regressions were run for each of the three trade areas, each of the four regressions having a different dependent variable, that is, variable to be predicted. The four variables were (1) dollar checking deposits, (2) dollar savings deposits, (3) number of checking accounts, and (4) number of savings accounts. The results of the regression runs were encouraging. The explanatory variables (as collected for the third type of trade area) were able to explain 73 percent of the variations among two of the variables to be predicted—branch dollar savings deposits and number of branch checking accounts. For the other two dependent variables—number of branch savings accounts and branch dollar checking deposits—71 percent and 50 percent of the variation were explained. Before the regressions were run, a sample was randomly selected and removed from the data. The models will be tested using this sample.

(See also G. David Hughes, "Predicting Bank Deposits and Loans," *Journal of Marketing Research,* Vol. 7, No. 1 (February 1970), pp. 95–100.)

Chapter 5
Suggested answers to the first six discussion questions

1. Price elasticity equals

$$e_{qp} = \frac{\partial s}{\partial P} \cdot \frac{P}{s}$$

$$= -0.0488 \cdot \frac{122.8}{8.081}$$

$$= -0.742$$

Income elasticity equals

$$e_{qI} = \frac{\partial s}{\partial I} \cdot \frac{I}{s}$$

$$= 0.0255 \cdot \frac{580.6}{8.081}$$

$$= 1.83$$

These coefficients may be interpreted as follows. Given a 1 percent increase in the price index of automobiles, the desired stock of automobiles will decline 0.742 of 1 percent. Given a 1 percent increase in permanent income, the desired stock of automobiles will increase 1.83 percent.

2. Price elasticity is -0.792, and income elasticity is 3.951, which may be read directly from Equation 5–8 because it is a log-log function. The coefficients in this function yield a direct estimate of constant elasticity.

3. $$\begin{aligned} \text{Log sales} &= -0.60 - 0.60(\log 3.01)^2 - 0.85 \log 0.44 \\ &\quad +0.28(\log 2.99)^2 + 0.31 \log 2.82 \\ &\quad +0.65(\log 10.19) - 0.16(\log 10.19)^2 \\ &\quad +0.44(\log 0.70) + 0.23(1.68) \\ &= -0.60 - 0.60(0.48)^2 - 0.85(-0.36) \\ &\quad +0.28(0.48)^2 + 0.31(0.45) \\ &\quad +0.65(1.01) - 0.16(1.01)^2 \\ &\quad +0.44(-0.15) + 0.23(0.23) \\ &= 0.255 \end{aligned}$$

Antilog of $0.255 = 1.8$ (100 million servings).

4. During the early stages of a product's life cycle, promotional elasticity exceeds price elasticity for several reasons. Because the product is new, its comparative advantages and availability must be communicated to buyers. Advertising is most effective when the product has a definite comparative advantage over its competitors. As the product becomes known to the buyers, the marginal cost of informing additional buyers increases. During later stages of the life cycle, competitive products have narrowed or eliminated the comparative advantage of the new product. As products become homogeneous in the minds of buyers, they tend to buy on price.

5. This question should be disturbing to economists who argue that advertising is a waste and also subscribe to the need for rational behavior within the firm. If advertising elasticity exceeds price elasticity, the rational manager should advertise, even if he only increases his market share. The only social gain in this case is to the stockholders. Like most philosophical questions regarding advertising, this question has no one answer. Answers reflect personal systems of value.

6. If a company uses advertising for offensive and defensive strategies, the short-run relationship between sales and advertising will be positive for the offensive situation and negative for the defensive situation. If all data are combined, the coefficient for advertising will probably not be significant, which could lead to an incorrect conclusion that advertising was not effective.

Chapter 9
Suggested answer to question 9, parts (a) and (b).[2]

This problem involves an understanding of the ideal point model of preferences (and hence probabilities of purchase using the psychological model of demand).

---
[2] These solutions were developed by Professor Vithala R. Rao.

The various steps involved in answering the questions (a) and (b) are:

1. Compute d_{ij} using the Euclidean distance formula for $i = 1$ and $j = 1$, 2, . . . , 6.
2. Compute $1/(1 + 2d_{ij}^2)$ for $i = 1$ and $j = 1, 2, . . . , 6$.
3. Normalize the value obtained in (2) for deriving probabilities of purchase, (P_{ij}) for $i = 1$, and $j = 1, 2, . . . , 6$. The above three steps yield the answer to question (a).
4. For answering (b), the steps 1–3 must be repeated for all other segments.
5. Market share for brand B (i.e., $j = 2$), denoted by S_2 is computed using:

$$S_2 = \sum_{i=1}^{5} P_{i2} m_i$$

where m_i is the market share of the i-th segment.

These computations are shown below:

Brand	j	d_{1j}^2	$1 + 2d_{1j}^2$	$1/(1 + 2d_{1j}^2)$	P_{1j}
			Market segment $1(i = 1)$		
A	1	1.0	3.0	0.3333	0.477
B	2	5.0	11.0	0.0909	0.130
C	3	9.0	19.0	0.0526	0.075
D	4	9.0	19.0	0.0526	0.075
E	5	8.0	17.0	0.0588	0.084
F	6	4.0	9.0	0.1111	0.159
Total.			78.0	0.6993	1.000

Thus, the probability of purchase of the institutional market segment for brand B is 0.130.

Similar calculations for other segments yield the following probabilities:

Brand	j	2	3	4	5
			Segment number		
A	1	0.033	0.659	0.561	0.644
B	2	0.243	0.094	0.146	0.102
C	3	0.567	0.051	0.071	0.055
D	4	0.027	0.051	0.059	0.055
E	5	0.090	0.051	0.062	0.052
F	6	0.040	0.094	0.101	0.092

The expected market share for brand **B** is:

$$0.130 \times 30\% +$$
$$0.243 \times 20\% +$$
$$0.094 \times 15\% +$$
$$0.146 \times 10\% +$$
$$0.102 \times 25\%$$

$$= 3.90 + 4.86 + 1.41 + 1.46 + 2.55 = 14.18\%.$$

Similarly the market shares of other brands will work out to be:

Brand		Market share
A	S_1	46.56%
B	S_2	14.18
C	S_3	16.46
D	S_4	5.52
E	S_5	7.00
F	S_6	10.28

Bibliography

AAKER, DAVID A. (ed.). *Multivariate Analysis in Marketing: Theory and Application.* Belmont, Calif.: Wadsworth Publishing Co., Inc., 1971.

ABBOTT, J. C. "The Role of Marketing in the Development of Backward Agricultural Economies," *Journal of Farm Economics,* Vol. 44 (May 1962), pp. 349–62.

ABRAMS, J. "An Evaluation of Alternative Rating Devices for Consumer Research," *Journal of Marketing Research,* Vol. 3 (May 1966), pp. 189–93.

ACHENBAUM, A. A. "Knowledge Is a Thing Called Measurement," in *Attitude Research at Sea* (eds. L. Adler and I. Crespi), pp. 111–26. Chicago: American Marketing Association, 1966.

ACKOFF, RUSSELL L. *A Concept of Corporate Planning.* New York: John Wiley & Sons, Inc.,—Interscience Publishers, 1970.

"Ad Recall? P&G Couldn't Care Less," *Marketing/Communications,* August 1971, pp. 22–26.

ADELMAN, IRMA. "An Econometric Analysis of Population Growth," *American Economic Review,* Vol. 53 (June 1963), pp. 314–39.

AGOSTINI, J. M. "Analysis of Magazine Accumulative Audience," *Journal of Advertising Research,* Vol. 2 (December 1962), pp. 24–27.

AJZEN, I., and FISHBEIN, M. "The Prediction of Behavior from Attitudinal and Normative Variables," *Journal of Experimental Social Psychology,* Vol. 6 (October 1970), pp. 466–87.

ALDERSON, W. *Marketing Behavior and Executive Action.* Homewood, Ill.: Richard D. Irwin, Inc., 1957.

263

ALEXIS, M. "Some Negro-White Differences in Consumption," *The American Journal of Economics and Sociology,* Vol. 21 (January 1962), pp. 11–28.

ALEXIS, M.; HAINES, G. H., JR.; and SIMON, L. "Consumer Information Processing: The Case of Women's Clothing," *Marketing and the New Science of Planning* (ed. R. L. King), pp. 197–205. 1968 Fall Conference Proceedings, Series No. 28. Chicago, American Marketing Association.

ALKER, H. A. "Is Personality Situationally Specific or Intrapsychically Consistent?" *Journal of Personality,* Vol. 29 (March 1972), in press.

———, and HERMANN, MARGARET G. "Are Bayesian Decisions Artificially Intelligent? The Effect of Task and Personality on Conservatism in Processing Information," *Journal of Personality and Social Psychology,* Vol. 19 (July 1971), pp. 31–41.

ALLPORT, G. W. "Attitudes," in *Handbook of Social Psychology* (ed. C. Murchison). Worcester, Mass.: Clark University Press, 1935. Excerpted in Fishbein (1967), pp. 3–13.

ALLVINE, F. C. "Diffusion of a Competitive Innovation," in *Marketing and the New Science of Planning* (ed. R. L. King), pp. 341–51. 1968 Fall Conference Proceedings. Chicago, American Marketing Association.

ALPERT, LEWIS, and GATTY, RONALD. "Product Positioning by Behavioral Life-Styles," *Journal of Marketing,* Vol. 33, No. 2 (April 1969), pp. 65–69.

ALPERT, M. I. "Identification of Determinant Attributes: A Comparison of Methods," *Journal of Marketing Research,* Vol. 8 (May 1971), pp. 184–91.

AMSTUTZ, A. E. *Computer Simulation of Competitive Market Response.* Cambridge, Mass.: The M.I.T. Press, 1967.

ANDERSON, N. J. "A Simple Model for Information Integration," in *Theories of Cognitive Consistency: A Sourcebook* (eds. Robert P. Abelson et al.), pp. 732–33. Skokie, Ill.: Rand McNally & Co., 1968.

ANDERSON, W. T. JR. "Identifying the Convenience-Oriented Consumer," *Journal of Marketing Research,* Vol. 8 (May 1971), pp. 179–83.

ANDREASEN, A. R. "Attitudes and Customer Behavior: A Decision Model," in *New Research in Marketing* (ed. L. E. Preston), pp. 1–16. Berkeley: Institute of Business and Economic Research, University of California, 1965.

ANDREWS, F. M.; MORGAN, J. N.; and SONQUIST, J. A. *Multiple Classification Analysis.* Ann Arbor: Survey Research Center, University of Michigan, 1967.

ARGYRIS, C. *Integrating the Individual and the Organization.* New York: John Wiley & Sons, Inc. 1964.

ASPINWALL, L. V. "The Parallel Systems Theory," in *Managerial Marketing: Perspectives and Viewpoints* (eds. W. Lazer and E. J. Kelley), pp. 644–52. Rev. ed. Homewood, Ill.: Richard D. Irwin, Inc., 1962.

ASSAEL, H. "Segmenting Markets by Group Purchasing Behavior: An Application of the AID Technique," *Journal of Marketing Research,* Vol. 7 (1970), pp. 153–58.

ATKINSON, J. W. *An Introduction to Motivation.* Princeton, N.J.: D. Van Nostrand Co., Inc., 1964.

————, and FEATHER, N. T. (eds.). *A Theory of Achievement Motivation.* New York: John Wiley & Sons, Inc., 1966.

AXELROD, J. N. "Attitude Measures that Predict Purchase," *Journal of Advertising Research,* Vol. 8 (March 1968), pp. 3–17.

BACK, KURT W. "New Frontiers in Demography and Social Psychology," *Demography,* Vol. 4 (1967), pp. 90–97.

BAIER, MARTIN. "ZIP Code: New Tool for Marketers," *Harvard Business Review,* Vol. 45 (January–February 1967), pp. 136–40.

BARCLAY, GEORGE W. *Techniques of Population Analysis.* New York: John Wiley & Sons, Inc., 1958.

BARNETT, NORMAN L. "Beyond Market Segmentation," *Harvard Business Review,* Vol. 46, No. 5 (January–February 1969), pp. 152–66.

BASS, F. M. "A Simultaneous Equation Regression Study of Advertising and Sales of Cigarettes," *Journal of Marketing Research,* Vol. 6 (August 1969), pp. 291–300.

————. "A New Product Growth Model for Consumer Durables," *Management Science,* Vol. 15 (January 1969), pp. 215–27.

————, and BECKWITH, N. E. *A Multivariate Regression Analysis of the Responses of Competing Brands to Advertising.* Marketing Science Institute, February, 1971. Mimeographed.

————; KING, C. W.; and PESSEMIER, E. A. (eds.). *Applications of the Sciences in Marketing Management.* New York: John Wiley & Sons, Inc., 1968.

————, and KING, C. W. *The Theory of First Purchase of New Products.* Institute for Research in the Behavioral, Economic, and Management Sciences, Paper No. 213. Purdue University, July 1968.

————, and TALARZYK, W. W. "A Study of Attitude Theory and Brand Preference." Working Paper No. 252, Institute for Research in the Behavioral, Economic, and Management Sciences, Purdue University, July 1969, p. 8.

BATTEN, BARTON, DURSTINE, AND OSBORN ADVERTISING AGENCY. *The Repetition of Advertising: A Survey of Eighty Years of Research on Repetition and its Effect on the Consumer.* New York, 1967.

BAUER, R. A. "Consumer Behavior as Risk Taking." Proceedings of the 43rd National Conference of the American Marketing Association (ed. R. S. Hancock), June 15–17, 1960, pp. 389–98.

———— (ed.). *Social Indicators.* Cambridge, Mass.: The M.I.T. Press, 1966.

————, and CUNNINGHAM, S. M. *Studies in the Negro Market.* Cambridge, Mass.: Marketing Science Institute, 1970.

————; CUNNINGHAM, S. M.; and WORTZEL, L. H. "The Marketing Dilemma of Negroes," *Journal of Marketing,* Vol. 29 (July 1965), p. 2.

————, and GERGEN, K. J. *The Study of Policy Formation.* New York: The Free Press, 1968.

BAUMOL, W. J. *Business Behavior, Value and Growth.* Rev. ed. New York: Harcourt, Brace & World, Inc., 1967.

BEAL, G. M., and ROGERS, E. M. "Informational Sources in the Adoption Process of New Fabrics," *Journal of Home Economics,* Vol. 49 (October 1957), pp. 630–34.

BEATTIE, D. W. "Marketing a New Product," *Operational Research Quarterly,* Vol. 20, No. 4 (December 1969), pp. 429–35.

BECKER, G. M., and McCLINTOCK, C. G. "Value: Behavioral Decision Theory," *Annual Review of Psychology,* Vol. 18 (1967), pp. 239–86.

BECKER, BORIS W., and MYERS, JOHN G. "Yeasaying Response Style," *Journal of Advertising Research,* Vol. 10, No. 6 (December 1970), pp. 31–37.

BELL, G. D. "Self-Confidence and Persuasion in Car Buying," *Journal of Marketing Research,* Vol. 4 (February 1967), pp. 46–52.

BENJAMIN, BERNARD. *Demographic Analysis.* London: George Allen & Unwin Ltd., 1968.

BERDY, DAVID. "Order Effects in Taste Tests," *Journal of the Market Research Society,* Vol. 11, No. 4 (October 1969), pp. 361–71.

BERENSON, CONRAD. "Marketing Information Systems," *Journal of Marketing,* Vol. 33 (October 1969), pp. 16–23.

BERKOWITZ, L. "Social Motivation," in *The Handbook of Social Psychology,* (eds. G. Lindzey and E. Aronson), Vol. 3. 2d ed. Reading, Mass.: Addison-Wesley Publishing Co., Inc., 1969.

BETTMAN, JAMES R. "Information Processing Models of Consumer Behavior," *Journal of Marketing Research,* Vol. 7 (August 1970), pp. 370–76.

————. "Methods for Analyzing Consumer Information Processing Models," in Gardner (1971), pp. 197–207.

————. "The Structure of Consumer Choice Processes," *Journal of Marketing Research,* Vol. 8 (November 1971), pp. 465–71.

BIRDWELL, A. E. "A Study of the Influence of Image Congruence on Consumer Choice," *Journal of Business,* Vol. 41 (January 1968), pp. 76–88.

BLACKETT, G. H. "Measuring Raw Materials Needs to the Year 2000," *The Conference Board RECORD,* January 1971, pp. 23–28.

BLACKWELL, R. D.; ENGEL, J. F.; and KOLLAT, D. T. *Cases in Consumer Behavior.* New York: Holt, Rinehart, & Winston, Inc., 1969.

————; HENSEL, J. S.; and STERNTHAL, B. "Pupil Dilation: What Does it Measure?" *Journal of Advertising Research,* Vol. 15 (August 1970), pp. 15–18.

BLAKE, B.; PERLOFF, R.; and HESLIN, R. "Dogmatism and Acceptance of New Products," *Journal of Marketing Research,* Vol. 7, No. 4 (November 1970), pp. 483–86.

BLAKE, J., and DAVIS, K. "Norms, Values, and Sanctions," in *Handbook of Modern Sociology* (ed. R. E. L. Faris), pp. 456–84. Skokie, Ill.: Rand McNally & Co., 1964.

BLALOCK, H. M. JR. "The Measurement Problem: A Gap between the Languages of Theory and Research," in *Methodology in Social Research* (eds. H. M. Blalock and Ann B. Blalock), chap. 1. New York: McGraw-Hill Book Co., 1968.

———. *Theory Construction: From Verbal to Mathematical Formulations.* Englewood Cliffs, N.J.: Prentice-Hall, Inc., 1969.

BLISS, PERRY (ed.). *Marketing and the Behavioral Sciences.* 2d ed. Boston: Allyn & Bacon, Inc., 1967.

BLUMEN, ISADORE; KOGAN, MARVIN; and MCCARTHY, PHILIP J. *The Industrial Mobility of Labor as a Probability Process.* Ithaca, N.Y.: New York State School of Industrial and Labor Relations, Cornell University, 1955.

BOGARDUS, E. S. "Measuring Social Distances," *Journal of Applied Sociology,* Vol. 9 (1925), pp. 299–308. Reprinted in Fishbein (1967), pp. 71–76.

BOONE, L. E. "The Search for the Consumer Innovator," *The Journal of Business,* Vol. 43 (April 1970), pp. 135–40.

BOULDING, K. E. "General Systems Theory—The Skeleton of Science," *Management Science,* Vol. 2 (April 1956), pp. 197–208.

———. *The Image.* Ann Arbor: University of Michigan Press, 1956.

BOURNE, F. S. "Different Kinds of Decisions and Reference-Group Influence," in *Some Applications of Behavioral Science Research* (ed. R. Likert and S. P. Hayes, Jr.), pp. 217–24. Paris: UNESCO (1957). Reprinted in Bliss (1967), pp. 270–78.

BOYD, H. W. JR., and DAVIS, R. T. *Marketing Management Casebook.* Homewood, Ill.: Richard D. Irwin, Inc., 1971.

BRAITHWAITE, R. B. *Scientific Explanation.* New York: Harper & Row, Publishers, 1953.

BREYER, R. *Quantitative Systemic Analysis and Control.* Study No. 1, Channel and Channel Group Costing. Philadelphia: College Offset Press, 1949.

BRITTS, S. H. (ed.). *Consumer Behavior and the Behavioral Sciences.* New York: John Wiley & Sons, Inc., 1966.

———. *Psychological Experiments in Consumer Behavior.* New York: John Wiley & Sons, Inc., 1970.

BROGDEN, H. E. "The Primary Personal Values Measured by the Allport-Vernon Test, 'A Study of Values,'" *Psychological Monographs,* No. 348 (1952).

BROSS, I. D. J. *Design for Decision.* New York: The Macmillan Co., 1961.

BRZEZINSKI, A. K. "America in the Technotronic Age," *Encounter,* January 1968, pp. 16–26.

BUCKLIN, L. P. "Retail Strategy and the Classification of Consumer Goods," *Journal of Marketing,* Vol. 27 (January 1963), pp. 50–55.

———. "Testing Propensities to Shop," *Journal of Marketing,* Vol. 30 (January 1966), pp. 22–27.

BURCH, S. W., and STEKLER, H. O. "The Forecasting Accuracy of Consumer Attitude Data," *Journal of the American Statistical Association,* Vol. 64, No. 328 (December 1969), pp. 1225–33.

BURK, M. C. *Consumption Economics: A Multidisciplinary Approach.* New York: John Wiley & Sons, Inc., 1968.

BURSK, E. C. *Cases in Marketing Management.* Englewood Cliffs, N.J.: Prentice-Hall, Inc., 1965.

———, and GREYSER, S. A. *Advanced Cases in Marketing Management.* Englewood Cliffs, N.J.: Prentice-Hall, Inc., 1968.

BUSH, V. "Science Pauses," *Fortune,* Vol. 71 (May 1965), pp. 116–19, 167, 172.

BUTLER, W. F., and KAVESH, R. A. *How Business Economists Forecast.* Englewood Cliffs, N. J.: Prentice-Hall, Inc., 1966.

BYRNES, J. C. "An Experiment in the Measurement of Consumer Intentions to Purchase," in *American Statistical Association 1964 Proceedings of the Business and Economics Section,* pp. 265–79. Washington, D.C.: American Statistical Association, 1965.

CAMPBELL, B. O. *Population Change and Building Cycles.* Bulletin No. 91. Urbana, Ill.: Bureau of Economic and Business Research, University of Illinois, 1966.

CARMAN, J. M., and NICOSIA, F. M. "Analog Experiments with a Model of Consumer Attitude Change." Proceedings of the American Marketing Association, December 1964, pp. 246–57.

———. *The Application of Social Class in Market Segmentation.* Berkeley, Calif.: Institute of Business and Economic Research, University of California, 1965.

CARROLL, J. D. "Individual Differences and Multidimensional Scaling." 1969, mimeographed.

———. "An Overview of Multidimensional Scaling Methods Emphasizing Recently Developed Models for Handling Individual Differences," in King and Tigert (1971), pp. 235–62.

———, and CHANG, J. J. "Relating Preference Data to Multidimensional Scaling Solutions via a Generalization of Coombs' Unfolding Model." Murray Hill, N.J.: Bell Telephone Laboratories, 1967. Mimeographed.

CHAMBERLAIN, N. W. *Beyond Malthus: Population and Power.* New York: Basic Books, Inc., Publishers, 1970.

CHAMBERS, JOHN C. "Management Science Tools for the Marketer," *Decision Making in Marketing, a Colloquium,* pp. 31–39. New York: The Conference Board, 1971.

————; MULLICK, S. K.; and SMITH, D. D. "How to Choose the Right Forecasting Technique," *Harvard Business Review,* Vol. 49 (July–August 1971), pp. 45–74.

CHE, MO-HUNG. "A Treatment of Distributed Lags in the Measurement of Advertising Effectiveness." Ph.D. dissertation, Cornell University, 1971.

CHIPMAN, J. S. "The Nature and Meaning of Equilibrium in Economic Theory," in *Functionalism in the Social Sciences* (ed. D. Martindale). Monograph 5, The American Academy of Political and Social Science, 1965, pp. 35–64.

CHOW, G. C. "Statistical Demand Function for Automobiles and Their Use for Forecasting," in *The Demand for Durable Goods* (ed. A. C. Harberger), p. 158. Chicago: The University of Chicago Press, 1960.

CHUNG, K. H. "Toward a General Theory of Motivation and Performance," *California Management Review,* Vol. 11 (Spring 1969), pp. 81–88.

CLANCY, K. J., and GARSEN, R. "Why Some Scales Predict Better," *Journal of Advertising,* Vol. 10 (October 1970), pp. 33–38.

CLAWSON, J. C. "How Useful Are 90-Day Purchase Probabilities?" *Journal of Marketing,* Vol. 35 (October 1971), pp. 43–47.

CLAYCAMP, H. J., and AMSTUTZ, A. E. "Simulation Techniques in the Analysis of Marketing Strategy," in Bass, King, and Pessemier (1968), pp. 113–50.

————, and LIDDY, LUCIEN E. "Prediction of New Product Performance: An Analytical Approach," *Journal of Marketing Research,* Vol. 6, No. 4 (November 1969), pp. 414–20.

COALE, ANSLEY J. "Population Change and Demand, Prices, and the Level of Employment," in Universities-National Bureau Committee for Economic Research, *Demographic and Economic Change in Developed Countries* (Special Conference 11), pp. 352–71. Princeton, N.J.: Princeton University Press (for the National Bureau of Economic Research), 1957.

————, and DEMENY, PAUL. *Methods of Estimating Basic Demographic Measures from Incomplete Data.* Manual IV, Population Studies No. 42, pp. 31–37. New York: Department of Economic and Social Affairs, United Nations, 1967.

————, and ZELNIK, MELVIN. *New Estimates of Fertility and Population in the United States.* Princeton, N.J.: Princeton University Press, 1963.

COHEN, J. B. "The Role of Personality in Consumer Behavior," in *Perspectives in Consumer Behavior* (eds. H. H. Kassarjian and T. S. Robertson). Glenview, Ill.: Scott, Foresman and Co., 1966.

————, and AHTOLA, O. T. "An Expectancy X Value Analysis of the Relationship between Consumer Attitudes and Behavior," in Gardner (1971), pp. 344–64.

————, and BARBAN, A. M. "An Interactive Consumer-Product Typological System: A Progress Report and Partial Evaluation." A paper presented to the First Annual Meeting of the Association for Consumer Research, University of Illinois, August 23–30, 1970.

————, and GOLDEN, E. "Informational Social Influence and Product Evaluation." Faculty Working Papers, No. 4, College of Commerce and Business Administration, University of Illinois at Urbana-Champaign, January 1971. Mimeographed.

————, and HOUSTON, M. "Some Alternatives to a Five-Point Likert Scale." Paper at the Workshop on Attitude Research and Consumer Behavior, University of Illinois, December 3–5, 1970.

COLEMAN, J. S. "Measures of Structural Characteristics," *Introduction to Mathematical Sociology,* pp. 430–68. New York: The Free Press of Glencoe, The Macmillan Co., 1964.

————; KATZ, E.; and MENZEL, H. "The Diffusion of an Innovation among Physicians," *Sociometry,* Vol. 20 (December 1957), p. 253.

————; ————; and ————. *Medical Innovation, a Diffusion Study.* Indianapolis, Ind.: The Bobbs-Merrill Co., Inc., 1966.

COLEMAN, R. P. "The Significance of Social Stratification in Selling," Proceedings of the American Marketing Association (ed. M. L. Bell) (December 1960), pp. 171–84. Republished in Bliss (1967), pp. 179–94.

COLLEY, R. H. *Defining Advertising Goals for Measured Advertising Results.* New York: Association of National Advertisers, 1961.

COLLINS, L., and MONTGOMERY, C. "Whatever Happened to Motivation Research? End of the Messianic Hope," *Journal of the Market Research Society,* Vol. 12 (January 1970), pp. 1–11.

COLVIN, L.; NILSON, H. S.; and RASHMIR, L. *The College Market, 1967–68,* p. 15. North Hollywood, Calif.: Market Compilation and Research Bureau, 1967.

COOMBS, C. H. *A Theory of Data.* New York: John Wiley & Sons, Inc., 1964.

————; DAWES, R. M.; and TVERSKY, M. *Mathematical Psychology,* chap. 10, "Information Theory," pp. 307–50. Englewood Cliffs, N.J.: Prentice-Hall, Inc., 1970.

COOMBS, L., and FREEDMAN, RONALD. "Use of Telephone Interviews in a Longitudinal Fertility Study," *Public Opinion Quarterly,* Vol. 28 (Spring 1964), pp. 112–17.

COPELAND, M. T. "Relation of Consumers' Buying Habits of Marketing Methods," *Harvard Business Review,* Vol. 1 (April 1923), pp. 282–89.

CORDTZ, D. "Autos: A Hazardous Stretch Ahead," *Fortune* (April 1971), pp. 69ff.

Cox, D. F. (ed.). *Risk Taking and Information Handling in Consumer Behavior.* Cambridge, Mass.: Division of Research, Graduate School of Business Administration, Harvard University, 1967.

Cox, K. K., and ENIS, B. M. *Experimentation for Marketing Decisions.* Scranton, Pa.: Intext, 1969.

CRANE, E. *Marketing Communications: A Behavioral Approach to Men, Messages, and Media.* New York: John Wiley & Sons, Inc., 1965.

CRAVENS, D. W. "An Exploratory Analysis of Individual Information Processing," *Management Science,* Vol. 16 (June 1970), pp. B656–670.

CRESPI, I. "Use of a Scaling Technique in Surveys," *Journal of Marketing,* Vol. 25 (July 1961), pp. 69–72.

CROSSMAN, E. R. F. W. "Information Processes in Human Skill," *British Medical Bulletin,* 1964, pp. 32–37.

————. "Information Theory in Psychological Measurement," in *Encyclopaedia of Linguistics, Information and Control* (ed. M. A. Roger), pp. 232–38. New York: Pergamon Press, Inc., 1969.

CUMMINGS, L. L.; SCHWAB, D. P.; and ROSEN, M. "Performance and Knowledge of Results as Determinants of Goal-Setting," *Journal of Applied Psychology,* in press.

DANCE, F. E. X. (ed.). *Human Communication Theory.* New York: Holt, Rinehart & Winston, Inc., 1967.

DAVIS, HARRY L. "Dimensions of Marital Roles in Consumer Decision Making," *Journal of Marketing Research,* Vol. 7, No. 2 (May 1970), pp. 168–77.

————. "Measurement of Husband-Wife Influence in Consumer Purchase Decisions," *Journal of Marketing Research,* Vol. 8 (August 1971), pp. 305–12.

DAVIS, KINGSLEY. "The Sociology of Demographic Behavior," in *Sociology Today: Problems and Prospects* (eds. R. K. Merton, L. Broom, and L. S. Cottrell, Jr.), pp. 309–33. New York: Basic Books, Inc., Publishers, 1959.

DAY, G. S. "Mathematical Models of Attitude Change for Evaluating New Product Introductions," in *Proceedings,* pp. 78–87. Washington, D.C.: American Statistical Association, 1969.

————. *Buyer Attitudes and Brand Choice Behavior.* New York: The Free Press, 1970.

DAY, G. S. "Changes in Attitudes and Intentions as Predictors of New Product Acceptance," in King and Tigert (1971), pp. 92–110.

DeFLEUR, M. L., and WESTIE, F. R. "Attitude as a Scientific Concept," *Social Forces,* Vol. 42 (October 1963), p. 30.

DEMBY, E. H. "Psychographics: Who, What, Why, When, Where and How," in King and Tigert (1971), pp. 196–99.

DOEHLERT, D. H. "Similarity and Preference Mapping: A Color Example," *Marketing and the New Science of Planning.* Proceedings of the American Marketing Association, 1969.

DOHRENWEND, B. S. "Some Effects of Open and Closed Questions on Respondents' Answers," *Human Organization,* Vol. 24 (Summer 1965), p. 183.

DOLICH, I. J. "Congruence Relationships between Self Images and Product Brands," *Journal of Marketing Research,* Vol. 6 (February 1969), pp. 80–84.

DORFMAN, R., and STEINER, P. O. "Optimal Advertising and Optimal Quality," *The American Economic Review,* Vol. 44 (December 1954), pp. 826–35.

DORN, HAROLD F. "Pitfalls in Population Forecasts and Projections," *Journal of the American Statistical Association,* Vol. 45 (September 1950), pp. 311–34.

DOUGLAS, P. H., and COBB, C. W. "A Theory of Production," *American Economic Review,* Vol. 18 (1928), supplement review.

DOWNING, J. A. "A Study of Brand Images: An Experimental Approach to Attitude Measurement," in *Attitude Scaling,* pp. 57–67. Publication 4 of the Market Research Society. London: The Oakwood Press, 1960.

DRUCKER, P. F. *The Practice of Management.* New York: Harper & Row, Publishers, 1954.

———. "Long-Range Planning," *Management Science,* Vol. 5 (April 1959), pp. 238–49.

———. "The Surprising Seventies," *Harper's Magazine,* July 1971, pp. 35–39.

DUNCAN, O. D. "Path Analysis: Sociological Examples," *American Journal of Sociology,* Vol. 72 (1966), pp. 1–16.

———. "Contingencies in Constructing Causal Models," in *Sociological Methodology* (ed. E. F. Borgatta). San Francisco: Jossey-Bass, Inc., 1969.

DUSSENBERRY, J. *Income, Savings and the Theory of Consumer Behavior.* Cambridge, Mass.: Harvard University Press, 1949.

DYCKMAN, T. R. "An Aggregate-Demand Model for Automobiles," *The Journal of Business,* Vol. 38 (July 1965).

EASTERLIN, RICHARD A. "The American Baby Boom in Historical Perspective," *American Economic Review,* Vol. 51 (December 1961), pp. 869–911.

———. "Long Swings in U.S. Demographic and Economic Growth: Some Findings on the Historical Pattern," *Demography,* Vol. 2 (1965), pp. 490–507.

———. "Economic-Demographic Interactions and Long Swings in Economic Growth," *American Economic Review,* Vol. 56 (December 1966a), pp. 1063–1104.

———. "On the Relation of Economic Factors to Recent and Projected Fertility Changes," *Demography,* Vol. 3 (1966b), pp. 131–53.

———. "The Effects of Population Growth on the Economic Development of Developing Countries," *The Annals of the American Academy of Political and Social Science,* Vol. 369 (January 1967), pp. 98–108.

———. *Population, Labor Force, and Long Swing in Economic Growth: The American Experience,* pp. 9–18. New York: National Bureau of Economic Research, 1968.

ECKSTRAND, G., and GILLILAND, A. R. "The Psycholgalvanometric Method for Measuring the Effectiveness of Advertising," *Journal of Applied Psychology,* Vol. 32 (August 1948), pp. 415–25.

EDWARDS, A. L. *Techniques of Attitude Scale Construction.* New York: Appleton-Century-Crofts, 1957.

EDWARDS, WARD. "Behavioral Decision Theory," in *Annual Review of Psychology* (eds. P. R. Farnsworth, O. McNemar, and Q. McNemar), pp. 473–98. Palo Alto, Calif.: Annual Reviews, Inc., 1961.

EGERTON, HENRY C., and BROWN, JAMES K. "Some Perspectives on Business Planning," *The Conference Board RECORD* (August 1971), pp. 32–36.

EGGERT, R. J., and MCCRACKEN, P. W. "Forecasting the Automobile Market," in *How Business Economists Forecast* (eds. W. F. Butler and R. A. Kavesh), pp. 313–33. Englewood Cliffs, N.J.: Prentice-Hall, Inc., 1966.

EHRENBERG, A. S. C. "The Discovery and Use of Laws of Marketing," *Journal of Advertising Research,* Vol. 9, No. 2 (June 1969), pp. 11–17.

———. "Towards an Integrated Theory of Consumer Behavior," *Journal of the Market Research Society,* Vol. 11 (October 1969), pp. 308–23.

———. "Models of Fact: Examples from Marketing," *Management Science,* Vol. 16, No. 7 (March 1970), Theory Series, pp. 435–45.

ELLIOTT-JONES, M. F. "An Introduction to Input-Output Analysis," *The Conference Board RECORD,* January 1971, pp. 16–19.

EMSHOFF, JAMES R., and MERCER, ALAN. "Aggregate Models of Consumer Purchases," *Journal of the Royal Statistical Society, Series A. General,* Vol. 133, Part 1 (1970), pp. 14–32.

ENGEL, J. F. "Communicating Religious Truth in a Changing World." Paper delivered at the 1970 Fall Conference of the American Marketing Association, Boston.

———; BLACKWELL, ROGER D.; and KEGERREIS, ROBERT J. "How Information Is Used to Adopt an Innovation," *Journal of Advertising Research,* Vol. 9, No. 4 (December 1969), pp. 3–8.

———; KOLLAT, D. T., and BLACKWELL, R. D. *Consumer Behavior.* New York: Holt, Rinehart & Winston, Inc., 1968.

————, and WALES, H. G. "Spoken versus Pictured Questions on Taboo Topics," *Journal of Advertising Research,* Vol. 2 (March 1962), p. 17.

ESKIN, G. J. "Marketing Information Systems, a Model Builder's View." Paper read at a Workshop: Marketing Information Systems, TIMS/ORSA Joint Meeting, San Francisco, Calif., May 1–3, 1968.

ESTES, H. M. "Will Managers Be Overwhelmed by the Information Explosion?" *Armed Forces Management,* Vol. 13 (December 1966), pp. 75–84. In *Readings in Marketing Information Systems* (eds. S. V. Smith, R. H. Brien and J. E. Stafford), pp. 178–86. Boston: Houghton Mifflin Co., 1968.

EYSENCK, H. J. "Organization, Nature and Measurement of Attitudes," *Attitude Scaling.* London: The Market Research Society and The Oakwood Press, 1960.

FARLEY, JOHN U ."Brand Loyalty and the Economics of Information," *Journal of Business,* Vol. 37 (October 1964), pp. 370–79.

————, and HINICH, MELVIN J. "Spectral Analysis," *Journal of Advertising Research,* Vol. 9, No. 4 (December 1969), pp. 47–50.

————, and LEAVITT, H. J. "A Model of the Distribution of Branded Personal Products in Jamaica," *Journal of Marketing Research,* Vol. 5 (November 1968), pp. 362–68.

————, and ————. "Marketing and Population Problems," *Journal of Marketing,* Vol. 35 (July 1971), pp. 28–33.

————, and RING, L. W. "An Empirical Test of the Howard-Sheth Model of Buyer Behavior," *Journal of Marketing Research,* Vol. 7 (November 1970), pp. 427–38.

FEATHER, N. T. "The Study of Persistence," *Psychological Bulletin,* Vol. 59 (1962), pp. 94–115. Reprinted in J. W. Atkinson and N. T. Feather (1966), pp. 31–48.

FEDERAL AVIATION ADMINISTRATION. *Aviation Forecasts Fiscal Years 1970–1981.* New York: Department of Transportation, Federal Aviation Administration, Office of Aviation Economics, Aviation Forecast Division. 1970.

FEDERAL HOUSING ADMINISTRATION, DEPARTMENT OF HOUSING AND URBAN DEVELOPMENT. *Analysis of the Tulsa, Oklahoma, Housing Market as of May 1, 1967.* Washington, D.C.: Federal Housing Administration, 1967.

FENDRICH, J. M. "A Study of the Association among Verbal Attitudes, Commitment, and Overt Behavior in Different Experimental Situations," *Journal of Social Forces,* Vol. 45 (1967), pp. 347–55.

FERBER, R. "Research on Household Behavior," *American Economic Review,* Vol. 52 (March 1962), pp. 19–63.

————. "Anticipations Statistics and Consumer Behavior," *The American Statistician,* Vol. 20 (October 1966), pp. 20–24.

————, and WALES, H. G. (Eds.). *Motivation and Market Behavior.* Homewood, Ill.: Richard D. Irwin, Inc., 1958.

FERTAL, M. J., et al. *Modal Split, Documentation of Nine Methods for Estimating Transit Usage,* p. 1. U.S. Department of Commerce, Bureau of Public Roads, Office of Planning. Washington, D.C.: U.S. Government Printing Office, 1966.

FESTINGER, L. A. *A Theory of Cognitive Dissonance.* Stanford, Calif.: Stanford University Press, 1957.

————. "Behavior Support for Opinion Change," *Public Opinion Quarterly,* Vol. 27 (Fall 1964), pp. 404–17.

FISHBEIN, M. "A Behavior Theory Approach to the Relations between Beliefs about an Object and the Attitude Toward the Object," in *Readings in Attitude Theory and Measurement* (ed. M. Fishbein), pp. 394–96. New York: John Wiley & Sons, Inc., 1967.

———— (ed.). *Readings in Attitude Theory and Measurement.* New York: John Wiley & Sons, Inc., 1967.

————. "The Search for Attitudinal-Behavioral Consistency," in *Behavioral Science Foundations of Consumer Behavior* (ed. J. B. Cohen). New York: The Free Press, 1971.

————, and RAVEN, B. H. "The AB Scales: An Operational Definition of Belief and Attitude," *Human Relations,* Vol. 15 (1962), pp. 35–44. Republished in Fishbein (1967), pp. 183–89.

FISK, G. *Marketing Systems.* New York: Harper & Row, Publishers, 1967.

FOOTE, N. N. "Asking the Right Questions." Paper presented to Second National Conference on Research Design, American Marketing Association, New York City, March 11, 1965.

FRANK, R. E. "Market Segmentation Research: Findings and Implications," in Bass, King, and Pessemier (1968), pp. 39–68.

————; MASSY, W. F.; and WIND, Y. *Market Segmentation.* Englewood Cliffs, N.J.: Prentice-Hall, Inc., 1972.

FREEDMAN, J. L., and SEARS, D. O. "Selective Exposure," in *Advances in Experimental Social Psychology* (ed. L. Berkowitz), Vol. 2, pp. 57–97. New York: Academic Press, Inc., 1965.

FREEDMAN, RONALD; COOMBS, LOLAGENE C.; and BUMPASS, LARRY. "Stability and Change in Expectations about Family Size: A Longitudinal Study," *Demography,* Vol. 2 (1965), pp. 250–75.

FRIEDLANDER, STANLEY, and SILVER, MORRIS. "A Quantitative Study of the Determinants of Fertility Behavior," *Demography,* Vol. 4 (1967), pp. 30–70.

FROST, W. A. K., and BRAINE, R. L. "The Application of the Repertory Grid Technique to Problems in Market Research," *Commentary,* Vol. 9 (July 1967), pp. 161–75.

GARDNER, D. M. (ed.). Proceedings of 2d Annual Conference of the Association for Consumer Research. College Park, Md., September 1–3, 1971.

GARFINKLE, NORTON. "The Value and Use of Psychographic Information in Decision Making," in King and Tigert (1971), pp. 206–10.

GATTY, R. "Multivariate Analysis for Marketing Research," *Applied Statistics,* Vol. 15 (1966), pp. 151–72.

GERRA, M. J. *The Demand, Supply, and Price Structure for Eggs.* Technical Bulletin No. 1204, U.S. Department of Agriculture. Washington, D.C.: U.S. Government Printing Office, 1959.

GERSON, MARTIN L., and MAFFEI, RICHARD B. "Technical Characteristics of Distribution Simulators," *Management Science,* Vol. 10 (October 1963), pp. 62–69.

GOLDBERG, M. E. "A Cognitive Model of Innovative Behavior: The Interaction of Product and Self-Attitudes," in Gardner (1971), pp. 313–30.

GOLDSTUCKER, J. L. "The Influence of Culture on Channels of Distribution." Proceedings of the American Marketing Association, Fall 1968, pp. 468–73.

GOLIN, E., and LYERLY, S. B. "The Galvanic Skin Response as a Test of Advertising Impact," *Journal of Applied Psychology,* Vol. 34 (December 1950), pp. 440–43.

GOULD, J. M. "Sales Analysis and the Data Processing Revolution," *Sales Management,* June 10, 1963, pp. 66–73.

GRAFFAM, D. T. "Brief Historical Introduction to Motivation," in *Understanding Human Motivation* (eds. C. L. Stacey and M. F. DeMartino), pp. 4–11. Cleveland, Ohio: Howard Allen, Inc., 1963.

GRAHAM, S. "Class and Conservatism in the Adoption of Innovations," *Human Relations,* Vol. 9 (1956), pp. 91–100. Republished in Bliss (1967), pp. 195–207.

GREEN, D. M., and SWETS, J. A. *Signal Detection Theory and Psychophysics.* New York: John Wiley & Sons, Inc., 1966.

GREEN, P. E. "Consumer Use of Information," in *On Knowing the Consumer,* (ed. J. W. Newman), pp. 67–80. New York: John Wiley & Sons, Inc., 1966.

———, and CARMONE, F. J. "The Performance of the Computer Market. A Multivariate Approach," *Economics and Business Bulletin,* Vol. 21 (1968), pp. 1–11.

———, and ———. "Multidimensional Scaling: An Introduction and Comparison of Nonmetric Unfolding Techniques," *Journal of Marketing Research,* Vol. 6 (August 1969), pp. 330–41.

———, and ———. *Multidimensional Scaling and Related Techniques in Marketing Analysis.* Boston: Allyn & Bacon, Inc., 1970.

————, and RAO, VITHALA R. "A Note on Proximity Measures and Cluster Analysis," *Journal of Marketing Research,* Vol. 6, No. 3. (August 1969), pp. 359–64.

————, and ————. "Nonmetric Approaches to Multivariate Analysis in Marketing." Working Paper, Marketing Science Institute, April 1970a.

————, and ————. "Rating Scales and Information Recovery—How Many Scales and Response Categories to Use?" *Journal of Marketing,* Vol. 34 (July 1970b), pp. 33–39.

————, and ————. *Applied Multidimensional Scaling.* New York: Holt, Rinehart & Winston, Inc., 1972.

————; ROBINSON, P. J.; and FITZROY, P. T. *Experiments on the Value of Information in Simulated Marketing Environments.* Boston: Allyn & Bacon, Inc., 1967.

————, and TULL, D. S. *Research for Marketing Decisions.* Englewood Cliffs, N.J.: Prentice-Hall, Inc., 1966.

GREENBERG, M. G. "Some Applications of Nonmetric Multidimensional Scaling." Proceedings of the American Statistical Association, August 19–22, 1969, pp. 104–9.

GROSSACK, MARTIN M. (ed.). *Understanding Consumer Behavior.* Boston: The Christopher Publishing House, 1964.

————. *Consumer Psychology: Theory and Practice,* p. 32. Boston: Branden Press, Inc., 1971.

GRUBB, E. L., and HUPP, G. "Perception of Self, Generalized Stereotypes and Brand Selection," *Journal of Marketing Research,* Vol. 5 (February 1968), pp. 58–63.

GUILFORD, J. P. *Psychometric Methods.* New York: McGraw-Hill Book Co., 1954.

————. *The Nature of Human Intelligence.* New York: McGraw-Hill Book Co., 1967.

HAINES, G. H. JR. "A Theory of Market Behavior after Innovation," *Management Science,* Vol. 10 (July 1964).

————. *Consumer Behavior: Learning Models of Purchasing.* New York: The Free Press, 1969.

HALEY, R. I. "Benefit Segmentation." Lecture given at Cornell University, March 2, 1972.

————. "Benefit Segmentation: A Decision-oriented Research Tool," *Journal of Marketing,* Vol. 32 (July 1968), pp. 30–35.

HALL, A. D., and FAGEN, R. E. "Definition of System," in *General Systems Yearbook of the Society for the Advancement of General Systems Theory,* Vol. 1, p. 18. The Society for General Systems Research, 1956.

HALL, E. T. "The Silent Language in Overseas Business," *Harvard Business Review*, Vol. 38 (May–June 1960), pp. 87–96. For details, see E. T. Hall. *The Silent Language.* Garden City, N.Y.: Doubleday & Co., Inc., 1959.

HANSEN, FLEMING, and BOLLAND, THOMAS. "The Relationship between Cognitive Models of Choice and Non-Metric Multidimensional Scaling," in Gardner (1971), pp. 376–88.

HARBERGER, ARNOLD C. (ed.). *The Demand for Durable Goods.* Chicago: University of Chicago Press, 1960.

HARP, H. H., and MILLER, M. "Convenience Foods: The Relationship between Sales Volume and Factors Influencing Demand." Agricultural Economic Report No. 81, Economic Research Service, U.S. Department of Agriculture, revised October 1965.

HARRIS, RICHARD J. "Dissonance or Sour Grapes? Post-'Decision Changes' in Ratings and Choice Frequencies," *Journal of Personality and Social Psychology*, Vol. 11, No. 4 (April 1969), pp. 334–44.

HEIDER, F. "Attitudes and Cognitive Organization," *Journal of Psychology* Vol. 21 (January 1946), pp. 107–12.

———. "The Gestalt Theory of Motivation," in *Nebraska Symposium on Motivation* (ed. M. R. Jones), pp. 145–72. Lincoln, Nebr.: University of Nebraska Press, 1960.

HEINECKE, H. H. "Sales Quotas." *Marketing Research in Action.* National Industrial Conference Board Studies in Business Policy No. 84, p. 64. New York, 1957.

HEISE, DAVID R. "Some Methodological Issues in Semantic Differential Research," *Psychological Bulletin*, Vol. 72, No. 6 (December 1969), pp. 406–22.

———. "The Semantic Differential and Attitude Research," in *Attitude Measurement* (ed. G. Summers). Skokie, Ill.: Rand McNally & Co., 1970.

HENRY, NEIL W.; McGINNIS, ROBERT; and TEGTMEYER, HEINRICH W. "A Finite Model of Mobility." Paper delivered at the meetings of the Population Association, Boston, Mass., April 18, 19, 20, 1968. Mimeographed.

HESS, E. H. "Attitude and Pupil Size," *Scientific American*, Vol. 212 (April 1965), pp. 46–54.

HESS, J. M. "Group Interviewing," Proceedings of the American Marketing Association, 1968 (ed. R. L. King), pp. 193–96.

HEYMAN, T. R. "Use of Census Data in Interregional Marketing," *Sloan Management Review*, Vol. 12 (Winter 1971), pp. 17–31.

HILGARD, E. R. *Theories of Learning.* 2d ed. New York: Appleton-Century-Crofts, 1956.

———, and BOWER, G. H. *Theories of Learning.* New York: Appleton-Century-Crofts, 1966.

HILTON, PETER. *Planning Corporate Growth and Diversification.* New York: McGraw-Hill Book Co., 1970.

HINKLE, J. *Life Cycles.* Chicago: A. C. Nielsen, 1966.

HOINVILLE, G. W. "Transport Research for Town Planning," *Commentary (The Journal of the Market Research Society),* Vol. 9 (July 1967), pp. 147–60.

HOLTON, R. H. "The Distinction between Convenience Goods, Shopping Goods, and Specialty Goods," *Journal of Marketing,* Vol. 23 (July 1958), pp. 53–56.

HOOVER, D. F. "Models for Campaign Planning," Abstracts of the 1970 Fall Conference of the American Marketing Association (ed. D. L. Sparks), p. 87.

HOPKINS, DAVID S., and BAILEY, EARL L. "New Product Pressures," *The Conference Board RECORD,* June 1971, pp. 16–20.

HOUTHAKKER, H. S., and TAYLOR, L. D. *Consumer Demand in the United States: Analyses and Projections.* 2d ed. Cambridge, Mass.: Harvard University Press, 1970.

HOVLAND, C. I.; JANIS, I. L.; and KELLEY, H. H. *Communication and Persuasion.* New Haven, Conn.: Yale University Press, 1953.

HOWARD, J. A. *Marketing Theory.* Boston: Allyn & Bacon, Inc., 1965.

———, and MORGENROTH, W. M. "Information Processing Model of Executive Decisions," *Management Science,* Vol. 14 (March 1968), pp. 416–28.

———, and SHETH, J. N. *The Theory of Buyer Behavior.* New York: John Wiley & Sons, Inc., 1969.

HUGHES, G. D. "Selecting Scales to Measure Attitude Changes," *Journal of Marketing Research,* Vol. 4 (February 1967), pp. 85–87.

———. "Measurement, the Neglected Half of Marketing Theory," in *Marketing and the New Science of Planning* (ed. R. L. King), pp. 151–53. Fall Conference Proceedings, American Marketing Association, August 28–30, 1968.

———. "Some Confounding Effects of Forced-Choice Scales," *Journal of Marketing Research,* Vol. 6 (May 1969), pp. 223–26.

———. *Attitude Measurement for Marketing Strategies.* Glenview, Ill.: Scott, Foresman and Co., 1971.

———, and GUERRERO, J. L. "Simultaneous Concept Testing with Computer-Controlled Experiments," *Journal of Marketing,* Vol. 25 (January 1971a), pp. 28–33.

———, and ———. "Automobile Self-Congruity Models Reexamined," *Journal of Marketing Research,* Vol. 8 (February 1971b), pp. 125–27.

———, and ———. "Testing Models through Computer-Controlled Experiments," *Journal of Marketing Research,* Vol. 8 (August 1971c), pp. 291–97.

————; ————; and SMITH, D. B. "A Computer-Controlled Experiment in Executive Information Processing." Working paper. Graduate School of Business and Public Administration, Cornell University, August, 1970.

————, and NAERT, P. A. "A Computer-Controlled Experiment in Consumer Behavior," *Journal of Business,* Vol. 43 (July 1970), pp. 354–72.

————; TINIC, S. M.; and NAERT, P. A. "Analyzing Consumer Information Processing." Proceedings of the Fall Meetings of the American Marketing Association, Cincinnati, August 25–27, 1969, pp. 235–40.

HULL, C. L. *Principles of Behavior.* New York: Appleton-Century-Crofts, 1943.

HUSTAD, T. P., and PESSEMIER, E. A. *Segmenting Consumer Markets with Activity and Attitude Measures.* Institute for Research in the Behavioral, Economic, and Management Sciences, Purdue University, Working Paper No. 298, March 1971.

HYRENIUS, HANNES, et al. *A Fertility Simulation Model.* Reports Nos. 2 to 5. Goteborg, Sweden: University of Goteborg, 1964 to 1967.

INGLIS, J., and JOHNSON, D. "Some Observations on, and Developments in, the Analysis of Multivariate Survey Data," *Journal of the Market Research Society,* Vol. 12, No. 2 (April 1970), pp. 75–98.

INSKO, C. A. *Theories of Attitude Change.* New York: Appleton-Century-Crofts, 1967.

THE INSTITUTE FOR INTERINDUSTRY DATA AND THE INPUT/OUTPUT COMMITTEE OF THE AMERICAN MARKETING ASSOCIATION. *An Industry and Government Review of the Standard Industrial Classification System.* Symposium, June 28, 1968. Mimeographed.

JACOBY, J. "Innovation Proneness as a Function of Personality," Abstracts, Fall Conference, American Marketing Association, 1970, (ed. D. L. Sparks), p. 121.

————. "Personality and Innovation Proneness," *Journal of Marketing Research,* Vol. 8 (May 1971), pp. 244–47.

JAFFE, L. J., and SENFT, H. "The Roles of Husbands and Wives in Purchasing Decisions," *Attitude Research at Sea* (eds. L. Adler and I. Crespi), pp. 95–110. Chicago: American Marketing Association, 1966.

JOHNSON, R. M. "Market Segmentation—A Comparison of Techniques." A paper delivered at the 16th International Meeting of the Institute of Management Science, New York, March 27, 1969.

————. "Techniques of Market Segmentation: Cluster Analysis vs. Q Analysis." Paper delivered at the 1969 International Marketing Congress, American Marketing Association, June 1969. Mimeographed.

————. "Relationships between Product Attributes and Preferential Choice Behavior." Proceedings of the American Statistical Association, 1969, pp. 97–103.

————. "Market Segmentation: A Strategic Management Tool," *Journal of Marketing Research,* Vol. 8 (February 1971), pp. 13–18.

JOHNSTON, J. *Econometric Methods.* New York: McGraw-Hill Book Co., 1963.

JONES, A.; WILDINSON, J.; and BRADEN, I. "Information Deprivation as a Motivational Variable," *Journal of Experimental Psychology,* Vol. 62 (August 1961), pp. 126–37.

JONES, J. MORGAN. "A Comparison of Three Models of Brand Choice, *Journal of Marketing Research,* Vol. 7, No. 4 (November 1970), pp. 466–73.

JUSTER, F. T. *Consumer Buying Intentions and Purchase Probability.* Occasional Paper 99, National Bureau of Economic Research. New York: Columbia University Press, 1966.

KAMEN, JOSEPH M. "Quick Clustering," *Journal of Marketing Research,* Vol. 7, No. 2 (May 1970), pp. 199–204.

KAPLAN, A. *The Conduct of Inquiry.* San Francisco, Calif.: Chandler Publishing Co., 1964.

KASSARJIAN, H. H. "Personality and Consumer Behavior: A Review," Abstracts (ed. D. L. Sparks), p. 19. Fall Conference. Chicago: American Marketing Association, 1970.

————. "Incorporating Ecology into Marketing Strategy: The Case of Air Pollution," *Journal of Marketing,* Vol. 35 (July 1971a), pp. 61–65.

————. "Personality and Consumer Behavior: A Review," *Journal of Marketing Research,* Vol. 8 (November 1971b), pp. 409–18.

KATONA, GEORGE. *Aspiration and Affluence.* New York: McGraw-Hill Book Co., 1971.

————. "Measurement and Predictive Value of Attitudes and Expectations," in King and Tigert (1971), pp. 331–38.

————; DUNKELBERG, W.; SCHMIEDESKAMP, J.; and STAFFORD, F. *1968 Survey of Consumer Finances.* Ann Arbor: Survey Research Center, Institute for Social Research, The University of Michigan, 1969.

KATZ, D., and KAHN, R. L. *The Social Psychology of Organizations.* New York: John Wiley & Sons, Inc., 1965.

KATZ, E., and LAZARSFELD, P. F. *Personal Influence.* New York: The Free Press, 1955.

KEGERREIS, R. J. "Diffusion of Innovations: Implications for Decision-Making in Marketing." Paper delivered at the Second Midwest Meeting of the American Institute for Decision Sciences, Bowling Green State University, Bowling Green, Ohio, April 2–3, 1971.

KELLEY, EUGENE J. *Marketing Planning and Competitive Strategy.* Englewood Cliffs, N.J.: Prentice-Hall, Inc., 1972.

————. "Marketing's Changing Social/Environmental Role," *Journal of Marketing,* Vol. 35 (July 1971), pp. 1–2.

KERLINGER, F. N. *Foundations of Behavioral Research.* New York: Holt, Rinehart & Winston, Inc., 1965.

KERNAN, J. B. "Graph Theoretic Models in Marketing," *Scientific Business,* Vol. 3 (Spring 1966), pp. 331–43.

———. "The CAD Instrument in Behavioral Diagnosis," in Gardner (1971), pp. 307–12.

———, and HAINES, G. H. "Environmental Search, an Information-Theoretic Approach," *Decision Sciences,* Vol. 2 (April 1971), pp. 161–71.

KEYFITZ, NATHAN. "On the Interaction of Populations," *Demography,* Vol. 2 (1965), pp. 276–88.

KIESLER, C. A.; COLLINS, B. E.; and MILLER, N. *Attitude Change.* New York: John Wiley & Sons, Inc., 1969.

———. *The Psychology of Commitment.* New York: Academic Press, 1971.

KING, C. W. "Fashion Adoption: A Rebuttal to the 'Trickle Down' Theory," *Proceedings of the American Marketing Association,* December 1963, pp. 108–25.

———. "Adoption and Diffusion Research in Marketing: An Overview," Proceedings of the American Marketing Association, Fall 1966, pp. 665–84.

———, and RYAN, G. E. "Identifying the Innovator as a Consumer Change Agent," in Gardner (1971), pp. 446–51.

———, and SUMMERS, J. O. "Generalized Opinion Leadership in Consumer Products: Some Preliminary Findings." Institute for Research in the Behavioral, Economic, and Management Sciences, Institute Paper No. 224 (January 1969). Krannert Graduate School of Industrial Administration, Purdue University.

———, and TIGERT, D. J. (eds.). *Attitude Research Reaches New Heights.* Marketing Research Techniques, Bibliography Series No. 14. Chicago: American Marketing Association, 1971.

KINNEAR, T. C., and TAYLOR, J. R. "Multivariate Methods in Marketing Research: A Further Attempt at Classification," *Journal of Marketing,* Vol. 35 (October 1971), pp. 56–59.

KISH, LESLIE. "Variances for Indexes from Complex Samples." Proceedings of the American Statistical Association, Social Statistics Section, 1962, pp. 190–99.

KLAHR, DAVID. "Decision Making in a Complex Environment: The Use of Similarity Judgments to Predict Preferences," *Management Science,* Vol. 15, No. 11 (July 1969), pp. 595–618.

KLAPPER, J. T. *The Effects of Mass Communication.* New York: The Free Press, 1961.

KLEINMUNTZ, B. *Personality Measurement: An Introduction.* Homewood, Ill.: Dorsey Press, 1967.

KNIGHT, F. H. *The Ethics of Competition.* New York: Harper & Row, Publishers, 1935.

KOLLAT, DAVID T.; ENGLE, JAMES F.; and BLACKWELL, ROGER D. "Current Problems in Consumer Behavior Research," *Journal of Marketing Research,* Vol. 7, No. 3 (August 1970), pp. 327–32.

KOOPMANS, T. "Statistical Estimation of Simultaneous Economic Relationships," *American Statistical Association Journal,* Vol. 49 (1945), pp. 448–66.

KOTLER, P. "Competitive Strategies for New Product Marketing Over the Life Cycle Curve," *Management Science,* Vol. 12 (December 1965), pp. 104–19.

———. "Mathematical Models of Individual Buyer Behavior," *Behavioral Science,* Vol. 13 (1968), pp. 274–87.

———. "New Directions for Marketing." Abstracts of the 1970 Fall Conference of the American Marketing Association (ed. D. L. Sparks), p. 1.

———. *Marketing Decision Making: A Model Building Approach.* New York: Holt, Rinehart & Winston, Inc., 1971.

———, and LEVY, S. "Broadening the Concept of Marketing," *Journal of Marketing,* Vol. 33 (January 1969), pp. 10–15.

———, and ZALTMAN, G. "Social Marketing: An Approach to Planned Social Change," *Journal of Marketing,* Vol. 35 (July 1971), pp. 3–12.

KOYCK, J. M. *Distributed Lags and Investment Analysis.* Amsterdam: North-Holland Publishing Co., 1954.

KRAUSS, R. M. "Language as a Symbolic Process in Communication," *American Scientist,* Vol. 56 (Autumn 1968), pp. 265–78.

KRECH, D.; CRUTCHFIELD, R. S.; and BALLACHEY, E. L. *Individual in Society.* New York: McGraw-Hill Book Co., 1962.

KUEHN, A. A. "Consumer Brand Choice—A Learning Process?" *Quantitative Techniques in Marketing Analysis* (eds. R. E. Frank, A. A. Kuehn, and W. F. Massy), pp. 390–403. Homewood, Ill.: Richard D. Irwin, Inc., 1962.

LADINSKY, JACK. "Sources of Geographic Mobility among Professional Workers: A Multivariate Analysis," *Demography,* Vol. 4 (1967), pp. 293–309.

LAMBIN, J. J. "Optimal Allocation of Competitive Marketing Efforts: An Empirical Study," *The Journal of Business,* Vol. 43 (October 1970), pp. 468–84.

LANCASTER, K. J. "A New Approach to Consumer Theory," *Journal of Political Economy,* Vol. 74 (April 1966), pp. 132–57.

LANZILLOTTI, R. F. "Pricing Objectives in Large Companies," *American Economic Review,* Vol. 47 (December 1958), pp. 921–40.

LAVIDGE, R. J., and STEINER, G. A. "A Model for Predictive Measurements of Advertising Effectiveness," *Journal of Marketing,* Vol. 25 (October 1961), pp. 59–62.

LAVINGTON, MICHAEL R. "A Practical Microsimulation Model for Consumer Marketing," *Operational Research Quarterly,* Vol. 21, No. 1 (March 1970), pp. 25–45.

LAZARSFELD, P. F. *Mathematical Thinking in the Social Sciences.* New York: The Free Press, 1954.

LAZER, WILLIAM. "Life Style Concepts and Marketing," Proceedings of the American Marketing Association, December 1963, pp. 130–39.

————, and BELL, W. E. "The Communication Process and Innovation," *Journal of Advertising Research,* Vol. 6 (September 1966), pp. 2–7.

LEHMANN, D. R. "A Basis for a Marketing Information System," Abstracts, Fall Conference, American Marketing Association, 1970 (ed. D. L. Sparks), p. 39.

————; FARLEY, J. U.; and HOWARD, J. A. "Testing of Buyer Behavior Models," in Gardner (1971), pp. 232–42.

LEIBENSTEIN, H. *Economic Theory and Organizational Analysis,* Part IV. New York: Harper & Row, Publishers, 1960.

LEONTIEF, W. "The Structure of the U.S. Economy," *Scientific American,* April 1965.

LEVITT, T. "Exploit the Product Life Cycle," *Harvard Business Review,* November–December 1965, pp. 81–94.

————. *The Marketing Mode—Pathways to Corporate Growth.* New York: McGraw-Hill Book Co., 1969.

LEVY, S. J. "Symbols by Which We Buy." Proceedings of the American Marketing Association, December 1958, pp. 409–16.

————. "Social Class and Consumer Behavior," *On Knowing the Consumer* (ed. J. W. Newman), p. 153. New York: John Wiley & Sons, Inc., 1966.

LEWIN, KURT. *Field Theory in Social Sciences: Selected Theoretical Papers* (ed. Dorwin Cartwright). New York: Harper & Row, Publishers, 1951.

LINDEN, FABIAN. "The Family Market-Young and Old," *The Conference Board RECORD,* Vol. 7 (August 1970), pp. 26–30.

————. "Young Adults," *The Conference Board RECORD,* April 1971, pp. 53–56.

————. "Age by Income—1980," *The Conference Board RECORD,* June 1971, pp. 25–27.

LIONBERGER, H. F. *Adoption of New Ideas and Practices.* Ames, Iowa: Iowa State University Press, 1960.

LIPSET, S. M. *Political Man.* Garden City, New York: Anchor Publishing Co., 1959.

LIPSTEIN, B. "A Mathematical Model of Consumer Behavior," *Journal of Marketing Research,* Vol. 2 (August 1965), pp. 259–65.

————. "Modeling and New Product Birth," *Journal of Advertising Research,* Vol. 10, No. 5 (October 1970), pp. 3–11.

LITTLE, A. D., INC. *The Market for Postal Services. Report to the President's Commission on Postal Organization.* Cambridge, Mass., 1968.

LLOYD, P. J. "American, German and British Antecedents to Pearl and Reed's Logistic Curve," *Population Studies,* Vol. 21 (September 1967), pp. 99–108.

LUCE, R. D., and SUPPES, P. "Preference, Utility, and Subjective Probability," in *Handbook of Mathematical Psychology; Vol. III* (eds. R. D. Luce, R. R. Bush, and E. Galanter), pp. 249–410. New York: John Wiley & Sons, Inc., 1965.

LUCK, D. J. "Interfaces of a Product Manager," *Journal of Marketing,* Vol. 33 (October 1969), pp. 32–36.

LUNN, J. A. "Empirical Techniques in Consumer Research," in *Industrial Society* (ed. D. Pym), pp. 401–25. Baltimore, Md.: Penguin Books, Inc., 1968.

————. "Prospectives in Attitude Research: Methods and Applications," *Journal of the Market Research Society,* Vol. 11 (1969), pp. 201–13.

MACDONALD, M. B. JR. *Appraising the Market for New Industrial Products,* chap. 3. Business Policy Study, No. 123. New York: National Industrial Conference Board, 1967.

McFALL, JOHN. "Priority Patterns and Consumer Behavior," *Journal of Marketing,* Vol. 33 (October 1969), pp. 50–55.

McGUIRE, W. J. "An Information-Processing Model of Advertising Effectiveness." Paper read at the *Symposium on Behavior and Management Science in Marketing,* Center for Continuing Education, the University of Chicago, June 11, 1969.

————. "Theory of the Structure of Human Thought." Paper presented at the Symposium on Behavioral and Management Science in Marketing, Center for Continuing Education, The University of Chicago, June 1969.

————. "The Guiding Theories Behind Attitude Change Research," in King and Tigert (1971), pp. 26–48.

McKITTERICK, J. B. "What Is the Marketing Management Concept?" *The Frontiers of Marketing Thought and Science* (ed. F. M. Bass). Chicago: American Marketing Association, 1957.

McNEAL, J. U. (ed.). *Dimensions of Consumer Behavior.* 2d ed. New York: Appleton-Century-Crofts, 1969.

————, and STOTERAU, T. L. "The Census Bureau's New Survey of Consumer Buying Expectations," *American Statistical Association 1967 Proceedings of the Business and Economic Statistics Section,* pp. 79–113. Washington, D.C.: American Statistical Association, 1968.

MAHER, B. A.; WATT, N.; and CAMPBELL, D. T. "Comparative Validity of Two Projective and Two Structured Attitude Tests in a Prison Population," *Journal of Applied Psychology,* Vol. 44 (August 1960), p. 284.

MANSFIELD, E. "Intrafirm Rates of Diffusion of an Innovation," *The Review of Economics and Statistics,* Vol. 45 (November 1963), pp. 348–59.

———. *Industrial Research and Technological Innovation.* New York: W. W. Norton & Co., Inc., 1968.

MARCHANT, L. "Attitudes of Individuals and the Purchasing Behaviour of Populations," in *The Thomson Medals and Awards for Advertising Research 1970,* pp. 51–74. Manchester, England; Withy Grove Press Limited, 1971.

MARGENAU, H. *The Nature of Physical Reality.* New York: McGraw-Hill Book Co., 1950.

Marketing Insights, November 28, 1966, p. 10.

MARRIS, R. *The Economic Theory of Managerial Capitalism.* New York: The Free Press of Glencoe, 1964.

MARSCHNER, D. C. "Dagmar Revisited—Eight Years Later," *Journal of Advertising Research,* Vol. 11 (April 1971), pp. 27–33.

MARTIN, A. "Empirical and A Priori in Economics," *The British Journal for the Philosophy of Science,* Vol. 15 (August 1964), pp. 123–36.

MARTINEAU, P. "Social Classes and Spending Behavior," *Journal of Marketing,* Vol. 23 (October 1958), pp. 121–30.

MASLOW, A. H. *Motivation and Personality.* New York: Harper & Row, Publishers, 1954.

MASSY, W. F. "Discriminant Analysis of Audience Characteristics," *Journal of Advertising Research,* Vol. 5 (March 1965), pp. 39–48.

———; FRANK, R. E.; and LODAHL, T. *Purchasing Behavior and Personal Attributes.* Philadelphia, Pa.: University of Pennsylvania Press, 1968.

———, and SAVVAS, J. D. "Logical Flow Models for Marketing Analysis," *Journal of Marketing,* Vol. 28 (January 1964), pp. 30–37.

———; MONTGOMERY, D. B.; and MORRISON, D. G. *Stochastic Models of Buying Behavior.* Cambridge, Mass.: The M.I.T. Press, 1970.

MATHEWS, H. L.; SLOCUM, J. W. JR.; and WOODSIDE, A. G. "Perceived Risk, Individual Differences, and Shopping Orientations," in Gardner (1971), pp. 299–306.

MAYER, LAWRENCE A. "Why the U.S. Population *Isn't* Exploding," *Fortune,* Vol. 75 (April 1967), p. 162.

———. "New Questions about the U.S. Population," *Fortune* (February 1971), pp. 80ff.

Merchandising Week, May 18, 1970, p. 17; and April 19, 1971, p. 8.

MICKWITZ, GOSTA. *Marketing and Competition: The Various Forms of Competition at the Successive Stages of Production and Distribution.* Societas

Scientiarum Fennica Commentationes Humanarum Litterarum XXIV. 2. Helsingfors, 1959.

MINDAK, W. A., and BYBEE, H. M. "Marketing's Application to Fund Raising," *Journal of Marketing,* Vol. 35 (July 1971), pp. 13–18.

MINOR, R. B. "Distribution Costs," in *Marketing Handbook* (ed. A. W. Frey). 2d ed. New York: The Ronald Press Co., 1965.

MISCHEL, W. *Personality and Assessment.* New York: John Wiley & Sons, Inc., 1968.

———. "Continuity and Change in Personality," *American Psychologist,* Vol. 24 (1969), pp. 1012–18.

MOINPOUR, REZA, and MACLACHLAN, D. L. "The Relations among Attribute and Importance Components of Rosenberg-Fishbein Type Attitude Model: An Empirical Investigation," in Gardner (1971), pp. 365–75.

MONSEN, R. J. JR., and DOWNS, A. "A Theory of Large Managerial Firms," *Journal of Political Economy,* Vol. 72 (June 1965), pp. 221–36.

MONTGOMERY, D. B., and SILK, A. J. "Patterns of Overlap in Opinion Leadership and Interest for Selected Categories of Purchasing Activity." *Marketing Involvement in Society and the Economy.* Proceedings of the American Marketing Association, August 1969, pp. 377–86.

———, and URBAN, G. L. *Management Science in Marketing.* Englewood Cliffs, N. J.: Prentice-Hall, Inc., 1969.

MORGAN, N., and PURNELL, J. "Isolating Openings for New Products in a Multidimensional Space," *Journal of the Market Research Society,* Vol. 11 (July 1969), pp. 255–60.

MOWRER, O. H. "Q-Technique—Description, History, and Critique," in *Psychotherapy: Theory and Research* (ed. O. H. Mowrer). New York: The Ronald Press Co., 1953.

MUELLER, E. "Ten Years of Consumer Attitude Surveys: Their Forecasting Record," *Journal of the American Statistical Association,* Vol. 58 (December 1963).

MURRAY, J. ALEX. "Canadian Consumer Expectational Data: An Evaluation," *Journal of Marketing Research,* Vol. 6 (February 1969), pp. 54–61.

———. "Utilizing Consumer Expectational Data to Allocate Promotional Efforts," *Journal of Marketing,* Vol. 33 (April 1969), pp. 26–33.

MYERS, G. C., and ROBERTS, J. M. "A Technique for Measuring Preferential Family Size and Composition," *Eugenics Quarterly,* Vol. 15 (September 1968), pp. 164–72.

MYERS, JOHN G. "Patterns of Interpersonal Influence in Adoption of New Products," in *Science Technology and Marketing* (ed. Raymond M. Hass). Proceedings of the Fall Conference, American Marketing Association, 1966.

————, and YEN, J. Y. "Diffusion Models and Advertising Effectiveness: A Shortest Path Approach." Paper delivered at the Western Section of the Operations Research Society, Monterey, Calif., February 6–7, 1969.

MYERS, J. H., and REYNOLDS, W. H. *Consumer Behavior and Marketing Management.* Boston: Houghton Mifflin Co., 1967.

NAGEL, E. *The Structure of Science.* New York: Harcourt, Brace & World, Inc., 1961.

NAKANISHI, MASSAO. "Consumer Learning in Awareness and Trial of New Products," in Gardner (1971), pp. 186–96.

NATIONAL CENTER FOR HEALTH STATISTICS, U.S. PUBLIC HEALTH SERVICE, U.S. DEPARTMENT OF HEALTH, EDUCATION, AND WELFARE. *Natality Statistics Analysis.* Series 21, No. 1. Washington, D.C.: U.S. Government Printing Office, 1964.

————. *Fertility Measurement.* Series 4, No. 1. Washington, D.C.: U.S. Government Printing Office, 1965.

————. *Methods and Response Characteristics, National Natality Survey, United States, 1963.* Series 22, No. 3. Washington, D.C.: U.S. Government Printing Office, 1966.

"National Income and Product Tables," *Survey of Current Business,* Vol. 51 (February, 1971).

NEIDELL, L. A. "The Use of Nonmetric Multidimensional Scaling in Marketing Analysis," *Journal of Marketing,* Vol. 33 (October 1969), pp. 37–43.

————, and TEACH, R. D. "Preference and Perceptual Mapping of a Convenience Good," in Proceedings of the American Marketing Association, 1969 (ed. P. R. McDonald), pp. 188–93.

NELSON, A. R. "Psyching Psychographics: A Look at Why People Buy," in King and Tigert (1971), pp. 181–88.

"New Focus on Potential Markets," *Printers' Ink,* March 12, 1965, p. 33.

NEWMAN, J. W. *Marketing Management and Information.* Homewood, Ill.: Richard D. Irwin, Inc., 1967.

————, and STAELIN, R. "Multivariate Analysis of Differences in Buyer Decision Time," *Journal of Marketing Research,* Vol. 8 (May 1971), pp. 192–98.

NICOSIA, F. M. *Consumer Decision Processes.* Englewood Cliffs, N.J.: Prentice-Hall, Inc., 1966.

————, and GLOCK, C. Y. "Marketing and Affluence: A Research Prospectus." Proceedings of the American Marketing Association, 1968 Fall Conference pp. 510–27.

NIESSER, U. *Cognitive Psychology.* New York: Appleton-Century-Crofts, 1967.

NORMAN, D. A. *Memory and Attention: An Introduction to Human Information Processing.* New York: John Wiley & Sons, Inc., 1969.

NORTH, HARPER Q., and PYKE, D. L. " 'Probes' of the Technological Future," *Harvard Business Review,* May–June 1969, pp. 68–82.

NUNNALLY, J. *Psychometric Theory.* New York: McGraw-Hill Book Co., 1967.

O'BRIEN, TERRENCE. "Stages of Consumer Decision Making," *Journal of Marketing Research,* Vol. 8 (August 1971), pp. 283–89.

O'CONNOR, R. W. "An Approach to Information Flow in a Public Family Planning Program." *Abstracts* of the 1970 Fall Conference of the American Marketing Association (ed. D. L. Sparks), p. 17.

ORCUTT, GUY H., et al. *Microanalysis of Socio-economic Systems: A Simulation Study.* New York: Harper & Bros., 1961.

OSBORNE, D. K. "On the Goals of the Firm," *Quarterly Journal of Economics,* Vol. 78 (November 1964), pp. 592–603.

OSGOOD, C. E.; SUCI, G. J.; and TANNENBAUM, P. H. *The Measurement of Meaning.* Urbana, Ill.: University of Illinois Press, 1957.

―――, and TANNENBAUM, P. "The Principle of Congruity in the Prediction of Attitude Changes," *Psychological Review,* Vol. 62 (1955), pp. 42–55.

OSHIKAWA, S. "Can Cognitive Dissonance Theory Explain Consumer Behavior?" *Journal of Marketing,* Vol. 33 (October 1969), pp. 44–49.

―――. "Learning and Behavior Without Awareness," *California Management Review,* Vol. 12 (Summer 1970), pp. 61–69.

OSTLUND, L. E. "Applications of Tree-Diagram Analysis to the Study of Innovative Behavior." Paper presented at the meetings of the Association for Consumer Research, The University of Massachusetts, Amherst, Mass., August 29, 1970.

OXENFELDT, A. R. "A Marketing Manager Looks at Attitude Research," in King and Tigert (1971), pp. 13–25.

OZANNE, U. B., and CHURCHILL, G. A. "Adoption Research: Information Sources in the Industrial Purchasing Decision," in *Marketing and the New Science of Planning* (ed. R. L. King), pp. 352–59. 1968 Fall Conference Proceedings, Series No. 28, American Marketing Association.

PALDA, K. S. *The Measurement of Cumulative Advertising Effects.* Englewood Cliffs, N.J.: Prentice-Hall, Inc., 1964.

―――. "The Hypothesis of a Hierarchy of Effects: A Partial Evaluation," *Journal of Marketing Research,* Vol. 3 (February 1966), pp. 13–24.

PAYNE, S. L. "Are Open-ended Questions Worth the Effort?" *Journal of Marketing Research,* Vol. 2 (November 1965), p. 418.

―――. "Return to Quantification," in *Attitude Research at Sea* (eds. L. Adler and I. Crespi), pp. 85–91. Chicago: American Marketing Association, 1966.

PEARL, RAYMOND, and REED, LOWELL J. "On the Rate of Growth of the Population of the United States since 1790 and Its Mathematical Representation," *Proceedings National Academy of Science,* Vol. 6 (1920), pp. 275–88.

PERLE, E. D. *The Demand for Transportation: Regional and Commodity Studies in the United States.* Department of Geography Study No. 95. Chicago: University of Chicago, 1964.

PERLOFF, ROBERT. *"Consumer Analysis,"* in *Annual Review of Psychology* (eds. Paul R. Farnsworth, Mark R. Rosenzweig, and Judith T. Polefka), pp. 437–66. Palo Alto, Calif.: Annual Reviews Inc., 1968.

PERRY, MICHAEL. "Discriminant Analysis of Relations between Consumers' Attitudes, Behavior, and Intentions," *Journal of Advertising Research,* Vol. 9 (April 1969), pp. 34–39.

PESSEMIER, E. A. *New-Product Decisions.* New York: McGraw-Hill Book Co., 1966.

———. "Measuring Stimulus Attributes to Predict Individual Preference and Choice." Institute for Research in the Behavioral, Economic, and Management Sciences, Krannert Graduate School of Industrial Administration, Purdue University, Working Paper No. 318, July 1971.

———, and BRUNO, ALBERT. "An Empirical Investigation of the Reliability and Stability of Selected Activity and Attitude Measures," in Gardner (1971), pp. 389–403.

———; DEBRUICKER, F. S.; and HUSTAD, T. P. "The 1970 Purdue Consumer Behavior Research Project." Krannert Graduate School of Industrial Administration, Purdue University, Working Paper, June 1971.

———; BURGER, P. C.; and TIGERT, D. J. "Can New Product Buyers be Identified?" *Journal of Marketing Research,* Vol. 4 (November 1967), pp. 349–54.

PETERS, WILLIAM H. "Relative Occupational Class Income: A Significant Variable in the Marketing of Automobiles," *Journal of Marketing,* Vol. 34, No. 2 (April 1970), pp. 74–77.

———. "Using MCA to Segment New Car Markets," *Journal of Marketing Research,* Vol. 7, No. 3 (August 1970), pp. 360–63.

PETERSEN, WILLIAM. *Population.* 2d ed. New York: The Macmillan Co., 1969.

PIERSOL, R. J. "Accuracy of Estimating Markets for Industrial Products by Size of Consuming Industries," *Journal of Marketing Research,* Vol. 5, No. 2 (May 1968), pp. 147–54, Table 2.

PITTEL, S. M., and MENDELSOHN, G. A. "The Measurement of Moral Values," *Psychological Bulletin,* Vol. 66 (1966), pp. 22–35.

PLATO. *The Republic.* Baltimore, Md.: Penguin Books, 1955.

PLATTES, CYRIL W. "Strategic and Tactical Decision Making in Marketing," in *Decision Making in Marketing, A Colloquium,* pp. 14–20. New York: The Conference Board, 1971.

POLLAK, O. "Social Adjustment in Old Age." *Social Science Research Council,* Bulletin 59 (1948).

————. "The Family for the Future," *Wharton Quarterly,* Spring, 1971, pp. 25–29.

POLLI, R., and COOK, V. "Validity of the Product Life Cycle," *Journal of Business,* Vol. 42 (October 1969), pp. 385–400.

PORT OF NEW YORK AUTHORITY, AVIATION DEPARTMENT, FORECAST AND ANALYSIS DIVISION. *Air Travel Forecasting, 1965–1975.* Saugatuck, Ct.: The Eno Foundation for Highway Traffic Control, 1957.

————. *Forecast of the United States Domestic Air Passenger Market,* 1960.

QUANDT, R. E. "Estimating the Effectiveness of Advertising: Some Pitfalls in Econometric Methods," *Journal of Marketing Research,* Vol. 1 (May 1964).

QUINN, JAMES BRIAN. "Next Big Industry: Environmental Improvement," *Harvard Business Review,* September–October 1971, pp. 120–31.

RAIFFA, H. *Decision Analysis.* Reading, Mass.: Addison-Wesley Publishing Co., Inc., 1968.

RAISBECK, G. *Information Theory: An Introduction for Scientists and Engineers.* Cambridge, Mass.: The M.I.T. Press, 1964.

RAMSAY, J. O., and CASE, B. "Attitude Measurement and the Linear Model." *Psychological Bulletin,* Vol. 74, No. 3 (September 1970), pp. 185–92.

RAO, V. R. "The Salience of Price in the Perception and Evaluation of Product Quality." Ph.D. dissertation, University of Pennsylvania, 1970.

RAPOPORT, A., and WALLSTEN, T. "Individual Decision Making," in *Annual Review of Psychology,* Vol. 23. Palo Alto, Calif.: Annual Reviews, Inc., 1972.

"Reasons for Moving: March 1962 to March 1963." *Current Population Reports, Population Characteristics,* Series P-20, No. 154 (August 22, 1966), U.S. Bureau of the Census, U.S. Department of Commerce. Washington, D.C.: U.S. Government Printing Office, 1966.

REILLY, W. J. *The Law of Retail Gravitation.* Austin, Tex.: University of Texas Press, 1931.

REITMAN, W. R. *Cognition and Thought.* New York: John Wiley & Sons, Inc., 1965.

REYNOLDS, F. D., and DARDEN, W. R. "Mutually Adaptive Effects of Interpersonal Communication," *Journal of Marketing Research,* Vol. 8 (November 1971), pp. 449–54.

RICH, S. U., and JAIN, S. C. "Social Class and Life Cycles as Predictors of Shopping Behavior," *Journal of Marketing Research,* Vol. 5 (February 1968), pp. 41–49.

ROBERTSON, R. S., and MYERS, J. H. "Personality Correlates of Opinion Leadership and Innovative Buying Behavior," *Journal of Marketing Research,* Vol. 4 (May 1969), pp. 164–68.

ROBERTSON, T. S. "Social Factors in Innovation Behavior," in *Perspectives in Consumer Behavior* (eds. H. H. Kassarjian and T. S. Robertson). Glenview, Ill.: Scott, Foresman and Co., 1968.

————. *Consumer Behavior.* Glenview, Ill.: Scott, Foresman and Co., 1970.

————. *Innovation and the Consumer.* New York: Holt, Rinehart, & Winston, Inc., in press.

ROBINSON, J. P., and SHAVER, P. R. *Measures of Social Psychological Attitudes.* Ann Arbor, Mich.: Institute for Social Research, The University of Michigan, 1969.

ROBINSON, PATRICK J., and LUCK, DAVID J. *Promotional Decision Making: Practice and Theory.* New York: McGraw-Hill Book Co., 1964.

————, et al. *Advertising Measurement and Decision Making.* Boston: Allyn & Bacon, Inc., 1968.

ROGERS, ANDREI. "The Multiregional Matrix Growth Operator and the Stable Interregional Age Structure," *Demography,* Vol. 3 (1966).

ROGERS, E. M., and STANFIELD, J. D. "Adoption and Diffusion of New Products: Emerging Generalizations and Hypotheses," in *Applications of the Sciences in Marketing Management* (eds. F. M. Bass, C. W. King, and E. A. Pessemier), pp. 228–29. New York: John Wiley & Sons, Inc., 1968.

ROKEACH, M. "The Consumer's Changing Image," *Trans-action* (July 1964), pp. 7ff. Reprinted in *Marketing and the Behavioral Sciences* (ed. P. Bliss), pp. 79–90. Boston: Allyn & Bacon, Inc., 1967.

————. "Attitude Change and Behavioral Change," *Public Opinion Quarterly,* Vol. 30 (1967), pp. 529–50.

————. *Beliefs, Attitudes, and Values: A Theory of Organization and Change.* San Francisco: Jossey-Bass, Inc., Publishers, 1968.

————. "The Role of Values in Public Opinion Research," *Public Opinion Quarterly,* Vol. 32 (Winter 1968–69), pp. 547–59.

ROSENBERG, M. J. "Cognitive Structure and Attitudinal Affect," *Journal of Abnormal and Social Psychology,* Vol. 53 (1956), pp. 367–72. Reprinted in Fishbein (1967), pp. 325–331.

ROTTER, J. B. "Generalized Expectances for Internal versus External Control of Reinforcement," *Psychological Monographs: General and Applied,* Vol. 80 (1966), pp. 1–28.

RUCKMICK, C. A. "The Electrodermal Response to Advertising Copy," *Psychological Bulletin,* Vol. 36 (1939), p. 627.

RUSS, F. A. "Evaluation Process Models and the Prediction of Preference," in Gardner (1971), pp. 256–61.

RYDER, NORMAL B. "The Character of Modern Fertility," *The Annals of the American Academy of Political and Social Science,* Vol. 369 (January 1967), pp. 26–36.

SALZMAN, LAWRENCE. *Computerized Economic Analysis.* New York: Mc-Graw-Hill Book Co., 1968.

SAMPSON, PETER. "Can Consumers Create New Products?" *Journal of the Market Research Society,* Vol. 12, No. 1 (January 1970), pp. 40–52.

———. "The Repertory Grid and Its Application to Market Research," in King and Tigert (1971), pp. 71–91.

SCANLAN, B. K. "Anthropology's Potential Role in Gauging Consumer Desires," *Business and Society,* Spring 1965, pp. 28–32. Reprinted in *Marketing Insights* (eds. R. C. Andersen and P. R. Cateora), pp. 171–76. New York: Appleton-Century-Crofts, 1968.

SCHLINGER, M. J. "Cues on Q-Technique," *Journal of Advertising Research,* Vol. 9 (September 1969), pp. 53–60.

SCHMIDT, W. H. *Organizational Frontiers and Human Values.* Belmont, Calif.: Wadsworth Publishing Co., Inc., 1970.

SCHNEIDER, L. M. *Marketing Urban Mass Transit.* Cambridge, Mass.: Division of Research, Graduate School of Business Administration, Harvard University, 1965.

SCHREIRER, F., and NICOSIA, F. M. *Marketing Research: A Behavioral Approach.* Belmont, Calif.: Wadsworth Publishing Co., Inc., in press.

SCHRIEVER, BERNARD A., and SEIFERT, WILLIAM W. *Air Transportation 1975 and Beyond: A Systems Approach.* Cambridge, Mass.: The M.I.T. Press, 1968.

SCHRODER, H. M.; DRIVER, M. J.; and STREUFERT, S. *Human Information Processing.* New York: Holt, Rinehart & Winston, Inc., 1967.

SCHULTZ, R. L. "Market Measurement and Planning with a Simultaneous-Equation Model," *Journal of Marketing Research,* Vol. 8 (May 1971), pp. 153–64.

SCOTT, W. A. "Attitude Measurement," in *The Handbook of Social Psychology* (eds. G. Lindzey and E. Aronson), Vol. II, pp. 204–73. 2d ed. Reading, Mass.: Addison-Wesley Publishing Co., Inc., 1968.

SELLTIZ, C.; JAHODA, M.; DEUTSCH, M.; and COOK, S. W. *Research Methods in Social Relations.* New York: Holt, Rinehart & Winston, Inc., 1959.

SELOVER, W. C. "Experts Agape at Baby Lag," *The Christian Science Monitor,* Vol. 63 (September 18, 1971), pp. 1 and 7.

SEVIN, CHARLES H. *Marketing Productivity Analysis.* New York: McGraw-Hill Book Co., 1965.

SHANNON, C. E., and WEAVER, W. *Mathematical Theory of Communication.* Urbana, Ill.: University of Illinois Press, 1949.

SHAW, M. E., and WRIGHT, J. M. *Scales for the Measurement of Attitudes.* New York: McGraw-Hill Book Co., 1967.

SHETH, J. N. "Multivariate Analysis in Marketing," *Journal of Advertising Research,* Vol. 10 (February 1970), pp. 29–39.

————. "The Multivariate Revolution in Marketing Research," *Journal of Marketing,* Vol. 34 (January 1971), pp. 13–19.

SIEGEL, S. *Nonparametric Statistics for the Behavioral Sciences.* New York: McGraw-Hill Book Co., 1956.

SILBERMAN, C. E. "The U.S. Economy in an Age of Uncertainty," *Fortune* (January 1971), pp. 72ff.

————. " 'Identity Crisis' in the Consumer Markets," *Fortune* (March 1971), pp. 92ff.

SILK, A. J. "Overlap among Self-Designated Opinion Leaders: A Study of Selected Dental Products," *Journal of Marketing Research,* Vol. 2 (August 1966), pp. 255–60.

SILK, L. S. *Forecasting Business Trends.* New York: McGraw-Hill Book Co., 1963.

————. *A Primer on Business Forecasting, with a Guide to Sources of Business Data.* New York: Random House, Inc., 1970.

SILVER, MORRIS. "Births, Marriages, and Business Cycles in the United States," *The Journal of Political Economy,* Vol. 73 (June 1965), pp. 237–55.

SIMON, H. A. *Models of Man, Social and Rational.* New York: John Wiley & Sons, Inc., 1957.

SIMON, J. L. "A Huge Marketing Research Task—Birth Control," *Journal of Marketing Research,* Vol. 5 (February 1968), pp. 21–27.

————. "Some 'Marketing Correct' Recommendations for Family Planning Campaigns," *Demography,* Vol. 5 (1968), pp. 504–7.

SKINNER, B. F. *Beyond Freedom and Dignity.* New York: Alfred A. Knopf, Inc., 1971.

SMITH, G. H. *Motivation Research in Advertising and Marketing.* New York: McGraw-Hill Book Co., 1954.

SMITH, GAIL. "How GM Measures Ad Effectiveness," *Printers' Ink* (May 14, 1965), p. 22.

SMITH, S. V.; BRIEN, R. H.; and STAFFORD, J. E. *Readings in Marketing Information Systems.* Boston: Houghton Mifflin Co., 1968.

SMITH, V. E. "Linear Programming Models for the Determination of Palatable Human Diets," *Journal of Farm Economics,* Vol. 41, No. 2 (May 1959), pp. 273–83.

SNOWBARGER, M., and SUITS, D. B. "Consumer Expenditures for Durable Goods," *Determinants of Investment Behavior* (ed. R. Ferber). New York: National Bureau of Economic Research, 1967.

Social Class Definition in Market Research Objectives and Practice. First Report. London: Market Research Society, 1963.

Sonquist, J. A. *Multivariate Model Building.* Ann Arbor: Institute for Social Research, University of Michigan, 1970.

————, and Morgan, J. N. *The Detection of Interaction Effects.* Monograph No. 35. Ann Arbor: Survey Research Center, University of Michigan, 1964.

Spence, K. W. *Behavior Theory and Conditioning.* New Haven: Yale University Press, 1956.

Stapel, J. "Predictive Attitudes," *Attitude Research on the Rocks* (eds. L. Adler and I. Crespi), pp. 96–115. Chicago: American Marketing Association, 1968.

Starbuck, W. H., and Bass, F. M. "An Expanded Study of Risk Taking and the Value of Information in a New Product Context." Institute Paper 117, Krannert Graduate School of Industrial Administration, 1965.

Starch, D. *Measuring Advertising Readership and Results.* New York: McGraw-Hill Book Co., 1966.

Stasch, S. F. *Systems Analysis for Marketing Planning and Control.* Glenview, Ill.: Scott, Foresman and Co., 1972.

Stefflre, V. J. "Some Implications of Multidimensional Scaling to Social Science Problems," in King and Tigert (1971), pp. 300–11.

Stephenson, W. *The Study of Behavior: Q-Technique and Its Methodology.* Chicago: University of Chicago Press, 1953.

Stevens, S. S. "Measurement, Psychophysics, and Utility," in *Measurement: Definitions and Theories* (eds. C. W. Churchman and P. Ratoosh), pp. 29–30. New York: John Wiley & Sons, Inc., 1959.

Stidsen, Bent. Some Thoughts on the Advertising Process, *Journal of Marketing,* Vol. 34, No. 1 (January 1970), pp. 47–53.

Stone, Bob. "Zip Codes Assist Marketers in Matching Products, Services to Market Segments," *Marketing Insights,* October 9, 1967, pp. 10–11.

Stout, Roy G. "Developing Data to Estimate Price-Quantity Relationships," *Journal of Marketing,* Vol. 33, No. 2 (April 1969), pp. 34–36.

Sturdivant, F. D., et al. *Managerial Analysis in Marketing.* Glenview, Ill.: Scott, Foresman and Co., 1970.

Suits, D. B. "The Determinants of Consumer Behavior Expenditures: A Review of Present Knowledge," in *Impacts of Monetary Policy* (eds. D. B. Suits et al.), pp. 1–57. Englewood Cliffs, N.J.: Prentice-Hall, Inc., 1963.

Summers, J. O. "The Identity of the Women's Clothing Fashion Opinion Leader." Institute for Research in the Behavioral, Economic, and Management Sciences, Herman C. Krannert Graduate School of Industrial Administration, Purdue University, Working paper No. 245, May 1969.

————, and King, C. W. "Opinion Leadership and New Product Adoption." Institute for Research in the Behavioral, Economic, and Management Sciences, Krannert Graduate School of Industrial Administration, Purdue University, Working Paper No. 243, April 1969.

Sunset Magazine, Western Marketing Almanac, 1967–68, pp. 7–8. Lane Magazine & Book Co., 1967.

SWAN, J. E. "Experimental Analysis of Predecision Information Seeking," *Journal of Marketing Research,* Vol. 6 (May 1969), pp. 192–97.

SWANSON, C. E. "The Frontiers of Consumer Psychology, 1964–70," in *The Frontiers of Management Psychology* (ed. George Fisk), pp. 188–208. New York: Harper & Row, Publishers, 1964.

SWETT, D. H. "Anthropology and the Business Community." Mimeographed and prepared for presentation to the Northern California Business Liason Committee, Barrows Hall, University of California, Berkeley, February 25, 1967.

TANNENBAUM, P. H., and GREENBERG, B. S. "Mass Communication," in *Annual Review of Psychology* (eds. P. R. Farnsworth, M. R. Rosenzweig, and J. T. Polefka), pp. 351–86. Palo Alto, Calif.: Annual Reviews, Inc., 1968.

TARVER, JAMES D., and GURLEY, WILLIAM R. "A Stochastic Analysis of Geographic Mobility and Population Projections of the Census Divisions in the United States," *Demography,* Vol. 2 (1965), pp. 134–39.

TAYLOR, D. W. "Toward an Information Processing Theory of Motivation," in *Nebraska Symposium on Motivation* (ed. M. R. Jones), pp. 51–79. Lincoln, Nebr.: University of Nebraska Press, 1960.

TAYLOR, J. R. "Management Experience with Applications of Multidimensional Scaling Methods." Marketing Science Institute Working Paper, May 1970. Mimeographed.

THEIL, HENRI. *Principles of Econometrics.* John Wiley & Sons, Inc., 1971.

————; BOOT, J. C. G.; and KLOCK, T. *Operations Research and Quantitative Economics.* New York: McGraw-Hill Book Co., 1965.

THOMAS, R. E.; SMITH, J. M.; and SPENCE, P. A. "Wheeling and Dealing. . . ," *Journal of the Market Research Society,* Vol. 10 (April 1968) pp. 78–86.

THOMPSON, WARREN S. *Population Problems.* New York: McGraw-Hill Book Co., 1953.

THORELLI, H. B. "Concentration of Information Power among Consumers," *Journal of Marketing Research,* Vol. 8 (November 1971), pp. 427–32.

THURSTON, PHILIP H. "Make TF Serve Corporate Planning," *Harvard Business Review,* September–October 1971, pp. 98–102.

THURSTONE, L. L. "Law of Comparative Judgment," *Psychological Review,* Vol. 34 (1927), pp. 273–86.

————. "The Indifference Function," *Journal of Social Psychology,* Vol. 2 (1931), pp. 139–67. Reprinted in *The Measurement of Values* (ed. L. L. Thurstone), pp. 123–44. Chicago: University of Chicago Press, 1959.

TIGERT, D. J. "A Research Project in Creative Advertising through Life Style Analysis," in King and Tigert (1971), pp. 223–27.

———, and ARNOLD, S. J. "Profiling Self-Designated Opinion Leaders and Self-Designated Innovators through Life Style Research," in Gardner (1971), pp. 425–45.

TINTERA, G. J. "A More Systematic Approach to Advertising Decisions." A paper delivered at the National Conference for University Professors of Advertising, University of Illinois, June 10, 1971.

TORGERSON, W. S. *Theory and Methods of Scaling.* New York: John Wiley & Sons, Inc., 1958.

URBAN, GLEN L. "Sprinter Mod III—A Model for the Analysis of New Frequently Purchased Consumer Products," *Operations Research* Vol. 18, No. 5 (September–October 1970), pp. 805–54.

———. "A Model for Strategic Planning of Family Planning Programs." Abstracts of the 1970 Fall Conference of the American Marketing Association (ed. D. L. Sparks), p. 18.

U.S. BUREAU OF THE BUDGET. *Standard Industrial Classification Manual.* Rev. ed. Washington, D.C.: Executive Office of the President, Bureau of the Budget, 1967.

U.S. BUREAU OF THE CENSUS. *County Business Patterns,* 1965, California CBP-65-6, p. 10. Washington, D.C.: U.S. Government Printing Office, 1966.

———. *Current Population Reports, Population Characteristics.* Current Population Reports, Series P-20, No. 154. Washington, D.C.: U.S. Government Printing Office, August 22, 1966.

———. *Consumer Buying Indicators: Buying Intentions for Automobiles, Housing, and Selected Household Equipment: Week of January 15, 1967.* Current Population Reports, Series P-65, No. 17, pp. 2–12. Washington, D.C.: U.S. Government Printing Office, 1967.

———. *Consumer Buying Indicators. Recent Purchases of Cars, and Other Durables and Expectations to Buy during the Months Ahead, Survey Data through 1969.* Current Population Reports, Series P-65, No. 25, March 11, 1969, p. 6. Washington, D.C.: U.S. Government Printing Office, 1969.

———. *Statistical Abstract of the United States: 1970.* 91st ed. (1970).

———. *Consumer Buying Indicators: Recent Purchases of Cars, Houses and Other Durables and Expectations to Buy during the Months Ahead, Survey Data through January, 1971.* Current Population Reports, Series P-65, No. 35, February 17, 1971.

U.S. DEPARTMENT OF AGRICULTURE, MARKETING ECONOMICS DIVISION, ECONOMIC RESEARCH SERVICE. *Evaluation of a Special Promotional Campaign for Frozen Concentrated Orange Juice.* Marketing Research Report No. 693, February 1965.

U.S. DEPARTMENT OF COMMERCE. *Measuring Markets.* Superintendent of Documents, GPO, 1966.

VAILE, R. S.; GRETHER, E. T.; and COX, R. *Marketing in the American Economy.* New York: The Ronald Press Co., 1952.

VENKATESAN, M. "Cognitive Dissonance," in *Handbook of Marketing Research* (ed. Robert Ferber). New York: McGraw-Hill Book Co., in press.

VILLIERS, A. "The Netherlands: Nation at War with the Sea," *National Geographic,* Vol. 133 (April 1968), pp. 530–71.

VITELES, M. S. *"Motivation and Morale in Industry.* New York: W. W. Norton & Co., Inc., 1953.

VOGEL, E. H. "Creative Marketing and Management Science," *Management Decision,* Vol. 3 (1969), pp. 21–25.

WASSON, C. R. *Product Management: Product Life Cycles and Competitive Marketing Strategy.* St. Charles, Ill.: Challenge Books, 1971.

WEBB, D. J.; CAMPBELL, D. T.; SCHWARTZ, R. D.; and SECHREST, L. *Unobtrusive Measures: Nonreactive Research in the Social Sciences.* Skokie, Ill.: Rand McNally & Co., 1966.

WEISS, E. H., AND COMPANY. *A Manual on the Use of the Semantic Differential in Advertising and Product Testing.* Weiss (December 1955), p. 5. Mimeo.

WELLS, W. D. "Personality and Buyer Behavior: What's Wrong? What Can We Do About It?" Abstract of a paper delivered at the meetings of the American Marketing Association, 1970 (ed. D. L. Sparks), p. 20.

———. "Segmentation by Attitude Types." 1968 Fall Conference Proceedings No. 28, American Marketing Association, p. 124.

———. "It's a Wyeth, not a Warhol, World," *Harvard Business Review,* January–February 1970, pp. 26–30.

———. "Group Interviewing." Mimeographed, December, 1970. Prepared for *The Handbook of Marketing Research* (ed. R. Ferber). New York: McGraw-Hill Book Co., in press.

———, and GUBAR, G. "Life Cycle Concept in Marketing Research," *Journal of Marketing Research,* Vol. 3 (November 1966), p. 360.

———, and SHETH, J. N. "Factor Analysis in Marketing Research," in *Marketing Research Handbook* (ed. R. Ferber). New York: McGraw-Hill Book Co., in press.

———, and TIGERT, D. J. "Activities, Interests and Opinions." Graduate School of Business, University of Chicago, Working Paper, September, 1969. Mimeographed.

WESTOFF, CHARLES F. "The Fertility of the American Population," in *Population: The Vital Revolution* (ed. R. Freedman). Garden City, N.Y.: Anchor Books, Doubleday & Co., Inc., 1964.

WHELPTON, P. K. "Why Did the United States' Crude Birth Rate Decline during 1957–1962?" *Population Index,* Vol. 29 (April 1963), pp. 120–25.

————. "Trends and Differentials in the Spacing of Births," *Demography,* Vol. 1 (1964), pp. 83–93.

————; CAMPBELL, ARTHUR A.; and PATTERSON, JOHN E. *Fertility and Family Planning in the United States.* Princeton, N.J.: Princeton University Press, 1966.

"Where We Go after 200-Million," *Business Week,* November 4, 1967, p. 97.

WHITE, L. S. "Models for the Delivery of Comprehensive Health Care to Large Populations," Abstracts of the 1970 Fall Conference of the American Marketing Association (ed. D. L. Sparks), p. 18.

WHITE, R. K. *Value Analysis: The Nature and Use of the Method.* Society for the Psychological Study of Social Issues, 1951.

WHITE, W. JAMES. "An Index for Determining the Relative Importance of Information Sources," *Public Opinion Quarterly,* Winter 1969–70, pp. 607–10.

"Why a Global Market Doesn't Exist," *Business Week,* December 19, 1970, pp. 140–44.

"Why New Products Fail," *Conference Board RECORD,* October 1964, pp. 11–18.

WICKER, A. W. "Attitudes versus Action: The Relationship of Verbal and Overt Behavioral Responses to Attitude Objects," *Journal of Social Issues,* Vol. 25 (1969), pp. 41–78.

WILLIAMS, CHARLES. "National and Corporate Goals," *TIMS Interfaces,* Vol. 1 (June 1971), pp. 1–9.

WILSON, C. L. "Homemaker Living Patterns and Marketplace Behavior, a Psychometric Approach." Proceedings of the American Marketing Association, 1966.

WILSON, D. T. "Industrial Buyers' Decision-Making Styles," *Journal of Marketing Research,* Vol. 8 (November 1971), pp. 433–36.

————, and MATHEWS, H. L. "Decision Patterns and Personality: 'A Study of Industrial Buyer Decision Making,' " March 1971. Mimeographed.

WINICK, C. "Anthropology's Contributions to Marketing," *Journal of Marketing,* Vol. 25 (July 1961), p. 59.

WISEMAN, FREDERICK. "A Segmentation Analysis on Automobile Buyers during the New Model Year Transition Period," *Journal of Marketing,* Vol. 35 (April 1971), pp. 42–49.

WITTENBORN, J. R. "Contributions and Current Status of Q Methodology," *Psychological Bulletin,* Vol. 58 (March 1961), pp. 132–42.

YANKELOVICH, DANIEL. "New Criteria for Market Segmentation," *Harvard Business Review,* March–April 1964, pp. 83–90.

―――. *The Changing Values on Campus.* New York: Simon & Schuster, Inc., 1972.

―――. "What New Life Styles Mean to Market Planners," *Marketing/Communications,* June 1971, pp. 38–45.

YOELL, W. A. "A Science of Advertising through Behaviorism." Behavior Research Institute, Working Paper, December, 1965.

ZALTMAN, GERALD, and DUBOIS, BERNARD. "New Conceptual Approaches in the Study of Innovation," in Gardner (1971), pp. 417–24.

―――, and VERTINSKY, I. "Marketing Health Services," Abstracts of the 1970 Fall Conference of the American Marketing Association (ed. D. L. Sparks), p. 16.

―――; ANGELMAR, REINHARD; and PINSON, CHRISTIAN. "Metatheory in Consumer Behavior Research," in Gardner (1971), pp. 476–97.

―――, and VERTINSKY, I. "Health Service Marketing: A Suggested Model," *Journal of Marketing,* Vol. 35 (July 1971), pp. 19–27.

ZIFF, RUTH. "Psychographics for Market Segmentation," *Journal of Advertising Research,* Vol. 11 (April 1971), pp. 3–9.

ZIKMUND, W. G., and STANTON, W. J. "Recycling Solid Wastes; A Channels-of-Distribution Problem," *Journal of Marketing,* Vol. 35 (July 1971), pp. 34–39.

Index

This book has been set in 10 and 9 point Times Roman, leaded 3 points. Chapter numbers are 30 point Helvetica and chapter titles are 18 point Helvetica. The size of the type page is 27 by 45^{11}⁄$_{12}$ picas.